Web Design with XML

Web Design with XML

Manfred Knobloch and **Matthias Kopp**
University of Tübingen

WILEY

Copyright © 2001 by dpunkt.verlag GmbH, Heidelberg, Germany.
Title of the German original: *Web-Design mit XML*. ISBN: 3-932588-96-7

English translation Copyright 2003 by John Wiley & Sons Ltd,
The Atrium, Southern Gate, Chichester,
West Sussex PO19 8SQ, England. All rights reserved

National   01243 779777
International (+44) 1243 779777
e-mail (for orders and customer service enquiries): cs-books@wiley.co.uk
Visit our Home Page on http://www.wileyeurope.com or http://www.wiley.com

Library of Congress Cataloging-in-Publication Data

(to follow)

British Library Cataloguing in Publication Data

A catalogue record for this book is available from the British Library

ISBN 0 470 84718 2
Translated and typeset by Cybertechnics Ltd, Sheffield
Printed and bound in Great Britain by Biddles Ltd., Guildford and Kings Lynn
This book is printed on acid-free paper responsibly manufactured from sustainable forestry for which at least two trees are planted for each one used for paper production.

Contents

Preface

With the emergence of the World Wide Web, the quantity of information that has been produced, stored, and used throughout the world in the form of HTML documents has increased unimaginably. There has been an enormous flow of information, and this has brought both problems and opportunities. Briefly, these include a lack of differentiation between presentation and content, lack of extensibility, and problems with indexing and searching. This makes the maintenance and processing of HTML difficult.

XML is invisible

In order to come up with a solution, a task force was established within the World Wide Web Consortium (W3C), whose activities in 1998 resulted in the recommendations for an eXtensible Markup Language (XML). This language is capable of arranging documents purely according to their content. Like HTML, XML works with markup elements. In contrast to what happens in HTML, however, these are used in XML to give the document a logical, content-based structure. XML itself cannot specify how a particular piece of content has to look on the screen, or how it appears on the printout. Graphical representations, visualization and rendering do not lie within the scope of XML. In this sense, XML is invisible.

Making XML documents visible

This book therefore deals with the remodelling of XML documents, using transformations, into visible and useful end-user documents. Hidden behind this uninspiring description are a multitude of possibilities for selecting, grouping, and displaying content in a variety of ways. Last but not least, by means of transformations, practical tools for everyday needs can be defined.

eXtensible Style Language

The tools that have been defined by the W3C for the conversion of XML data into user documents are grouped together under the generic name of an extensible representation language, the "eXtensible Style Language" (XSL). The standardization of XSL was completed in October 2001, and XML documents can already be processed with XSL: Web pages, PDF documents, and other diverse formats are generated through the use of appropriate XSL Style Sheets from XML documents.

Cascading Style Sheets

Cascading Style Sheets (CSS) are also available to render XML documents for display in Web browsers. Although it is possible to use each of the two forms of style sheets independently in order to make XML visible, the two designs should not be seen as mutually exclusive. For presentation in a Web browser, the combination of both stylesheet techniques has some advantages.

The opportunities afforded by XML technology are still difficult to assess, as are its risks and problems. At present, it is clear that, compared to "traditional" methods for creating HTML pages, production of just a few small Web documents is more labour intensive with XML. In this case, the use of a commercial HTML editor is probably more effective and straightforward. Appropriate tools for XML will change this situation.

It is also certain that this increased effort brings a higher degree of specialization into Web page development: the activities of content management, graphical layout and compilation of data into a cohesive set within the context of a site are becoming distinguished. This division of labour is an indication of the industrialization of the production process, which will become a central theme in the production and distribution of information for the coming years: the automated transfer of an application-neutral data source in a variety of practical contexts, such as, for example, printing, Web, sound, etc.

The basis for this is XML, and the tools are the transformation mechanisms that the W3C has defined for this purpose.

The technical design of Web documents "Web design with XML" therefore deals with aspects of the technique of designing documents and information for the WWW. The topics of structural or cognitive aspects of Web design are not covered in this book. These questions have to be dealt with independently from the technology used. Technical information or document modelling is subordinate to the question of aesthetics and presentation. The actual task of the technology here should be to implement requirements as closely as possible.

Many people have been involved in the production of this book: family members who have been somewhat neglected by the authors, friends, who are at the end of their tether from having to listen to the same topics (XML of course) over and over again, work colleagues, who see my grey face every morning and advise me to cut down on my night life a little. I would like to thank all these people for their patience, understanding, and for all their fascinating comments.

Important contributions in the form of exquisite suggestions on the wording of this book came from Mr. Osthof from the TVZ-Verlag and from Mr. Buck (Academy for Data Processing). Colleagues who read my book at dpunkt.verlag and various other publishers have provided much practical task-based advice, which has made the book more user-friendly. The numerous conversations about XML I have had with my colleague Dr. Stumpp have flowed into these pages. They have often made us aware of difficulties that we did not know about, and have been the catalysts for knowledge. Many thanks to everyone for their constructive intervention.

In particular, I would like to thank my co-author Dr. Matthias Kopp from the computing centre of the University of Tübingen, who wrote Chapter 4 and furthermore, with his suggestions, has enriched and furthered the subject matter of all the chapters.

Manfred Knobloch

Tübingen

Introduction

People often say that XML will revolutionize the Web, but they do not say how this will actually happen. The aim of this book is to show how XML can be used to create content for the WWW. The book is therefore aimed at users who want to present content on the WWW: Web designers, HTML developers, Web masters, content developers, and content providers. Readers of this book should at least be familiar with HTML. An expert knowledge of HTML is however not required; it is sufficient to know which HTML constructs can be used and where, in order to achieve the desired effects.

Similarly, some previous knowledge of XML makes it easier to understand how it works, but the book does not assume knowledge of XML as a prerequisite. The XML Recommendation is relatively short ([XML10] approx. 50 pages); even the most important XML topics can be explained briefly. The problems arise when XML is put into practice. In this book, therefore, definitions and recommendations are mostly introduced by means of examples.

1.1 Road map

In the following ten chapters, you will become familiar with the techniques that are used to produce legible documents from XML files.

Chapter 2: Overview of XML, XSL and CSS

A recurring example This chapter explains why and how the concept of the separation of content from presentation information requires the different components of XML and XSL or CSS. The chapter also shows how these components are connected to each other, the combinations that are possible for XML, and when these should be used. Read this chapter to get an overview of the topic and to become acquainted with the recurring example introduced here.

Chapter 3: A brief introduction to XML

You can skip this chapter if you are already familiar with XML. Since XML is only the basis for the work we do in this book, we will only mention the basic concepts of the language: what is meant by well-formed, and what is validity? What does the XML parser do? The topic of document type definition (DTD) is discussed using the following key concepts: elements, attributes, entities and notation. When should information be put into an attribute, and when should it be referred to as an element? What are entities and notations and what are they used for?

Chapter 4: XML and CSS

This chapter will show how display material can be produced by structuring content using Cascading Style Sheets (CSS). A brief summary of CSS follows the description of the syntax of style definitions. You can skip this chapter if you have already worked with Cascading Style Sheets for HTML. You can use this chapter as reference if you have any queries regarding the example data that is introduced. The chapter also contains advice on how to support different CSS concepts in various browsers.

Chapter 5: XSL

This chapter gives an overview of the three components of XSL (XSLT, XPath and XSL:FO). An insight into working with an XSL processor can help to show how these are used in more detail. The chapter gives tips on how to establish a working environment with freely available tools.

Chapter 6: Transformations using XSLT

This chapter is dedicated to the transformation of XML files into visible end-user documents. It will introduce the notation of the transformation language XSLT in stylesheet files and its data models. The chapter also contains several simple examples showing how the sample data is converted into HTML, and also introduces the language elements and basic abilities of XSLT.

Chapter 7: XPath

This chapter introduces the XPath navigation language, which is used within XSLT to identify and select parts of the input documents. The self-contained concepts of XPath are explained and demonstrated by means of a number of examples.

Chapter 8: Other XSLT language elements

Once you have learnt about XPath, other language elements will be introduced. The reorganization of the example documents into a single source document shows how a unified source of information can be built up. With the help of XSLT transformations, it can now be used as the starting point for creating subsets.

Chapter 9: Creating navigation structures

Starting with our example document, we show several ways in which transformations can create consistent link structures. To begin with, the result is a single file with internal links. To extend this, a variety of HTML files are generated from the one source file, which all contain a sequential forward-backward navigation structure. Another example will show the creation of a Web site containing hierarchical navigation.

Chapter 10: XSL Formatting Objects

If the result of an XSLT transformation cannot be or is not to be used immediately, a formatting process has to take place after the transformation. This is why Formatting Objects were developed. As an output-neutral definition, templates are used, which we already know from CSS. This chapter discusses the basic structure of an FO document. A PDF document, which is the slide document in PDF format, is used as an example. If you are only interested in the creation of HTML documents, you can skip this chapter.

Appendix A: Elements of the XSLT language

If the previous chapters aimed to provide readable text, this reference section will introduce short examples and solution templates, which no longer stick to the recurring example, exemplifying the different language elements and functions of XSLT.

1.2 Working environments and tools

All the examples in this book were produced using the free tools of the XML Apache project, which are available from

```
http://xml.apache.org
```

Java runtime environment For you to be able to follow the examples, you will need a Java runtime environment. You can find advice on how to set this up in Chapter 6. For the examples in the book, JDK 1.2.2 was used on Windows NT 4.0 and there were no problems with the transfer to JDK 1.1.7 under SuSE Linux 6.x. The same is expected for the Java runtime environment of other systems.

Browsers As far as was possible, the examples were viewed in various browsers. Immediate presentation of XML or CSS is supported by Microsoft Internet Explorer 5.x, the most recent Mozilla version, and version 4 and higher of the Opera browser.

Editors XML source texts were often (but not always) created using XML editors. For smaller documents, an ASCII editor was sufficient. So far, there has been no killer application. Java based systems are normally free, but users should be patient as the runtime is often very poor. On the other hand, many of these programs stand out from the others because they have very flexible functions (Xeena can be found on alphaworks.ibm.com).

Platform dependent programs (xmlspy, CLIP, ...) are fast, but do cost money. Not all these systems can be connected to XML parsers and XSLT processors for free.

Systems from large commercial providers such as Softquad XMetaL, or programs that come from the SGML world such as, for example, FrameMaker+SGML are much more complex and more expensive. As a rule, they can be adapted to specific uses by developers and are therefore aimed at use in the professional (publishing) field.

1.3 Further advice

The book by R. Tolksdorf "The Language of the Web: HTML and XHTML" [TOL00] can be used as an overview and reference book for HTML. At the end of the book there are detailed bibliographical details and further useful literature.

A freely available XML parser and XSLT processor, as well as the formatter "Formatting objects for PDF" (FOP) can be found under http://xml.apache.org.

You can search for other tools and editors on the sites of J. Tauber and L. van den Brink (http://www.xmlsoftware.com) and from IBM (http://alphaworks.ibm.com). On these sites you can find links to other sites which contain material on XML topics.

Overview of XML, XSL and CSS

This chapter explains how the Extensible Style Language (XSL) and Cascading Style Sheets (CSS) support the concept of the separation of content and presentation information in XML documents. The details of XML syntax, XSL and CSS are not looked at closely in this chapter, as this will be done in subsequent chapters. First of all you should get to know how these topics and the related terms are connected to each other, and which combinations are possible for design with XML. At this point we introduce an example that is used throughout the entire book.

2.1 An example document

The document we will use as an example is a presentation slide that is used as a handout for a lecture on Content Management Systems.

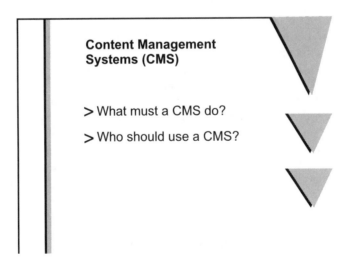

Figure 2.1 Slide in a presentation tool

The aim of this, and many similar documents, is to display small amounts of content clearly and concisely. You can see the content of the example at a glance. How is this achieved? The text that carries the content has been specially structured for this purpose: the function of each of the lines is characterized by different font sizes. The heading is larger and set in boldface, whilst the content elements are left-aligned as a list.

A different use, different layout information

The content therefore complies with a layout that is optimized for the special context of a "slide presentation". If the text is reused in another way – for example, if you want to give the audience some written notes – this layout information will need to be changed. To make this possible, current presentation programs allow you to print out slides. When you do this, a redesign is automatically carried out: since there is not a lot of information in each slide, several slides are normally printed out on one sheet.

A problem that arises when the context in which a document is used changes is that the visual appearance does not contain any readable information about the function and position of each part of the text. For human readers, this is done by changing the way the text is displayed (bold, enlarged, centred). It is a simple task for readers to identify the first element of the list in the example. It would be much more difficult to find the 37th element in a list.

For a computer program, processing the short text in our example, which may entail handling the first element of the list of topics in a special way, is quite difficult. There are no explicit indications of where a list item begins and where it ends. How does XML solve this problem?

2.2 Organizing documents

Separating structure and design

An important aim pursued during the development of XML has been the distinction between the structure of the document and its presentation. The organization of a document and its structure should, if possible, be carried out purely on the basis of the content.

The need to separate the structured content from its output on paper, on the monitor, or through a loudspeaker requires the author of the document to do a little rethinking. People intuitively imagine text as a display of characters on paper or on a screen. When writing a letter by hand, we imagine the salutation as a character string that is detached from the rest of the text. Thinking of this structural property separately from the content often means a break from conventional methods. When trying to introduce this into everyday life, you repeatedly find that the principle cannot be followed universally.

As an example, you can imagine that part of some text is to appear in italics, in between some characters that are not in italics. The italic part of the text must be marked appropriately, so that these characters are actually displayed like this in the printout. Some presentation information will have to be attached to the word that carries the content. Many such cases in everyday experience, show that, in practice, the distinction between structure and presentation does not survive. The aim of the separation of form and content, which is to reuse contents in other use contexts, does not become impossible because of this. Let's go back to our example. The XML version can look as follows:

```
<?xml version="1.0"?>
<slide>
    <title>Content Management Systems (CMS)</title>
    <topiclist>
      <topic>What must a CMS be able to do?</topic>
      <topic>Who should use a CMS?</topic>
    </topiclist>
</slide>
```

The example contains several markup elements, such as <slide> or <title>, which respectively have the ending </title> and </slide>, and are embedded into the actual content. The element <slide> provides an outer bracketing structure, within which a hierarchical partition is defined by means of other elements.

In the XML version of the example document, there are no hints as to which font, size, alignment etc. should be used for the display of the content between the element markers. This is deliberate, but unusual.

Tags and In general, the form of the markup elements is the same as those in HTML, the
elements only difference being that, in the case of XML, the structuring of the documents is carried out with the help of freely definable markup elements. As in HTML, these are called tags. A tag is a word that comes between angle brackets. In XML documents, tags almost always appear as a pair. As you can see in the above example, for every start tag there is an end tag. The actual content appears between these two tags.

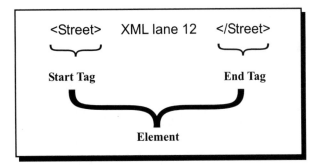

Figure 2.2 Structure of an element

In XML jargon, the combination of a start tag, content and an end tag is known as an element. (See Figure 2.2.) This is merely a simplified definition that will be expanded on in the next chapter. All the markup elements and all the tags of the language are known as markup. And since the name of the markup element is not predetermined, meaningful names should be used. Because the names of the tags are used as labels for the content, this form of markup is called semantic markup.

Qualified   It is certainly clear that we can carry out the search for a title for the slide in such
search   documents in a very specific way. The naming of the markup element (the tag
name) can be used to refine the search criteria. If a program is capable of reading
tags, it can also be used to search the text within particular tags for a specific pattern.
A document containing an element such as `<surname>James</surname>` can
be searched for references to people with this surname, even though James is usually a forename. This information cannot be taken from an HTML paragraph element such as, for example `<p>James</p>` reliably.

As a rule, this was not originally possible with conventional text systems, and –
as explained – not in the case of HTML pages either. In order to make things easier
for search engines on the WWW, the so-called `<META>` tags were therefore invented
for HTML pages, but these require authors to compile a kind of list of keywords, so
that the search for contents can be more specific than simply searching through the
whole of the HTML document.

It is easier for programs to search the XML version of the example using such criteria. If meaningful names are used for the markup elements during the creation of
the document, you can imagine that a program can be asked to search for specific
elements. This is difficult in an HTML document, because the markup elements say
little or nothing about the content that they hold.

Another way of searching through XML documents specifically is based upon
the hierarchical structure of XML. Because of this ordered, hierarchical structure, directions through the document can be given in order to identify a specific part
clearly. The XML 1.0 Recommendation describes how this kind of document structuring must be carried out for it to be labelled as "XML". These requirements are discussed in detail in the next chapter. To begin with, take note of the following: an
important feature is the strong hierarchical structure of the document. In simpler
terms, start tags that are nested within one another must be ended again in reverse
order. The overlapping of several start and end tags is forbidden.

Paths through   With these prerequisites, it is easy to understand which part of our example doc-
the document   ument is referred to by the following expression:

```
/slide/topiclist/topic[1]
```

This expression describes the path from the entrance point in the document via the
`<slide>` element, to the branch `<topiclist>` to the first `<topic>` element.
Why do we use this if we do not yet have a presentation for these contents (which
can be found so easily)? Precisely for this purpose: firstly, elements of XML documents have to be selected, and secondly, they have to be linked to design information.

1. It is the task of the XPath language to make this selection possible. The path expression shown above is a valid XPath expression. Using XPath, [XPath] the
   WWW Consortium defines a notation that describes how parts of an XML document can be found.

2. The assignment of layout information to these selected elements is the task of a
   conversion process that is usually called a transformation.

These two "components" of the use of XML, transformations and XPath, are discussed in detail in Chapters 6, 7 and 8. Transformations are used to create a readable product. The variants that are available during the transformation of undisplayed data into visible content are shown in the overview of the next section.

2.3 The presentation of XML

Combining content data and its layout with the help of transformations is a step in the direction of the automated production of information. This has only been a very abstract concept until now. How can this be implemented practically? How does an XML document become visible, legible or possibly audible?

Let's consider an HTML browser. An HTML browser knows how an `<h1>` element should be displayed and what `<br>` means. The number of HTML tags and their names are predetermined. This is not the case with XML data. A browser cannot possibly guess how a `<nickname>` or a `<menu>` element should be displayed.

Transformation programs

One way of displaying the contents is to write a program that reads the XML file and carries out special operations for certain markup elements. In this case, the instructions for the presentation are defined in the program code. A program that converts the XML data into another form is called a transformation program. The following schema shows the transformation of XML data into an HTML document. The transformation program "knows" which XML tags must be converted into which HTML tags.

Figure 2.3 Processing files with XML data sources

This fairly simple model has the obvious disadvantage that each change in the document leads to a change in the program code. If the name of a markup element changes, this must also be followed up by a change in the program code.

As limited as this processing model may appear at first glance, in many cases it is a very useful concept. If the structure of the document does not change that often, such a custom-built program probably offers the highest processing speed possible. In essence, a simple HTML browser works in the same way as this kind of application. The documents that have to be processed are all different, but still contain a fixed number of markup elements. If the HTML version changes, i.e. if new elements are added, new browser versions then have to be programmed.

It can also be said that in the case of this model, the document is not tied down to a specific processing program. It is possible for various programs to access the same document and from these create various kinds of transformations. The separation of the structured content from the presentation of the content still remains.

Configurable transformations

A simple extension of this kind of processing makes fixed coding of display instructions in the text of the program unnecessary.

Another file is passed to the transformation program as an input file. This file contains rules for the presentation of the elements of the source file. This control file is usually created by a user. In its simplest form, this file can be understood as a list, containing a description of how each element of the input is to be displayed. The authors of this control file must therefore know the structure of the source file that will be displayed and will need to formulate appropriate rules for its presentation. The difficulties connected with displaying the file are thus decoupled from the code of the transformation program.

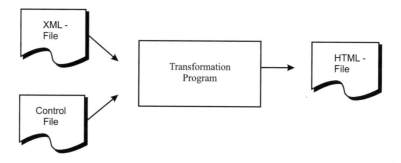

Figure 2.4 Processing files with a control file

The transformation program is thus much more complicated to create, although it can be used universally. If it is able to accept and analyze any XML document as input, and to assign display rules from a control file for each element, the transformation program can be used to create any output conceivable. What actually changes is the control file and the display rules that are contained within it.

Style sheets This is the same concept as style sheets: the content of a source file is displayed by using so-called format templates. The style sheet therefore contains a construction plan for the presentation of source data.

Cascading Style Sheets (CSS) were established for formatting HTML documents. They allow information about layout to be assigned to HTML tags. A declaration such as

```
H1 {font-family: "sans-serif";
    font-size: large;
```

```
text-align: center;

color: #FFFFFF;
background: #400040}
```

in a CSS file will result in any level 1 heading (H1) being centred, a purple background, white text, and a large font size. A browser that can process CSS uses this definition as control information for the creation of its presentation of the document.

This proven method is also used for formatting XML data; the tags of an XML document can be assigned formatting instructions in this way. The difference from HTML is that the XML tags can have any name at all. A browser that supports the display of XML with the help of CSS must therefore be able to cope with an unknown set of tags.

However, the use of CSS statements is limited to simple elements. Furthermore, CSS can only be used for documents that can be displayed in browsers. The implications of this will be discussed in more detail in the next chapter. Therefore we will only mention the limited use of CSS in XML.

2.4 XSL as a better style language

Since the limitations of Cascading Style Sheets had to be overcome, XSL was designed as an eXtensible Style Language for XML. The original aim for the definition of XSL was to offer a language that makes it possible to create formatting instructions for XML documents. However, during its development it soon became apparent that a further separation of the process into various intermediate steps was necessary. The transformation of original data into a formatted document was split into two separate steps:

1. The conversion of the original document into an intermediate document containing instructions as to how it is to be formatted.

2. The further processing of the intermediate documents by a formatting program, which leads to the creation of concrete pages, paragraphs etc. either on paper or on the monitor.

During conversion into the intermediate document, that is, during transformation, several operations can be carried out:

- A change to the layout of the document: outputting the data that was input in a different sequence.

- Repeated output: the multiple output of elements of the source file (e.g. contents, title of the chapter, entry in the register,...).

- The attachment of layout information to elements of the original document.

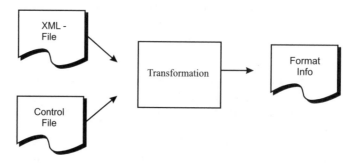

Figure 2.5   From the source to formatting

The outcome of a transformation is therefore a document that can be displayed in a browser or can be sent to the printer using a formatting program.

Why all this effort? Well, let us just imagine a long text which contains some headings. It is far easier for readers to navigate their way through the document if there is table of contents. But a table of contents is not a natural part of the text. It is an extract of parts of the text, normally the headings, which show information about the text, and which also depend on the text and must be able to change along with it.

For a transformation program, this means that it may need to be able to go through the source data several times. For example, when it runs through the data the first time, only the contents of certain elements are selected to create a table of contents. These are usually chapter and section headings. In further transformation operations, special contents (paragraphs, abstracts, tables) may be selected, or elements that are not required (directions and corrections) may be ignored. If all contents and references are created for the output document, in a further transformation step, special markup elements are entered into the output as instructions for the graphical layout of the document (bold typeface, alignment, pagination).

The XSL task force of the WWW Consortium has published several documents describing various operations.

XSLT, XPath   The part of XSL that is concerned with the transformation processes is called XSL Transformations, in short XSLT. The XSLT elements therefore describe how the transformations must be carried out. For this reason, XSLT is known as a control language for a transformation process. Within XSLT another subcomponent is used, which we have already seen briefly. This subcomponent is called XPath, as it describes paths in the source document that lead to elements or whole fragments of the document. XPath has the task of marking elements or parts of the source document so that they can be selected explicitly. Both XSLT and XPath were adopted as Recommendations by the W3C in November 1999.

XSL:FO   The aspect of XSL that is concerned with the assignment of layout information
Formatting is called XSL Formatting Objects, in short XSL:FO or just simply XSL. The Format-
Objects   ting Objects describe, for example, how a page of an output document is structured, in which direction the text runs, how wide the columns are, and so on.

To summarize, we can say that XSLT describes how the conversion of a document into another is carried out, and, in contrast, XSL:FO indicates what should be contained in the output document for it to be displayed correctly.

The control files that describe the transformation process are called XSLT style sheets, although their function goes beyond controlling format and therefore style. They are more accurately described as transformation scripts. The name style sheet is a left over from the time when XSL was thought to be a better replacement for CSS. A complete XSL processing chain from the XML document to the end user document thus includes the steps of transformation and formatting. The transformation produces a restructured intermediate document with inbuilt formatting information. From this, the formatting process produces a specific output format. This could be PostScript or RTF or PDF, as in the example shown in Figure 2.6.

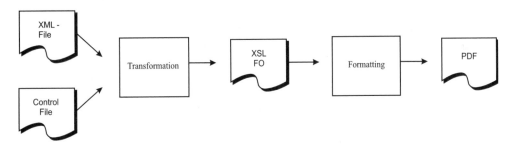

Figure 2.6 XSL processing chain

The advantage of this complex sequence of processes is, amongst other things, that the components involved can work independently of one another.

The formatter is completely independent of the input document. It is always given a data stream as input, and this data stream always conforms to the Formatting Objects specification. Its input data consists of content that is structured in accordance with the FO and is intertwined with FO layout instructions. The formatter has to convert this standardized FO input stream into a concrete output format (PDF, RTF, DOC,...).

2.5   The uses of transformations

The transformation process does not require any information about the format in which the final output is to be displayed. It works through a transformation script on the basis of the elements that are found when reading though the input document. The transformer just assumes that the input file conforms to XML. Information about the concrete elements of the input document is simply placed in the style sheet.

It seems reasonable to ask whether results other than formatting instructions can be created by means of a transformation. The fact that this is actually possible, gives transformation with XSLT a special purpose. However, the multiple use of

XML data in different contexts depends on whether this data has been prepared for the appropriate context. An XML-structured file alone is no use. If this had to be adapted for different uses "by hand" every time, then nothing would be gained over the current state of things. This is exactly the gap that the transformation language XSLT fills.

Generating HTML   An important and very clear example of this is the creation of HTML files from XML data. In this case, the not all of the processing chain that is shown above has to be run through. The intermediate format that has to be created is HTML; instead of a formatting program, a browser is used.

The WWW Consortium has defined the current version of HTML as an XML application. Because of this, the names of the HTML tags have not been changed, but they do have to take into account slightly changed rules, which conform to XML. Therefore, this up-to-date version of HTML is also called XHTML. (Henceforth, we will use the names HTML and XHTML interchangeably.) An XHTML document is therefore an XML document. XHTML can be created from an XML document with just one single transformation and can thus be made browsable.

Until browser manufacturers provide wide support for XML/XSL, this form of transformation will be the main mechanism for using XML as a source of Web pages.

To summarize, the following scenarios show the different uses of XSL and CSS.

- **XML and CSS**. XML data is displayed in the browser using CSS statements. CSS statements etc. are written by hand and referenced from the XML file.

- **An XSLT transformation creates XML and CSS**. An XML file is assigned an existing CSS file using an XSLT transformation script. It is also possible that CSS information can be inserted into the XML file via the transformation.

- **An XSLT transformation creates XHTML.** A transformation script creates an XHTML file from an XML file. As in the previous point, whether or not CSS information is created by the transformation depends on the application.

- **An XSLT transformation creates XSL:FO for a formatter.** The complete chain of XSL processing is run through. In a Web context, the creation of a PDF document can illustrate this case.

- **An XSLT transformation creates program code for dynamic Web pages.** Since the transformation, as already described, works independently from the formatter, it is also conceivable that an XSLT transformation script could output program code for script language interpreters. Used in combination with HTML, this can be JavaScript, VBScript, Perl or PHP for server-side processing, or others.

There are no hard and fast rules stating when each scenario should be used. Using XSL is much more time consuming than using Cascading Style Sheets. If you are dealing with small amounts of data and require quick and visible output, a visualization of XML through the use of Cascading Style Sheets is an attractive option. As well as Microsoft Internet Explorer from version 5.0, Netscape Navigator 6 (and other browsers based on the Mozilla project's Gecko engine) and the Opera browser version from 4.0 also support this, though they do so with various degrees of conformance to the standard.

It should also be taken into account that in all cases in which the structure of the input file cannot be taken on in the output file, CSS alone cannot be used. XSL or, even better, XSLT is always required if it is a question of creating navigation structures or overview information that require regroupings or sortings to be carried out.

The basis of all these auspicious opportunities is XML – the topic of the following chapter.

3

A brief introduction to XML

In the course of this book, eXtensible Markup Language is used as a tool and is itself only indirectly of interest. The aim of this chapter is to describe a basic subset of the language which is adequate to express information in a way that conforms to XML. This introduction therefore confines itself only to the most necessary details. The consequences that arise from the basic concepts of XML are also discussed here.

3.1 Well-formed XML

There are only a very few rules that a document has to follow in order to be an XML document. If something is described as being well-formed, this means that it meets some central requirements.

Tags and elements
At first glance, an XML document is very similar to an HTML document. It consists of elements with established rules concerning their notation. An element consists of content, and a start and end marker. These start and end markers are called tags. A start tag consists of an opening angle bracket, a name, some optional attributes and a closing angle bracket, for example, `<slide status="active">`. Here a tag called `slide` is opened, containing an attribute called `status`. As you can see from the example, the value of the attribute is assigned using an equals sign. In contrast to attributes in HTML, in XML each attribute value must be written between quotation marks.

End tags have a very similar construction to start tags, but must have a slash (/) after the opening angle bracket and may not contain any attribute details.

The content, i.e. the data, is entered between the start and end tags. A sequence of a start tag, content and end tag is described as an element.

```
<slide status="active"> any content </slide>
```

The names of the tags can be chosen freely. You just have to remember that the names themselves must not contain any blank spaces and that lower and upper case letters are distinguished between. Thus `<slide>` and `<Slide>` are two different tags.

An element can also contain other elements; in this case the embedded elements are described as child elements. The structure of XML documents can therefore be described as a tree structure (provided that you have no difficulties with the tree growing from top to bottom, as this is how documents are read, from top to bottom): the elements are branches that start from a root element from which other branches emerge if child elements are embedded. With regards to their structure-forming function in the document, the elements are also described as nodes. Each element can therefore be used as a node in the hierarchy of the branches or can be a leaf (terminal element) which is only of interest due to its content.

The presentation slide can be used as a brief example of this:

```
<slide>
    <title>Content Management Systems (CMS)</title>
    <topiclist>
      <topic>What must a CMS be able to do?</topic>
      <topic>Who should use a CMS?</topic>
    </topiclist>
</slide>
```

The elements `<title>` and `<topiclist>` are child elements of `<slide>`, `<topic>` is the child of `<topiclist>`. You should take care that hierarchically nested elements are closed in the reverse order to that in which they are opened. A tag sequence

```
<topiclist>
    <topic>What must a CMS be able to do?</topiclist>
</topic>
```

is not allowed, since the `<topic>` tag must be closed before the `<topiclist>`.

Document root   The slide document in the above example contains four elements. The `<slide>` tag forms a bracket for the whole document and is also called the document root.

The set of tags used in a document is called markup. In the case of XML, markup is not predefined but extensible. This is why it is called eXtensible Markup Language. But this is somewhat misleading. More precisely, XML is not a markup language, because the extent of the markup is not fixed. Instead, XML is a meta language for describing markup languages. Each document that uses a set of tags that is defined by a developer is in this sense an XML application written in the developer's own markup language.

Semantic markup   The possibility of creating your own markup language also means that the names of the tags can be chosen so that they describe the information that they enclose, for example <forename>, <telephonenumber>, ... Because of this feature, markup in XML is also called semantic markup. Whether this expression is an accurate description depends on how the developer of the document uses this possibility. You do not need to think up actual "meaningful" tag names, if you do not want to. Therefore, at this point, when developing documents, we suggest that you should weigh up the use of tag names that can be understood by everyone against names which describe the information that they enclose.

There are two consequences of the freedom with which tags can be named.

1. An application program (e.g. a browser) cannot know how to display an XML data stream correctly, as this information is not contained in the XML file itself. Since the names of the elements can be different in each document and are therefore unpredictable, the graphic representation cannot be fixed for each element, unlike in HTML.

   This also means that there are no constructs such as INPUT elements or control elements. As the developer of a document, you can use these names, but they do not have any consequences.

   All agents that create a presentation of XML data rely on additional information. In this sense, content and presentation are already separated in the basic concept of XML.

2. Access to elements in the document can be oriented to the structure of the content, to the semantic markup. Put in an abstract way, fragments of a document can be found and addressed. Because of this, in principle, there is the option of putting hyperlinks into parts of a document reserved for content.

   An expression such as `/slide/title` clearly refers to the the title element of the document, without there having to be a special marker, for example in the sense of an HTML anchor tag. This form of notation will be discussed in more detail in the chapter on XPath beginning on page 107.

   When searching in a document library, this also means that you can look specifically for the content of the `<title>` element. In contrast to the structure of traditional Web documents, it can be assumed that the name of the element has a meaning which makes it possible to specify search criteria. So, for example, a selection term such as `[forename='Hugo']` can be used to limit the search for Hugo to occurrences within `<forename>` elements – see *"Predicates and complete location paths"*, page 116. A piece of information that is put into an HTML tag such as `<center>` or `<h2>` can be much harder to identify as the title of an object.

Empty elements
Other criteria for "well-formedness" apply to empty elements, and the definition of attributes. For empty elements, an abbreviation in the form of `<title/>` is allowed. The title element is defined, but does not have any content.

Empty elements are often used to carry attributes. Each attribute name can only appear once in a tag.

```
<slide title="Content Management Systems (CMS)" />
```

In this example, the document is still empty, however the title has been set.

Comments
Comments are an important aid for human readers. They are written in the same way as in HTML.

```
<!-- There can be comments anywhere-->
```

There can be comments anywhere, except between the opening and closing angle brackets of a tag.

XML documents should satisfy another condition. Our previous example still lacks a prologue which can be as minimal as the following:

```
<?xml version= "1.0" ?>
<slide>
    . . . .
</slide>
```

In the first line, the version number of the XML specification being used has to be specified. This line is called the XML declaration. The name XML, or xml (in upper and lower case) and the version attribute ([XML10], Section 2.6) are reserved names. The XML declaration formally has the structure of what is known as a processing instruction, but it is not one. We will now look briefly at a processing instruction.

A processing instruction (in short PI) is written between an opening and closing angle bracket, with a question mark at the start and at the end. Processing instructions are used to provide information about the document to the application program that is processing it. The name of the application that is processing this instruction therefore appears at the start of the PI.

There is no certainty that a program will take notice of processing instructions as different instructions can be inserted into a document for different programs. The documentation of the processing system in question should specify which PIs are processed and what they effect. According to the guidelines of the XML standard, instructions that a program does not understand are simply ignored.

For example, the XML declaration is not dealt with as a normal processing instruction within XSLT because, unlike a normal processing instruction, it cannot be generated by means of a transformation. The XML prologue normally contains more information, which we will discuss later.

Summary of the rules for well-formed XML

1. XML documents consist of markup (tags) and content.

2. Each element has a start and an end tag.

3. In the start tag of an element, information that appears once can be entered in the form of attributes.

4. Each XML document has just one document root.

5. Elements can be nested hierarchically.

6. Elements can be empty.

7. A document may be and should be introduced by an XML prologue.

In the guidelines to XML, the WWW Consortium stated that the new language should be simple and Web-capable. A multitude of applications can therefore cope with XML data, which merely meet the criteria of being well-formed.

3.2 Validity

The structure of documents and DTDs Often, types of documents are developed that are to be used repeatedly. Companies often spend a lot of money structuring documents such as standardised business letters and reports. Even in the case of Web pages, more and more value is being placed upon corporate design. In order to make it easier for users to find their way through pages, pages should always be constructed in as uniform a way as possible. This ensures that when these types of documents are used, the fixed structure can be kept in every concrete document. For this purpose, XML provides support in the form of so-called Document Type Definitions (DTD).

A developer can specify which elements can appear in a document and how often they do so using a DTD. A DTD is a grammar, a set of rules that describes the structure of the document. Using the appropriate programs (parsers) it is possible to test whether a document follows the rules of the grammar that has been assigned to it. If the structure of the document is different from what the DTD specifies, an error message is produced. Special XML editors or application programs that have an integrated parser can pass on these error messages to the user or even disallow the faulty input. If the structure of the document agrees with the structure that was specified in the DTD, we call this a *valid* document.

The notation of a DTD follows a different syntax from that of XML itself. Predefined keywords are used for the formal description of the document model in a DTD. The form of the slide model that has just been described is defined using the following instructions in a DTD:

```
<!ELEMENT slide (title, topiclist)>
<!ELEMENT title (#PCDATA)>
<!ELEMENT topiclist(topic*)>
<!ELEMENT topic (#PCDATA)>
```

The first of these elements specifies that a slide must consist of two child elements, namely `<title>` and `<topiclist>`. The comma inside the bracket defines its sequence: the `<title>` element has to appear in front of the `<topiclist>` element. Both elements have no further indication as to how frequently they occur. The default value in this case is a single occurrence. A document with the following structure

```
<slide>
    <title>Content Management Systems (CMS)</title>
    <title>Document Management Systems (DMS)</title>
    <topiclist>
    ..
    </topiclist>
</slide>
```

would then be considered invalid, as the `<title>` element can only appear once. A slide without a `<title>` element would likewise be invalid.

The `<title>` element itself consists of *parsed character data* abbreviated to *(#PCDATA)*. This means that character strings of any kind are allowed here.

In contrast to this, the `<topiclist>` element cannot consist of arbritrary characters. The `(topic*)` rule means that its child elements must be `<topic>` elements; the asterisk signifies that there must be zero or more of them. A slide that is still being worked on therefore ought to have an empty `<topiclist>`. During processing, any number of `<topic>` elements can be added, according to the DTD.

If the above definition is saved in a file called `slide.dtd`, it can be integrated into our XML document as follows:

```
<?xml version="1.0" standalone="no" ?>
<!DOCTYPE slide SYSTEM "slide.dtd">
<slide>
    <title>Content Management Systems (CMS)</title>
    <topiclist>
        <topic>What must a CMS be able to do?</topic>
        <topic>Who should use a CMS?</topic>
    </topiclist>
</slide>
```

External DTDs The line with which the DTD (Document Type Definition) is assigned to the document is called the document type declaration. The name of the root tag has to come after the DOCTYPE keyword. Furthermore, this indicates where the description of the document model can be found.

The *SYSTEM* keyword indicates that the definition is not in the file itself, but in another place. The name that follows can be a filename, which refers to the local file system, or a URL. In this case, this is known as an external DTD. In a network, even on the WWW, it is thus possible to save a definition centrally on a server and to access the external DTD from any connected workstation through a document type declaration.

standalone In the above example, the XML declaration, which is the prologue of the document, has changed. As well as this, our document is accompanied by another object, i.e. it is not *standalone*. Programs that process the document are informed by this that the document may be correctly understood, though not fully validated, without reading the external parts of the DTD.

A document that is successfully checked against a DTD known as a *valid document.*

Internal DTDs A DTD does not have to be saved in the file system. It can be included as a part of the XML document itself, as an internal DTD. It then looks as follows:

```
<?xml version="1.0" standalone="yes" ?>
<!DOCTYPE slide [
<!ELEMENT slide (title, topiclist)>
<!ELEMENT title (#PCDATA)>
<!ELEMENT topiclist (topic*)>
<!ELEMENT topic (#PCDATA)>
```

```
]>
<slide>
....
</slide>
```

Although such an internal DTD may sometimes be more convenient, an external DTD makes it easy to reuse definitions for other files and applications and to make sure that the structure of the document is retained.

At this point we can remark that document type definitions have another use besides the description of the structure of the document. Internal DTDs are often used for the automated processing of documents. Since the two requirements of automation and the reuse of definitions coincide in the creation of a document, a mixture of internal and external definitions is often found. In the following section, we concentrate on the principle of validity.

Further content models for elements

The example that we have been using up till now is very simple, and so is the DTD. There are other ways of defining elements, pertaining to the more accurate description of the frequency of occurrence (cardinality) and the sequence of elements.

As well as the comma, which is used as a sequence operator, the OR-operator is often used in element descriptions. The line

```
<!ELEMENT slide (title | topiclist)>
```

would allow either just a `<title>` or a `<topiclist>` element to be entered in the slide (but not both). The OR-operator does not however in itself have an exclusive OR-function. In the line shown above, it is a result of the combination of the OR-operator with the restriction that the elements may only appear once in our example.

Adding an asterisk to this line (to show that any number of occurrences may appear, including zero) allows any number of `<title>` and `<topiclist>` elements to be contained within the slide in any order.

```
<!ELEMENT slide (title | topiclist)* >
```

Both examples are inappropriate for use in the document slide, but illustrate the effects that the smallest changes to the DTD can have on the structure of the document that is permitted.

The following shows some variants so that you can familiarise yourself with the notation:

```
<!ELEMENT slide (title? | topiclist*) >
```

No `<title>` element, or one `<title>` element, or alternatively any number of `<topiclist>` elements.

```
<!ELEMENT slide (title?, topiclist*) >
```

An optional `<title>` element, followed by any number of `<topiclist>` elements.

```
<!ELEMENT slide (title+, topiclist) >
```

At least one `<title>` element followed by just one `<topiclist>` element.

These are the most important tags for the contents of elements. As well as these, there are also the so-called 'content models' ANY and EMPTY and the 'entity declaration' NDATA.

The content model ANY allows character strings and arbitrary defined markup in the element. In the following lines, an empty `<topic>` element is embedded in the `<title>` element.

```
<title>
<topic/>Content Management Systems (CMS)
</title>
```

The title "Content Management Systems (CMS)" is, as already described, the content of the `<title>` element. The appropriate definition of the *title* element then has to look as follows:

```
<!ELEMENT title ANY >
```

If ANY is replaced by EMPTY, the element cannot have any content. By content, however, we mean content in the form of child elements. Such an element cannot be simply subdivided further and also may not contain any content text because text always has a child relationship to the appropriate nodes. As a rule, the EMPTY content model is used when an element is just going to contain attributes. An example of this is a file that is merely used as a directory, and which refers to other files that contain the content. This is a typical use for an empty element.

```
<slide status="active" source="cms-intr.xml" />
```

The NDATA entity declaration describes elements that do not consist of character strings, but of binary coded data such as sound or images.

Here is an overview of the content types for XML elements:

Table 3.1 Content model for elements

Identifier	Meaning
ANY	Any content: Character strings or defined markup
(#PCDATA)	Parsed character data: any characters
EMPTY	No content
NDATA	Non-XML data, binary data
|	Separator for selective list (OR)
,	Separator for lists with fixed sequence
( )	Grouping symbols

continues

Table 3.1 *(continued)*

Identifier	Meaning
	(Whitespace) Exactly one occurrence
?	Zero or one occurrence
+	One or more occurrences
*	Zero or more occurrences
(#PCDATA | <.>)	Mixed content: Character strings or specified markup

Definition of attributes In addition to the description of elements, types can also be specified for attributes. In our DTD examples, they have not however been used until now.

Attributes are pieces of information about the document that are intended both for automatic processing and for human readers. They are given in the start tag of an element as `name="value"` pairs. A `name` can only appear once per element. This is one reason why attributes are specified in a DTD by means of different content types from those applicable to elements. For example, the number of times an attribute occurs does not have to be indicated since this is set to one from the start. The definition of attributes generally has the following form:

```
<!ATTLIST Element-Name Attribute-Name Type valueindication>
```

If we decide that a slide is to contain information regarding the date that it was created, we can use an attribute to do so.

```
<slide created="3.1.2000">
    <title>.....</title>
    <topiclist>.......</topiclist>
</slide>
```

This version of slide is valid with respect to a DTD with the following structure:

```
<!ELEMENT slide (title, topiclist)>
<!ATTLIST slide created CDATA #IMPLIED>
<!ELEMENT title (#PCDATA)>
<!ELEMENT topiclist (topic*)>
<!ELEMENT topic (#PCDATA)>
```

ATTLIST The first thing that appears after the `ATTLIST` keyword in an attribute definition list declararation is the name of the element for which an attribute is to be defined; *CDATA* following this, the name of an attribute is given. The `CDATA` content description allows any kind of character string as content here and because of this is equivalent to the (`#PCDATA`) specification for elements. After the description of the content comes the valid range for the values that are entered. The `#IMPLIED` keyword that is used in the example has no restrictive effect – it means that the attribute may optionally be specified by giving it a CDATA value. The processing of the document depends on whether a value is entered or not. If the input of a value for the attribute that gives information about the creation date is to be enforced, #REQUIRED is used as a tag.

```
<!ELEMENT slide (title, topiclist)>
<!ATTLIST slide created CDATA #REQUIRED>
..
```

The ATTLIST entry does not have to appear directly after the definition of the element. By entering the element name, the attribute can even be assigned if it appears much later in the DTD. If several attributes are to be defined for an element, several separate ATTLIST entries can be made. It is shorter and more legible to enter several attributes' details inside the angle brackets.

```
<!ELEMENT slide (title, topiclist)>
<!ATTLIST slide created CDATA #IMPLIED
                author CDATA "Knobloch and Kopp">
<!ELEMENT title (#PCDATA)>
<!ELEMENT topiclist (topic*)>
<!ELEMENT topic (#PCDATA)>
```

In this case, a value was predetermined for the author attribute. This has two consequences: as with #IMPLIED, a value may optionally be provided; however, the predetermined value after CDATA is used if the author attribute is not supplied. In the following document, the author attribute is missing completely.

```
<?xml version="1.0" ?>
<!DOCTYPE slide SYSTEM "slide1.dtd">
<slide  created="3.1.2000">
    <title>Content Management Systems (CMS)</title>
    <topiclist>
       <topic>What must a CMS be able to do?</topic>
       <topic>Who should use a CMS?</topic>
    </topiclist>
</slide>
```

Nevertheless, the display in Microsoft Internet Explorer 5.0, using the default stylesheet (see page 42), looks as follows:

```
<?xml version="1.0" ?>
<!DOCTYPE slide (View Source for full doctype...)>
<slide created="3.1.2000" author="Knobloch and Kopp">
    <title>Content Management Systems (CMS)</title>
    <topiclist>
       <topic>What must a CMS be able to do?</topic>
       <topic>Who should use a CMS?</topic>
```

```
            </topiclist>
        </slide>
```

Before it was displayed, the author attribute was provided with a value according to the specification in the DTD. This value was provided by the XML parser built-in to the browser.

Content type ID　　　Another important attribute type is ID. An attribute of this type has to have some value, which is unique within the document. The value must be an XML name, essentially, a string beginning with a letter and not containing any spaces. A DTD with the following form enforces the input of an unambiguous identifier for the slide.

```
<!ELEMENT slide (title, topiclist)>
<!ATTLIST slide created CDATA #IMPLIED
               ident ID #REQUIRED
               author CDATA "Knobloch and Kopp">
  . . .
```

The uniqueness of ident values can then be checked by the XML parser. If there is an error, this is reported. Explicit names are normally used for the automatic creation of links. This was also the intention of the introduction of the ID attribute type to XML.

There are also IDREF and IDREFS types, which provide a complementary facility to ID. They are used to refer to elements that have explicit ID attributes. Although there are other ways of processing XML further with XSLT in order to select contents or elements from a document, in some cases the ID cannot be left out. By using the *key(), page 208*　　key() function in XSLT, you can access elements in an XML file directly without having to use ID attributes in the document, but, when used in this way, this function is merely a substitute for the much faster id() function that does require ID attributes and therefore a DTD.

If our example document from Section 4.1 contains not just one slide but several, the most obvious way of linking content is the use of ID and IDREF. A document that has an overview of the whole lecture can use ID and IDREF as a reference system.

```
<?xml version="1.0" ?>
<!DOCTYPE slide SYSTEM "slide.dtd">
<slides>
<slide created="3.1.2000" ident="slide1">
    <title>Slides Overview</title>
    ....
</slide>
<slide created="3.1.2000" ident="slide2"
                     contents="slide1">
    <title>Introduction to the criteria</title>
    ....
```

```
</slide>
</slides>
```

Here the `contents` attribute of slide 2 refers to slide 1, since the table of contents for all slides is found there. The appropriate definitions in the DTD could look as follows:

```
<!ELEMENT slides (slide*)>
<!ELEMENT slide (title, topiclist)>
<!ATTLIST slide created CDATA #REQUIRED>
<!ATTLIST slide author CDATA "Knobloch and Kopp">
<!ATTLIST slide ident ID #REQUIRED>
<!ATTLIST slide contents IDREF #IMPLIED>
<!ELEMENT title ANY>
<!ELEMENT topiclist (topic*)>
<!ELEMENT topic (#PCDATA)>
```

It is not yet clear whether and how this referencing is used within the document. We have not yet got an example or introduced a program that could use this linking information in the document, for example to create hypertext links. All definitions that have been discussed up till now have a merely declarative character. They are passive and do not effect any actions themselves. We will therefore not go any deeper into the possiblities of defining attributes at this point.

The following table, which is by no means complete, provides an overview of the rules that are used for defining attributes.

Table 3.2 Content models for attributes

Identifier	Meaning
CDATA	Character data: text
ID	Identifier that is unique within the document
IDREF	Value of an ID in the document
IDREFS	Value of several IDs of the document as a list. Each of the values is separated by whitespace
(VALUE1 | VALUE2)	List of possible (permitted) values that the attribute can take on
"VALUE"	Default value/ preset value
ENTITY	Name of an ENTITY (cf. Section 3.5)
NOTATION	Name of a NOTATION (cf. Section 3.5)

3.3 The role of the parser

Files that contain XML data can be created using any ASCII-capable editor. This is perfectly feasible, provided you are prepared to type in all the angle brackets and slashes. This is often the simplest way of trying out small examples. However, XML structures that are typed in are not really what we want. The reason for using XML is that we want to be able to process appropriately edited content in any form automatically. The most important program for processing XML files is the XML parser. This kind of parser is contained in every application program that processes XML data. Therefore, at this point we will briefly look at the basic features of XML parsers.

The task of a parser A parser is a program that can identify structural elements in a data stream. These are often called grammatical units, which are read by the parser. Grammatical units are connected to other parts of the data stream, i.e. they are connected to each other logically. The parser has to be able to reconstruct this combination and test it to see whether it is correct. An example of processing a file in which no markup is used should illustrate this.

In traditional file processing, a file from an application program is read a portion at a time. These portions can be lines, or simply a certain number of bytes. In order to organise the content of files, even in the past, control information was inserted into them. A very simple yet extrememly wide-spread method is that of interspersing separators between the logical units in files. This way of organising the content of files is often described as "delimited ASCII". Each of the values of a line is separated from the next by a delimiter. The semicolon is frequently used for this purpose. The example slide in this file format could look as follows:

Content Management Systems (CMS);What must a CMS be able to do?;Who should use a CMS?;
...

Each value contains a slide entry. Our program for reading the content of the slide – our example parser – would see all characters up to the next semicolon as a unit and then, depending on the position, would decide which function this unit has. The knowledge about the meaning of the position has to be coded into the program as logic. For example, if the title – that is, the first position – is empty the semicolon must still be used so that the slides parser does not get confused and print a list item as a bold heading. It is clear that this file format is very inflexible and temperamental. However, because it is easy to write processing programs for delimited ASCII files, it is often used as a data exchange format.

The tasks of an XML parser An XML parser, on the other hand, has to do a lot more than this. The units that an XML parser has to identify are elements, and these can be very complex. They can contain other arbitrary embedded elements. As already described, the names of the elements are not fixed, which is why specific keywords cannot be searched for. In a DTD, rules can also be specified, which stipulate how the individual elements and their attributes have to be constructed.

It is the task of an XML parser to "identify" and check these structures. The prerequisite that an XML parser needs in order to work is that the XML should be well-formed. Therefore, the first test that has to be carried out is to find out whether this condition has been met. If this test fails, the reading operation is aborted with an error. If this test is sucessful, the parser can access elements and subtrees of the document and manipulate them. An XML parser could, for example, then be instructed to read all the <topic> elements from a file.

Validating parser   When reading through a file, there is an additional task of checking whether the definitions of the DTD have been adhered to and of reporting errors. A parser that checks a document against its DTD is known as a validating parser.

It is not much use if the parser can only read and validate a file. The outcomes of the reading process have to be useful for other processing steps or for other programs. This is why parsers have interfaces that allow application programs to make use of these abilities. For example, the developers of XML editors do not normally write program code that parses XML files. Instead, they use an already existing parser and call its interface functions to get it to take care of this work. The XML parser isolates the XML document from the application program. An XML-capable program (browser, editor) therefore always establishes contact with the data via the built-in parser. In the process, the application program calls functions from the parser, and the output of the functions are processed further by the program.

This is not a radically new technique: each Web browser has a built-in HTML parser that analyses the data stream and passes on the contents to a component of the program that generates the presentation. Although HTML is a fixed language, and therefore has a defined number of tags, current HTML parsers as a rule do not validate. There are no error messages – at most, an incorrect display of the data is produced if the HTML code is not correct.

XML API   In the case of XML parsers, the availability of standard APIs (Application Programming Interfaces) is worth mentioning. This means that a collection of function calls can be used for the manipulation of XML data independently from any particular parser.

An application program can, for example, call a function that extracts certain elements of the XML document and then returns to the application. The following illustration shows the call of a method that requests all the contents of the <topic> elements to be returned by the parser.

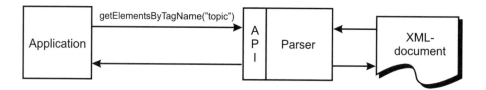

Figure 3.1 Call of an API method of the parser

The standardization of method calls as an API is one reason for the high acceptance and rapid distribution of XML technology in the field of data exchange. As a file format, XML is can accommodate arbitrary variations in the structure of the content. For the application program, defined access methods can be used. Since there are enough parsers already available, the complexity of the parsing is no longer a problem for the applications.

These days, many parsers offer two APIs for accessing XML documents. On the one hand there is the *Document Object Model* interface, or DOM API, and on the other there is the *Simple API for XML*, which is abbreviated to SAX API.

DOM

DOM-API The DOM API defines a set of interface functions that conform to the Document Object Model of the WWW Consortium. The DOM represents a document as a tree structure. These DOM definitions are not limited to XML, but can also be used to describe a HTML document. Anyone working with ECMAScript (JavaScript) can likewise use the DOM description to describe and manipulate parts of documents. A DOM-capable XML parser creates a representation of an XML file that is equivalent to a tree structure.

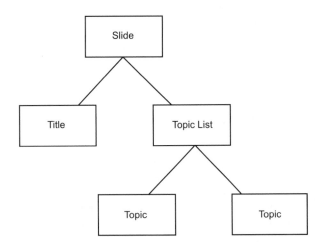

Figure 3.2 The DOM document model

A DOM parser also contains method calls that allow an application program to query whether, for example, an element has child elements, whether there are sibling nodes, whether it is the first, third or last element below the sibling and such like. These kinds of thing play an important part in the formatting process.

If, for example, a list consisting of the contents of all elements that are on one level is output, a comma has to be put after the content of each element; this comma can only be left out for the last element of the level. An application program that carries out this task will ask the parser for the position of the element that is being processed and will output a comma if one is required. This kind of information can be provided by the DOM parser because it builds up and controls the structure of the document itself in main memory. DOM parsers are handy for application programs, because the applications do not need to build up their own representation of the document. The effort and the memory requirement falls on the parser. As a result, DOM parsers tend to be memory-hungry and slow.

SAX

Simple API for XML – SAX The SAX API has a completely different view of an XML document. In contrast to DOM, it was developed especially for XML. When parsing the document, a number of events are created for each element node that is visited. A SAX parser represents an XML document as a sequence of (transient) events.

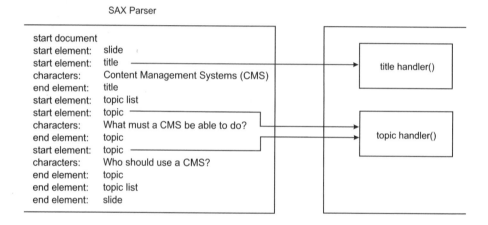

Figure 3.3 The SAX event chain

An application program that accesses a document using SAX methods initially registers itself with the parser and declares its interest to the data stream that is generated from the reading of the XML document. The program can provide a separate function for each element (`<slide>`, `<title>`, `<topiclist>`...). When reading through the XML document, the event "node found" occurs. The parser then calls the function registered by the application program, passing it the current element, and moves on.

For example, an application program may have the task of creating a DTD from an existing XML document. For this purpose, all the different elements that appear in the document are output once. The application program registers with the parser and instructs it to report each occurrence of an element. During the processing, the application program has to save element names that have already appeared once. If an element name already exists, the processing continues, if not, the new element is put into a buffer memory. When the parser reports that it has read to the end of the document, the application program can output or process the list of element names further.

This is a typical use of SAX, since a SAX parser does not have to expend resources managing a representation of the document in the form of a tree in memory; it merely has temporary access to single elements. Thus SAX parsers require less memory and can be executed more quickly than other kinds of parsers. The application program pays for this advantage with a higher level of effort on its part. It must save information from the document itself when it is passed by the parser as the corresponding event occurs.

Since this book is not a programming textbook, we will not pursue the question as to when and which API should be used, and we will not discuss the APIs themselves in more detail either. To summarise, any program that processes XML data must use a parser. The kind of parser that is used affects the behaviour of the application, its runtime, memory requirement, etc.

The type of API is not, however, the only factor that affects XML applications. Speed issues also depend on the programming language in which the parser was implemented. The majority of parsers are written in Java. Since the definition of XSL took place after the definition of XML, almost all the XSLT processors that are available at the moment are also in Java, since they must also use the parsers that are currently available.

3.4 Elements and attributes

A question that is often asked is whether elements or attributes should be used when creating documents. For example, should a <book> element be defined as follows

```
<book>
    <isbn>3-932588-13-4</isbn>
    . . .
</book>
```

or would this be better?

```
<book isbn="3-932588-13-4">
    . . .
</book>
```

Unfortunately, there is no conclusive answer to these questions. The answer depends on how the content of the document is to be structured. Also, the choice between an attribute or element often affects further processing. The following considerations may be helpful when making this decision in practical cases.

1. Attributes are suitable for placing information in the document such as, for example, author, date of creation, colour, status of the elements (e.g. "new", "freed", "checked"...).

2. Attributes are values that appear on their own and are not subdivided any further, i.e. it is less effort for the parser to test attributes. The judicious use of attributes can reduce the hierarchical depth of a document.

3. Attributes cannot be extended once they are set. Content that is to recur under the same name (e.g. <topic>) cannot be saved in attributes.

4. If XML data is to be formatted using a Cascading Style Sheet, no information that is to be displayed can be in the attributes. As is shown in the next chapter, attributes can only be used in conjunction with CSS to control formatting.

5. Attributes are more difficult than elements for a human reader and editor to use.

3.5 Using entities as abbreviations

General entity A DTD for a complex document can easily become confusing. So as not to have to rewrite recurring definitions every time, so-called entities can be used. Because of this, people usually use entities if they wish to abbreviate. Entities have a name and content. The name acts as a kind of dummy which tells the parser where the content that belongs to the name should be displayed. General entities are used to abbreviate the content of the *document,* and so-called parameter entities act as an abbreviation mechanism within the *DTD* itself. Here are two examples of this: a general entity for the definition of a copyright entry could be defined as follows:

```
<!ENTITY cr "(c) M. Knobloch February 2000" >
```

If a copyright specification is required in the XML file, the abbreviation &cr; can be entered into the data stream. The line

```
<footer> &cr; </footer>
```

is expanded by the parser to the following:

```
<footer>(c) M. Knobloch February 2000 </footer>
```

Parameter entity A parameter entity definition is used in order to make it possible to use an abbreviation within a DTD. It is written with a preceding % sign, which is followed by a blank space, and then the name.

```
<!ENTITY % xa "xml.apache.org">
<!ENTITY xaln "<link href='http://%xa;' name='%xa;'/>" >
```

In the first line, a parameter entity is defined. This is used inside the DTD in order to define a general entity (xaln). The line

```
<topic>You can find the program under &xaln; </topic>
```

is expanded by the parser to the following

```
<topic>You can find the program under
<link href='http://xml.apache.org' name='xml.apache.org'/>
</topic>
```

It is obvious that the line that has not been expanded is easier to read, but, on the other hand, the expanded version makes it easy to create a hyperlink in a transformation process.

Parsed entities   Both kinds of entities are expanded by the parser, and therefore parsed. They are described as "parsed entities". There are, however, cases when it is inappropriate for the parser to analyse the data stream. This always applies to binary data.

```
<!ENTITY myPhoto SYSTEM "smile_pig.gif"
NDATA GIF87A>
```

External entity   Here, an entity is defined that is not parsed and belongs to the category of external entities. External entities lie outside of the DTD in separate files. (An external DTD is, incidentally, an external entity.)

External and internal entities   Technically, external entities mean that to determine content, the parser has to access another file. An external entity therefore does not define replacement text, rather a file whose content is inserted in place of the entity reference. The difference between parsed and unparsed external entities is therefore important. There has to be an indication as to whether markup should be expected in the external file or not. When collections of documents are organised, the parts, e.g. the chapters of a book, are saved meaningfully as external parsed entities.

The NDATA keyword is provided for marking non-XML data in connection with a so-called NOTATION declaration. (Some tips on NOTATIONs can be found in the next section.) NDATA signals to the parser that the content of the entity is not within the scope of its operations. It cannot perform substitution of the entity name without starting a helper program that can cope with data in this format.

Important predefined internal entities are the substitutes for characters that play a part in the definition of markup. For the parser, an opening angle bracket signals the start or the end tag of an element. If this kind of symbol is to be used in the content of an XML file, this too must be coded appropriately.

Table 3.3 Codings for predefined internal entities

Symbol	Coding	numeric
<	< (less than) stands for left angle bracket	&#60;
>	> (greater than) stands for right angle bracket	&#62;
&	& (ampersand) stands for ampersand	&#38;
'	' (apostrophe) stands for apostrophe	&#39;
"	" (quote) stands for quotation marks	&#34;

In addition to the predefined abbreviations, numerical codings can always be used for all symbols. All XML parsers have to recognise these codings, even if they cannot be explicitly defined in a user DTD.

Control characters such as, for example
 for newline in Unix or   as the equivalent to   (non-breaking space) in HTML are important for transformation into text-oriented formats. Numeric entities can also be given in hexadecimal notation. For example, the predefined entity for the copyright symbol can be written hexadecimally as ©. Character coding is a very wide topic and is always particularly important if you are dealing with a non-European language. The standards for this can be found in Appendix A.4 of the XML Recommendation [XML10].

3.6   Notes on external applications with notations

What does an XML parser do with non-XML data? It does nothing. This is because a parser cannot know how an image should be displayed on the screen or how a sound file has to be processed. As described in the previous section, this is controlled with the help of non-parsed external entities. The external program that is to be used for this data (e.g. to listen to a WAV file) can be given in the following notation.

```
<slide created="3.1.2000" ident="UES" scroll="further" >
```

After this XML line describing the noise that is made when scrolling to the next slide, there is a DTD, which is quite difficult to read:

```
<!ELEMENT slides (slide*)>
<!ELEMENT slide (title,  topiclist)>
<!NOTATION WAV SYSTEM "player.exe" >
<!ENTITY further SYSTEM "clack.wav" NDATA WAV>
<!ATTLIST slide created CDATA #REQUIRED
            author   CDATA "Knobloch and Kopp"
            ident   ID #REQUIRED
            inh     IDREF #IMPLIED
            scroll ENTITY #IMPLIED>
<!ELEMENT title ANY>
<!ELEMENT topiclist (topic*)>
<!ELEMENT topic (#PCDATA)>
```

The NOTATION declaration in this DTD says that WAV files are to be processed with "player.exe". The unparsed internal ENTITY further refers to a WAV file. In our example, the entity further can then be found again as a value in the scroll attribute. From the definition of scroll as an attribute of the ENTITY type, the parser knows that the content is not a normal character string, but has to agree with the name of an external binary ENTITY declared in the DTD.

This information can be processed by applications (e.g. browsers) that have been instructed to do so. The role of the parser is merely to pass on the appropriate data to the application. Whether or not this information is used is completely up to the application. The XML specification does not stipulate that this data has to be evaluated.

A third way of describing non-XML data has already been mentioned in the discussion of processing instructions (see Section 3.1). In this case it is also up to the application program whether and how it is processed further.

3.7 XML in an XML file

A special problem arises if XML markup is to be documented in an XML file. This should be represented as a sequence of elements and therefore not be interpreted by the parser. For instance, if the text of this book is converted into XML, all the examples will have to be specially coded to prevent their being parsed. The examples can be put in a CDATA section for this purpose. This is because everything that appears in a CDATA section is ignored by the parser. This also means, however, that no entity references are interpreted. A CDATA section is embedded into the sequence <![CDATA[...]]>. An example for the description of XML topics can look as follows:

```
. . .
<topic>Examples of XML notation</topic>
<topic>
<![CDATA[
Comments begin with <!-- and end with -->
The Copyright symbol can be called with the entity
&#xA9;.
The root element of the slides document is <root>.
Not all of these are handled by the parser.
]]>
</topic>
. . . . .
```

A CDATA section thus behaves rather like a nameless, unparsed entity containing text, which can be used directly in the document.

3.8 Other ways of describing documents

The description of the structure of documents using DTDs leads, despite the possibility of outsourcing blocks using entities, to definitions that are difficult to read if the documents are complex. It is also interesting that the notation of DTD entries does not use the XML syntax, but has its own structure. Because of this, DTDs are often described as inadequate.

The WWW Consortium created a different method of description, in the form of the so-called XML schemata, which supplemented the capabilities of DTDs. An important task of schemata is to describe data types for XML, as is usual in common programming languages. When using programming languages and databases, a lot of work needs to be done if the datatype and format of a value cannot be checked automatically.

For example, many databases use a date datatype whose layout may be described by means of a format. If this kind of type were represented by an XML PCDATA element, it would not be clear whether it was actually a valid date at all, and in what format it is. Does the first figure represents a day, as is normal in European date specification, or does the year number appear at the front, like the American format? A DTD provides no way of answering these questions. Furthermore, DTDs neither set a restriction on the length of an element nor an arbitrary maximum or minimum number of times that an element can appear.

In order to eliminate these and other problems, alternatives are described in the two documents on XML schemata [XMLS1], [XMLS2], with which structures and datatypes within XML documents can be unambiguously defined using XML itself. We will not go into XML schemata any further in this book since they are not important for the understanding of transformation with XSL.

3.9 Namespaces

XML was designed for use on the Internet. Anybody can assign names of tags to elements of their own documents. Because there are so many documents from different origins on the Internet, there can easily be naming collisions. Tags such as <title> or <name> are assigned very frequently, and their use in documents that can be accessed world-wide are indistinguishable. The tag names or type names of elements or attributes are therefore as a rule only unambiguous locally, within a file.

The use of unambiguous names also plays an important part when documents or parts of documents are reused by different processing programs or when information from different sources is mixed. In order to be able to prevent ambiguity, the WWW Consortium created the possibility of declaring namespaces. A namespace is a collection of element and attribute names; the namespace itself has a name, which takes the form of a URI (Uniform Resource Identifier), and hence will be unique. A namespace thus describes an area in which a name is unique. A namespace is declared within a document by assigning the namespace's name (URI) as the value of an attribute. This attribute has a two-part name. It consists of an introductory xmlns:, which stands for XML namespace. Directly after the colon, a string which will be used as a prefix within the document is appended; this prefix can be chosen freely. This looks as follows:

```
xmlns:prefix="URI"
```

As an example, we take `<title>` from the slide. In the document we are dealing with, this tag is unique. It is more difficult if data from a list of personal descriptions is to be incorporated, for example, in order to present a set of slides about the employees of a department. How can a program decide whether the title of a slide is meant, or the title of a person? Adding a prefix such as, for example, `slide:title` or `person:title` provides a means of distinguishing. World-wide unambiguity is ensured through the use of the appropriate URI. Our definition for our slides namespace could for example look as follows:

```
xmlns:slide="http://www.Wiley.com/XML-WEB/2000/slide/1.0"
```

The namespace is valid for the element in which the attribute is given and therefore for all child elements, so long as they do not define their own namespaces.

The content of the attribute `xmlns:slide` does not have to refer to anything physical. It is not a URL, but simply a character string that is definitely unambiguous to the rest of the world. It is not practical to write this as an identifier for a namespace before each tag name. Therefore, the prefix represents the explicit name.

Namespaces play a major part in transformation scripts and we will meet them again in Chapter 6.

3.10 Further reading

A practical overview, in German, of the topic of entities can be found in [XMLSY]. Both [HAR99] and [NOR99] also contain worthwhile chapters on the topic of XML syntax, document structure, and the definition of DTDs.

Some brief information on many XML topics can be found in [ECK00], which is however no longer up-to-date for the topic of XSL.

The W3C document [XMLNS] gives information about the use of namespaces. An attempt to interpret this rather heavy document in a few pages is offered by J.Clark [CLA99].

XML and CSS

At various points in the previous chapters we mentioned that data that conforms to XML is initially "invisible" to the browser. The semantic markup does not contain any information about the presentation of the individual elements, merely details about their logical meaning. Unlike HTML, tag names can therefore be chosen freely. The price of this freedom is that these tags, unlike HTML tags, do not have fixed, typographical qualities built into browsers.

Nevertheless, there are two ways of specifying how XML elements are presented in browsers: one of these makes it possible to transform an XML document into an HTML document according to rules that have to be established specifically for each document. This procedure and its far-reaching implications are the subject matter of the following chapters in this book.

The second way, the use of Cascading Style Sheets (CSS), with which presentation features can be defined for XML elements, is dealt with in this chapter. Since we cannot cover all design methods in detail in this context, the central concepts are dealt with as examples. Particular attention is paid to the mechanisms which not only influence the appearance of elements, but can also change their content – dynamically, if necessary.

The apparatus defined by means of CSS, with which features for the presentation of individual components of a structured document can be fixed, can be used on XML documents as well as on HTML documents. In later chapters, this apparatus will be used to change the presentation of the outcome of transformations. In addition, it will become apparent that the syntax of CSS has strongly influenced that of Formatting Objects.

The mechanisms of *Cascading Style Sheets* were initially developed for HTML. They make it possible to define presentation features in addition to the minimal typographical features that are fixed and built into the browser. Presentation features are assigned to tags. This kind of assignment can be carried out not just by giving a tag's name, but also through the reference to two special attributes. This concept, which made possible a previously impossible distinction between presentation features and document structure for presentation of HTML files, can also be used on XML files. The difference is that in XML one is not restricted to the tag names defined in HTML.

4.1   The syntax of CSS statements

The information about layout that is required for rendering individual elements is usually saved in a separate file, the style sheet. You can also place style rules directly in the tag as attributes. This procedure, which is advantageous under some circumstances, is discussed briefly in Section 4.7; it results in the source code of the HTML page increasing considerably.

Container model,
cascade

The CSS specifications describe a large number of directives with which presentation features such as typeface and font size, font color and background color, positions, distances, etc. can be defined. Elements are seen as containers that can contain content – as a rule text – and/or further elements. Some of the style features that are defined for an element are passed on to its child elements. In other words, this means each element inherently has some of the style features of the element in which it is contained (background and box properties are not inherited). So that the presentation features that are defined by means of CSS can be used, the boundaries of the elements have to be clearly and explicitly defined: XML documents have to be well-formed, which implies, among other things, that the end tags must not be left out, unlike in HTML. The inheritance within the nested container is one aspect of the so-called *cascade*, which gives the *Cascading Style Sheets* their name.

Unlike XSL, the use of CSS can influence the layout, i.e. the *form* of the presentation. On the other hand, using CSS, you cannot change the *content* of a document, apart from preventing a component from being displayed. (However, since the emergence of CSS2 it has been possible to insert strings and attribute values and also to carry out computation on style attributes at the time of presentation.)

The multiple reproduction of different components (for example for an automatically generated table of contents) or a change in the relative sequence of components (such as that required for the creation of different output formats of a bibliography) is, on the other hand, not possible with CSS, which is not oriented to the manipulation of structure and content. Practical requirements have of course meant that the principles have not been adhered to: the content of an element can be supplemented via the mechanism of *generated content* (see Section 4.6).

If an XML document is loaded in Internet Explorer 5 for Windows (IE 5(Win)) without the specification of a style sheet, the browser uses a default style sheet that presents tags *and* the content of elements by using line breaks, indents, bullets and different text colors so that the structure of the document is discernible to the human eye.

```
<?xml version = "1.0"  encoding="ISO-8859-1" ?>
<slide>
  <title>Content Management Systems (CMS)</title>
  <topiclist>
   <topic>What must a CMS be able to do?</topic>
    <topic>Who should use a CMS?</topic>
```

```
</topiclist>
</slide>
```

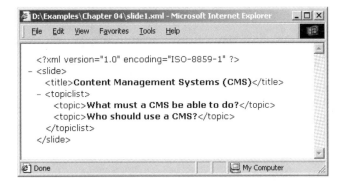

Figure 4.1 Slide 1 with the default stylesheet of IE 5(Win)

The default stylesheet of IE 5(Win) is based on XSL; it is therefore not discussed in any more detail here. If a browser is to use a user-defined style sheet for the presentation of an XML file, this must be specified using an appropriate processing instruction (PI):

PI for indicating
the stylesheet

```
<?xml-stylesheet type="text/css" href="slides1.css" ?>
```

The sequence `?xml` marks this line as a processing instruction; by adding the suffix `-stylesheet` this particular processing instruction is identified. (The form `xml:stylesheet` is also possible, cf. Chapter 3.) The specification of the `type` indicates the MIME type of the style sheet; as well as `text/css` the value `text/xsl` would also be possible. `href` refers to the style sheet file; any absolute or relative URL can be used.

If this file is loaded in an XML-capable browser, the result – providing that the style sheet file actually exists – is a presentation in which the individual elements are displayed according to the specifications of the style sheet.

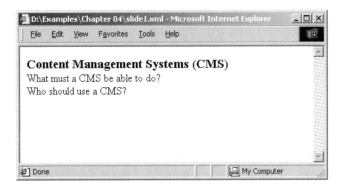

Figure 4.2 Slide 1 in IE 5(Win) using slide2.css

The style sheet responsible for Figure 4.2 contains the following details:

slide2.css
```
title {display:block; font-size:120%; font-weight:bold}
topic {display:block}
```

With these two lines, *rules* are established for the presentation of the `<title>` and `<topic>` tags.

Syntax of stylesheet instructions Each CSS rule consists of two parts: it starts with a *selector*. This specifies the tag or tags to which the rules apply. This is then followed by a *property:value* pair within curly brackets, or several separated from one another by a semicolon, which specify values for typographic and layout properties.

```
SELECTOR {PROPERTY:VALUE; [PROPERTY:VALUE; ...]}
```

In the above example, the properties `display`, `font-size` and `font-weight` were set for the `<title>` tag, and just `display` for `<topic>`. Before we talk about these properties and their values in the following section, we want to consider another style sheet and its effects:

slide3.css
```
slide  {font-family:sans-serif}
title  {display:block; font-size:120%; font-weight:bold}
topic  {display:block}
```

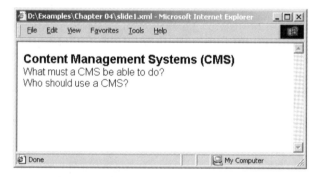

Figure 4.3   Slide 1 in IE 5(Win) using slide3.css

The `font-family` property of the `<slide>` element is defined in this example. The `<slide>` element does not contain any textual content, just the child elements `<title>` and `<topiclist>`, to which this definition is passed. This rule will have the effect of changing the font of the entire slide to a sans serif. (It will only have a visible effect if the default font of the user's browser is a serif font, as it usually is.)

If the style sheet that has been specified does not exist, IE 5(Win) uses default values for the presentation of the elements. The example slide is shown in the following:

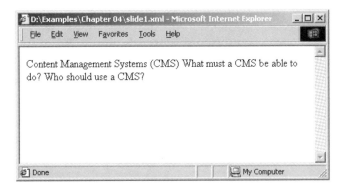

Figure 4.4 Slide 1 in IE 5(Win) using default values

Unlike the previous examples, all elements are now displayed in the default font and size without any structured line breaks.

4.2 Properties

In this section, the properties and values defined in the CSS specifications for the control and presentation of structural elements are described in overview, and explained using simple examples. Because until now there have been no browsers that support features defined in CSS1 and CSS2 completely, this section has a hybrid character. On the one hand, the specifications that are not yet completely implemented will be described on the basis of the underpinning theory. On the other, the basis of the practical examples and the illustrations are IE 5 and Opera 4.0, which can display XML files. (Netscape 6 and other browsers, such as Mozilla, which use the Gecko rendering engine can also interpret XML files). The CSS specifications are, as mentioned, partially implemented to varying degrees in the browsers that are currently available.

The possibilities provided by CSS for accessing structure elements (i.e. for the specification of selectors) are discussed in Section 4.3.

4.2.1 Classification: element type/display property

Using the `display` property, you can establish whether an element in the presentation is to be separated from its neighboring elements through a fixed text break and, if necessary, how this has to be done. In CSS1, the values `block`, `inline`, `none` and `list-item` are defined for this property. In CSS2, additional values are provided, with which an element can be characterized as a table or part of a table (column, line, cell, header, etc.).

The value `block` means that a line break is made before and after an element, whilst this does not happen in the case of `inline` elements. As the previous example shows, the default is the presentation as an inline element (this is always the case in IE 5(Win)). Elements that have the value `none` for `display` are invisible – but nevertheless still exist in the source text.

In order to show the effects these properties have, the slide that has been used till now is supplemented with lecture notes, which – depending on the style sheet used – are to be either visible or invisible:

```
<?xml version = "1.0" encoding = "ISO-8859-1" ?>
<?xml-stylesheet type="text/css" href="slide4.css"?>
<slide>
<notes>
<item>The use of CMS in the media</item>
<item>Predecessor technologies</item>
<item>Parallels in other areas</item>
<br>Coffee break</br>
<item>Strategies</item>
<item>Acquisition of content</item>
<item>Enriching content with information</item>
</notes>
<title>Content Management Systems (CMS)</title>
<topiclist>
<topic>What must a CMS be able to do?</topic>
<topic>Who should use a CMS?</topic>
</topiclist>
</slide>
```

The referenced style sheet (slide4.css) contains the following information:

```
slide      {font-family:sans-serif}
title      {display:block;
            font-size:120%; font-weight:bold}
topic      {display:block}
notes      {display:none}
```

Because the display property of the element notes is set to none, using this style sheet results in the presentation in the browser that has already been shown in Figure 4.3; <notes> and all the other elements that are contained are invisible and do not take up any space. (In contrast to the other values that are possible for display, none is inherited.) The following style sheet leads to a different presentation:

slide4.css
```
slide      {font-family:sans-serif}
title      {display:block; font-size:120%; font-weight:bold}
topic      {display:block}
notes      {font-size:80%}
item       {display:inline}
br         {display:block; font-weight:bold}
```

The default value is now used for the display property of the <notes> element, which is also assigned a font size (and through inheritance, all of its descendants are as well). The <item> elements have the display value inline and are consequently strung together without a line break. The <br> element is then detached from its environment and displayed in bold.

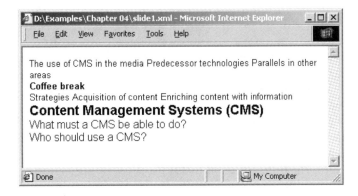

Figure 4.5   Slide 1 (amended) in IE 5(Win) using slide4.css

display:list-item   At the time of writing, the list-item value is supported adequately only by the Opera browser. Because of this, we will only give a summary of it here and then pick it up again in Section 4.7 in connection with style instructions in the tag (cf. Figure 4-23). Before and after elements with their display value set to list-item, a line break is introduced as in the case of the value block; as well as this, an additional component, a list symbol, is inserted before the element. There are four possibilities for the layout of this symbol, which can be controlled using the list-style-type or list-style-image property. Either a user-defined graphic is used, or a symbol (e.g. circle, square), which can be set using an appropriate value. The third possibility is that dynamically incremented letters or numbers are used. Finally, the list symbol can be left out. As well as this, the indentation of the new lines generated if the content of a list element is longer than the width of the screen (this can be caused if the browser window is reduced at any time) is variable (and can be changed using the list-style-position property). The three properties that have been mentioned can also be grouped together and abbreviated via the list-style property.

4.2.2   Font properties and text properties

font-family   The font-family property was used on different occasions in the previous examples. Using this property, it is possible to indicate which font is to be used for the presentation of an element and its descendants. One or several values can be given for font-family, which can be generic names (serif, sans-serif, cursive, fantasy, monospace) as well as names of actual font families (Times, Palatino, Helvetica, Verdana, Courier ...). If several values are given, these have to be separated from each other by commas and are processed from left to right, with the first one available on the client system being used by the browser to display the element's text. If there is no generic name available, and the font family that has been indicated is not available to the browser, another font family is used, but you cannot predict which one. It is therefore recommended that several actual and generic values are given for font-family.

font-weight   Using the font-weight property, the weight of the font in which the content of an element (and its descendants) are to be displayed is set. In addition to the values bold and normal, relative weights (bolder and lighter – respectively compared to the parent element) as well as a total of nine decimal values of 100, 200, 300 ... 900 can also be used.

font-size   font-size controls the size of the characters of an element its descendants. In addition to keywords, which have an effect relative to the default value of the browser that is displaying the data (xx-small, x-small, small, medium, large, x-large, xx-large), relative values referring to the parent element are also possible. These have to be either a keyword (smaller, larger) or percentages. The differentiation that is provided by specifying font-weight and font-size is not supported by all browsers.

font-style   The font-style property, with which an italic font can be activated if necessary, can be assigned one of the three values: normal, italic, and oblique. Whilst a personalized font can be used with italic (which of course has to be at the browser's disposal), the effect of oblique is generated from an automatic change of a normal font.

font-variant   By giving the value small-caps for the font-variant property, a small caps effect is obtained: All characters of an element are displayed as upper case, independently of whether they are upper or lower case letter; the font size that applies at the moment is reduced. When interpreting this style value, an attempt is made to make use of the browser's operating environment: If possible, an available smallcaps font is used, otherwise the corresponding minimized upper case letters are used by the browser. If we use the following lines in the style sheet

```
title {font-variant:small-caps;
       font-weight:bolder; font-size:larger}
```

we get the following result:

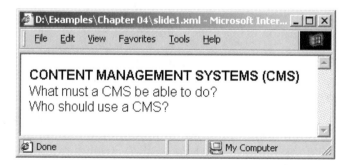

Figure 4.6 Small-caps in the <title> element

If the parent element was switched over to small-caps, its child elements can be changed back to the normal state by specifying normal.

font   Depending on the structure of the document and the depth of nesting, by using the font property you can, circumstances permitting, save yourself a lot of typing. Using this property, several font properties can be set in an abbreviated form. Since not all browsers implement this shorthand completely, it will only be mentioned briefly here. The syntax of this property is fixed as follows: values for the font-style, font-variant and font-weight properties can be entered in an arbitrary sequence. These values must be followed by a specification of the font-size. A value for line-height can be inserted after a / and an obligatory specification of the font-family concludes the shortened formulation of the font properties. Since this notation is not universally implemented, we advise against its use.

slide5.css
```
slide    {font:italic small-caps 20 verdana}
title    {font-weight:bolder}
topic    {display:block; font-variant:normal}
notes    {display:none}
```

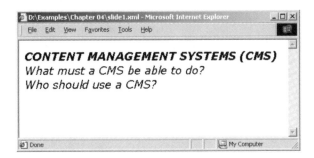

Figure 4.7 Slide 1 in IE 5(Win) using slide5.css

color Specifying the color property controls the color in which the text contained in the element is displayed. Either a defined keyword or a number triplet can be entered. The latter defines the desired color as a mixture of the three additive primary colors red, green and blue. The proportions of the mixture are defined using either decimal numbers, percentages, or hexadecimal values. In the first two cases, the values are separated from each other by whitespace, and the whole entry has to be enclosed by rgb (at the beginning, and) at the end; percentages are distinguished as such by entering the unit %. A hexadecimal triplet is characterized by a preceding #, and the three hexadecimal values come immediately after one another. Consequently, for the color *green* or *palegreen*, there are four different equally valid forms of notation:

```
color:green
color:rgb(0, 255, 0)
```

```
color:rgb(0%,100%, 0%)
color:#00FF00

color:palegreen
color:rgb(153, 250, 153)
color:rgb(65%,95%, 65%)
color:#99FA99
```

colors or mixtures of colors for which no keywords are defined can simply be entered by specifying the proportions of the mixture, that is, in one of the last three notations. When doing so, you must take into account the fact that the presentation of numerically specified colors depends on properties of the client system and is, in general, unpredictable.

In CSS2, additional abstract color specifications are provided in the form of *system colors*, with which colors that have been assigned certain functions on the client can be activated, for example: `activeborder`, the colors that contain the border of an active window, `background`, the color of the desktop, or `buttontext`, the color of the text on buttons. The use of these values therefore does not provide actual concrete colors, but instead they derive from the fact that meaningful effects can be achieved using the client-defined system colors. This makes it possible for an XML/HTML page to be displayed in harmony with the locally or personally defined preferences. In order to minimize the risk of an illegible, indiscernible presentation under these circumstances, on the one hand it is recommended never to mix system colors with other color notations, and, on the other, to use appropriate combinations of system colors for the font and background colours(e.g.: `Menu` and `MenuText` or `Window` and `WindowText`).

In the following, we will briefly point out some further properties with which the appearance of general text elements can be modified.

The `text-decoration` property can, in addition to its default value `none`, take on the – self explanatory – values `underline`, `overline`, `line-through` and `blink`. Further variations are possible with the use of the `text-transform` property (`none`, `capitalize`, `uppercase`, `lowercase`).

If the first preference of font is not available, alternative fonts can be specified, which may have other proportions. By means of `font-size-adjust` they can be adapted so that they are the same size as the font that was the first preference.

Using the `font-stretch` property, the length of a font can be changed. Possible values for this include `condensed` and `expanded`. The spaces between letters or words are varied using `letter-spacing` and `word-spacing` by using absolute or relative length specifications.

Giving `line-height` an absolute or relative measurement affects the distance between the lines. As well as these measurements, a factor can also be given. Unlike the specifications already mentioned, these are recalculated if there is any inheritance. Using `vertical-align`, the vertical alignment of individual characters and embedded illustrations can be controlled either by using keywords (i.e. `top`, `bottom`) or absolute specifications, or relative specifications referring to the current `line-height`.

Positive and negative first line indents can be obtained by means of absolute or relative specifications of the text-indent property. The alignment of the text is controlled through text-align (left, right, center, justify).

4.2.3 Box properties

All elements whose display property has the value block are considered to be in a box. This box contains – in addition to its content (which is generally textual) – presentation features, which can be changed using CSS declarations. The fundamental features of a box are three frames, which are described using the three properties padding, border and margin, which surround the text area of each block element – see Figure 4-8. (Do not confuse this sort of frame, which is analogous to a picture frame around the box, with the frames sometimes used to divide HTML pages into independent areas.) By default, they have a width of 0, and are therefore not visible. Other important features or properties of a box that can be changed using CSS are the (background) color, the dimensions, and the position.

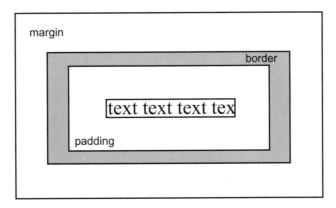

Figure 4.8 The three frames

Padding

Immediately surrounding the text of an element is the frame that is described by the *padding* specification, which fills the space between the text area and the proximate area – by default it has the width 0, so is therefore non-existent. By the proximate area we mean the border area, if a value larger than 0 has been given for border, otherwise, the margin area or, if the margin has the width 0, the surrounding element. The value of the padding property is either a number in absolute units or a relative specification referring to the parent element. In the following style sheet the value 10px is given for the padding property of the topic element. This specifies that there is a frame around the text zone with a width of 10 pixels (for the units of measurements, see Section 4.5. below). This displays on the screen as shown in Figure 4.9.

slide6.css
```
slide    {font-family:sans-serif}
title    {display:block;
          font-size:120%; font-weight:bold}
topic    {display:block; padding:10px}
```

Instead of the padding property, the padding-top, padding-left, padding-bottom and padding-right properties can also be used, with which the appropriate parts of the frames can be addressed individually. You can also explicitly address individual parts of the frame using the padding property: if two values are given, the first controls the top and bottom parts of the frame, and the second the left and right parts. If three values are given, the first applies to the top, the second to the right and the left part, and the third to the bottom parts of the frame. Finally, if four values are assigned, these are assigned in a clockwise direction, beginning at the top of the frame.

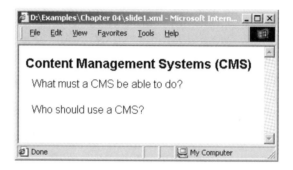

Figure 4.9   Slide 1 in IE 5(Win) using slide6.css

The interpretation of the padding property was not implemented fully in IE 5; as far as HTML is concerned, from version 3.6 and above, Opera almost completely meets the specifications.

Individual -top, -right, -bottom and -left properties are also defined in the same way for other properties of the three frames, which selectively access individual sides of the respective frames. It is also possible to set one or several sizes specifically by giving between one and three values, as described above.

border

Next, we will look at frames that are described using the border properties: the borders of the box. The border-width, border-color and border-style properties can be used to manipulate these. The CSS specifications prescribe that all kinds of elements – even those whose display property does not have the value block – have border properties available; in IE 5, however, this is only true for block elements.

border-width
The border-width property controls the width of border. Either numerical values, or one of the constants thin, medium or thick can be given as a value. If

nothing is entered as a value, a default comes into effect whose value depends on the browser. In Netscape, the width 0 is the default, whereas IE assumes the value `thin` (which is, however, only effective if the `border-style` has also been specified, since in IE 5 this property has no, or an empty default). It is recommended that, in any event, an explicit value should be given.

The width or stroke weight of a side of the border can also be specified using the properties: `border-top-width`, `border-right-width`, `border-bottom-width`, `border-left-width`. In the same way as you can for `padding`, you can also explicitly address individual sides of the frame by giving several values to `border-width`.

border-color   The `border-color` property is used to set the color of the border. The values that can be given to this property are the same as those that are used to specify the foreground or font color, which have already been discussed. Internet Explorer only interprets the values for `border-color` if a `border-style` has been specified (see below). Additionally, using this property, the color of each of the sides of the frame can be made different. This can be done either by giving between one and four values to `border-color`, or by using the properties `border-top-color`, `border-right-color` etc.

border-style   Using the `border-style` property, the style of the border is specified in more detail. There is no default for this value; one of the following constants can be given: `none`, `dotted`, `dashed`, `solid`, `double`, `groove`, `ridge`, `inset`, `outset`. In the case of HTML, Netscape only interprets `border-style` specifications if a `border-width` has also been specified (since the default for `border-width`, as already mentioned, is 0 in Netscape). By specifying one or several values (up to a maximum of four), it is also possible to selectively access individual sides of the border in the way described for the `padding` property.

The following style sheet defines a border around each <topic> element, with the width 1, the color `black` and the style `solid`.

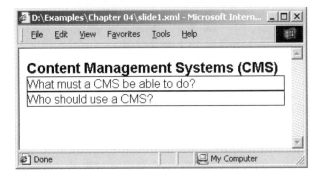

Figure 4.10   Slide 1 in IE 5(Win) using slide7.css

slide7.css
```
slide   {font-family:sans-serif}
title   {display:block;
         font-size:120%; font-weight:bold}
```

```
topic   {display:block;
         border-width:1;
         border-color:black;
         border-style:solid;
        }
```

The resultant display is unsatisfactory, since the borders of the two topic areas are touching and thus, at this point, there is a single, wide, black line. In the next section, we will be able to avoid this effect by using the margin property. A peculiarity of IE is, in contravention of the CSS standard, the fact that the borders stretch over the entire available width (which, in this case, is dictated by the width of the <title> element). A similar border specification in Netscape would be interpreted based on the width of the element in question and would lead to the expected result. In IE, the effect can be brought under control to some extent. This can be done by using the width property described further below, with which the width of an element can be set.

There is also a shortened notation for border, in which values for border-width, border-color and border-style can be given in any order and are separated by blank spaces. The same effect can therefore be achieved using the following statement:

```
topic{border:1 black solid;}
```

We now add another padding specification to the style sheet slide8.css in order to illustrate how the padding and border properties work together (using a graphically less convincing example):

```
topic{padding:20 10;}
```

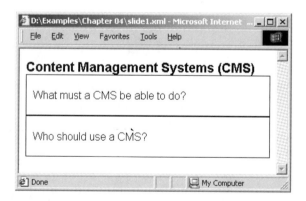

Figure 4.11   Slide 1 in IE 5(Win) using slide8.css

Before we improve the presentation of this example by using the margin property, the border-top, border-right, border-bottom and border-left properties should be mentioned, with which – in the same way as described with padding – declarations can be given for individual parts of the border zone.

margin

The outermost of the three frames surrounding the block elements is called the *margin*. The `margin` property indicates the width of this transparent frame. Either numerical values (units of measurement) or percentages referring to the parent element's box can be given as values. If no value is given, by default this frame has width 0. As is the case with the properties described previously, it is also possible to address individual sides of the margin frame specifically, either by giving one, two, three or four values to `margin` or by using the `margin-top`, `margin-left`, `margin-bottom` and `margin-right` properties. If we supplement the style sheet we used in the previous example with a `margin` declaration, the two border frames of the `<title>` elements no longer touch, since now there is a margin frame around both of them.

slide9.css

```
slide   {font-family:sans-serif}
title   {display:block;
         font-size:120%; font-weight:bold}
topic   {display:block;
         border:1 black solid;
         padding:20px 10px;
         margin:20px;
         }
```

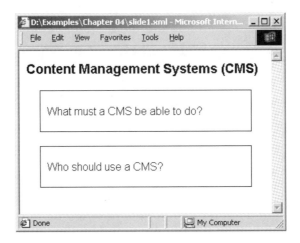

Figure 4.12 Slide 1 in IE 5(Win) using slide9.css

width and height

The *width* and *height* properties can be used to specify the dimensions of the box in which the content of an element is displayed. In addition to numbers that indicate absolute measurements, and percentages that refer to the parent element's box, the constant auto (which is the default) can also be given; this causes the browser to determine these dimensions depending on the content. If the values that are given here define a box that is too small to display the content, this box is enlarged so that it can. If the defined box is larger than is actually required, blank space is created. If we add the line width:250; to the above style sheet slide9.css for the declaration for the <topic> element, the width of the text area is explicitly fixed (and thus the undesirable effect that was seen in connection with the border property, which appears in IE 5 if the available space in the browser window is completely taken up by block elements, is avoided). If we also add the declaration height:100;, this leads to a correspondingly sized blank space under each topic.

slide10.css

```
slide{font-family:sans-serif}
title{display:block;
       font-size:120%; font-weight:bold}
topic{display:block;
       border:1 black solid;
       padding:20px 10px;
       margin:20px;
       width: 250px;
       height:100px;

     }
```

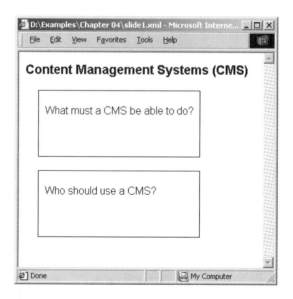

Figure 4.13 Slide 1 in IE 5(Win) using slide10.css

4.2.4 Background properties

Background properties are not inherited

The layout of the background for all elements is controlled using the background properties, which are not inherited. The background color of an element can be set using the background-color property, which can contain either the (default) value transparent or a color declaration (in the notation discussed for the color property).

If a background image is to be shown instead of a background color, the background-image property has to be used, which requires as its value the url constant followed by a URL in parentheses. The graphic identified by this URL is then used as a background for the box.

Whilst the size of a box is relative, and can change depending on the browser window, the size of an image cannot be changed. Using the background-position and background-repeat properties, you can therefore determine where the background image is positioned and, if necessary, how any empty space is to be dealt with.

Two values, separated from each other by a blank space, can be declared for background-position. These values – based on the box that was assigned the background graphic – determine the position of the top left corner of the graphic. As well as percentages and absolute measurements, the constants top, center, bottom or left, center, right can be used. These are equivalent to the percentages 0%, 50% and 100%, respectively. The default for the position of a background graphic is the top left corner of the box.

If a background graphic is larger than the element to which it was assigned, it is clipped after the declaration of background-position has been evaluated; if it is smaller, it is repeated if necessary, depending on the values that are given to background-repeat. The default for this property is repeat: the graphic is repeated horizontally and vertically so that the box in question is completely filled. Using the instructions repeat-x or repeat-y the graphic – also within the box – is repeated horizontally or vertically only. The instruction no-repeat means that the background graphic will only be output once at the position set using background-position. In all other cases, the value given to background-position determines the position from which it is repeated horizontally and/or vertically – this is important for the repetition of a large background graphic.

To illustrate the background properties we use a simple graphic, a red ball, that can be found in the file red-dot.gif, which will be used as the background of the <slide> element:

slide12.css

```
slide    {font-family:verdana;
          background-image:url(red-dot.gif);
          background-repeat:no-repeat}
title    {display:block; }
topic    {display:block;}
```

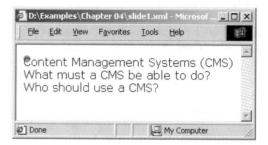

Figure 4.14   Slide 1 in IE 5(Win) using slide12.css

If the declaration `background-position:center` is added to the style sheet, the background graphic moves into the middle of the box for which it was declared. If the value `repeat-x` is given for background-repeat, this generates the following display, in which the background graphic is repeated horizontally starting from the middle of the browser window:

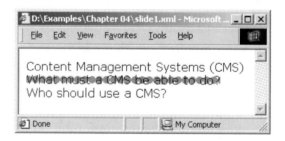

Figure 4.15   Slide 1 in IE 5(Win) using slide13.css

If the element for which a background graphic was determined is scrollable, there is the question of how the graphic should behave when the content of the element is being scrolled through. With the `background-attachment` property, which can have the value `scroll` or `fixed`, you can determine whether the graphic is to move along with the text or the box. In the first case (`scroll`), the graphic moves when the text is scrolled, in the second case (`fixed`), the content of the element, i.e. the text, scrolls over the background graphic.

Properties for controlling the position and relative movements of elements   The advanced techniques with which the position and the relative movement of elements can be controlled should merely be given a mention at this point. Using the `position` property and the `top`, `left`, `bottom` and `right` properties, which can be assigned different values, you can determine whether the position of an element is `static` or whether it will be controlled differently from the rest of the page (`relative` / `absolute` / `fixed`).

By moving their positions in these different ways, elements may end up overlapping each other. The ordering of overlapping elements in the 3rd dimension, can be controlled using the `z-index` property. By default, elements that are put into the source document later on overlap, if necessary, those that were put in earlier. Using the `z-index` property, a value (which may be negative) can be assigned to each element, which is used to determine the relative position of elements in the third dimension if there are overlaps. Elements with higher `z-index` values lie in front of those with lower values; elements with a positive `z-index` are in front of their parent, those with a negative `z-index` are behind it.

The `visibility` property can either assume the value `visible` or `hidden`. As you would expect, `hidden` makes an element invisible or transparent. Unlike the use of `display:none` the space that the element takes up is still there, but is displayed as blank space.

If an element has a defined size that is no longer adequate for its content, you can control whether the surplus is shown or whether it is ignored by using the `overflow` property (`visible` / `hidden`); furthermore, you can also have scroll bars to control the display of overflowing content, which are either on permanent display or are only shown when needed, by giving the value `scroll` or `auto` to the `overflow` property.

4.3 Selectors

In practice, the separation of content from form will only be attractive if the application and the syntax of the style sheet definition are both simple and flexible. Only if the different forms of presentation can be produced without a new and time consuming analysis and modification of the source document is a reduction of tagging to application-independent structures sensible.

In the previous section, the means that are available in CSS for controlling the display of selected components were discussed. In the following sections, we present the apparatus with which CSS makes the selection of individual components of application-independent structures possible.

In addition to the tag name that was used in all the previous examples for selection, attributes now make an appearance. These open up new possibilities for defining further "feature layers" or structure layers in a document. As well as using tag names, attributes can be used to select components and to assign specific display features to them. On the one hand, doing this makes it possible to refine the selection and its subsequent presentation: Elements that have the same name can be treated differently on the basis of their differing attribute values. On the other hand, elements with different names can be selected at the same time with less effort using one attribute and thus be treated and displayed in the same way.

The increased number of different display options which are made available by attributes such as `font`, `align`, etc. were and still are of great importance when using HTML, because these override the limitations that are imposed by the fixed restrictive stock of tag names. In an XML environment, the differentiation for which an HTML developer has to use attributes can be created by the use of appropriately differentiated tag names. Since in practice XML files will contain attributes for XSL purposes at any rate, their use in CSS will be dealt with here.

Flexible use of attributes in CSS2

Whilst CSS1 only permits the use of the attributes "class" and "ID" in selectors, there are no longer any limitations under CSS2. The names of attributes can be used freely. In addition to this, in CSS2 the values of the attributes can be called up in a more sophisticated way than is possible under CSS1.

4.3.1 Tag

In all the previous examples, structure elements were selected by declaring the corresponding tag name. In addition to this static access to single elements, CSS provides other, more flexible possibilities. To demonstrate, we first extend the slide example so that the element <notes>, which up until now only contained other elements, is supplemented with the text "Production notes, comments". In addition to this, together with the content, the <topic> elements are repeated within the <notes> element in order to form the production notes.

slide14.xml

```
<?xml version = "1.0" encoding = "ISO-8859-1" ?>
<?xml-stylesheet type="text/css" href="slide14.css"?>
<slide>
   <notes>Production notes, comments
      <topic>What must a CMS be able to do?</topic>
      <item>Use of CMS in the media</item>
      <item>Predecessor technologies</item>
      <item>Parallels in other areas</item>
      <br>Coffee break</br>
      <topic>Who should use a CMS?</topic>
      <item>Strategies</item>
      <item>Acquisition of content</item>
      <item>Enriching content with information</item>
   </notes>
   <title>Content Management System (CMS)</title>
   <topiclist>Program
      <topic>What must a CMS be able to do?</topic>
      <topic>Who should use a CMS?</topic>
   </topiclist>
</slide>
```

In order to obtain the effect show in Figure 4.16, we first use this style sheet:

```
slide      {font-family:verdana;}
title      {display:block; font-variant:small-caps;
            font-weight:bolder; font-size:larger;}
notes      {display: block; margin-top:15;
            font-style:italic}
topic      {display:block; font-weight:bold;
```

```
                           font-style:normal}
item           {display:block; font-style:normal}
br             {display:none}
topiclist      {display: block; margin-top:15;
                           font-style:italic}
```

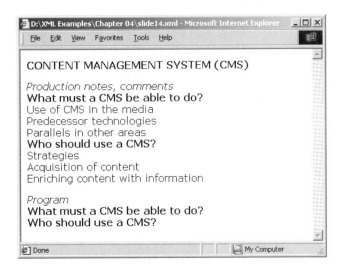

Figure 4.16 slide14.xml

Since the declarations for `<notes>` and for `<topiclist>` (the two blocks with the details regarding the program) are identical, we can choose an abbreviated notation for the description of the presentation of these two elements and, instead of two rules, simply give the following:

```
...
notes, topiclist {display: block; margin-top:15;
                           font-style:italic}
....
```

Element lists That is, instead of one element or tag, several that are to be dealt with in the same way can be given in the selector of a rule, separated by a comma.

`<topic>` elements appear in the notes block as well as in the topic list block and in both cases are displayed in the same way. We now want to display the `<topic>` element differently in the notes block and in order to do this we use the possibility of declaring the context of an element. To be more precise: we restrict the presentation features to elements that have to be contained in other defined elements.

Context The declaration of a context, i.e. of the parent element or the ancestors of an element, is carried out by means of a list of element names which are separated from one another by a blank space. The farthest element to the right meets the selection conditions if it is contained in the sequence that is given in the elements to the left of it. The selection condition

```
notes topic {color:red}
```

indicates the color in which the text of <topic> elements is to be displayed, if they are contained in a <notes> element. It augments the declaration

```
topic {display:block; font-weight:bold;
         font-style:normal}
```

and results in the display shown in Figure 4.17 (the difference between the original red and original bold black parts can also be seen in a black and white reproduction)

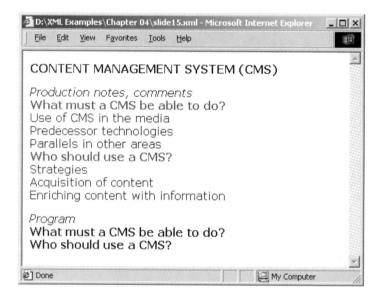

Figure 4.17   slide15.xml

In order to improve the presentation on the screen, we now add another two declarations to the style sheet:

```
notes {font-size:80%}
topiclist {font-size:120%; border-size:1;
            border-style:solid;
            border-color:black; padding:20}
```

The first – in addition to the previous definitions – determines that the entire notes block is to be displayed in a small font. The second defines the font size, borders and padding for the topic list block, which is shown in Figure 4.18.

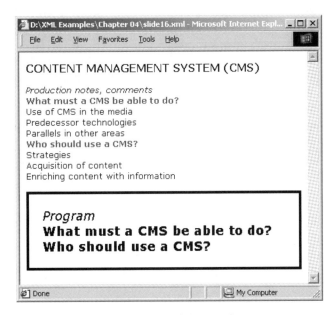

Figure 4.18 slide16.xml

The style sheet now looks as follows:

```
slide{font-family:verdana;}
title{display:block;
                    font-variant:small-caps;
                    font-weight:bolder;
                    font-size:larger;}
notes, topiclist{display: block; margin-top:15;
                    font-style:italic}
notes{font-size:80%}
topiclist{font-size:120%;
                    border-size:1; border-style:solid;
                    border-color:black; padding:20}
topic{display:block; font-weight:bold;
                    font-style:normal}
notes topic{color:red;}
item{display:block; font-style:normal}
br{display:none}
```

Classes

As we have already mentioned, like the ID attribute that is dealt with in the next section, the class attribute was developed in order to make a more sophisticated interpretation of HTML tags – and thus a more sophisticated display of HTML files –

possible. Whilst the evaluation of attributes, which is dealt with in Section 4.3.6, has only been described in the specifications and has not been widely implemented, mechanisms for the evaluation of the attributes class and ID are already available for the display of XML files in the browser. The notation used to access the class attribute in style sheets is dealt with in the next section.

We show the use of the class attribute by using two slides from the slide example. These contain the information about two blocks of a seminar and are to be displayed together. The <topic> elements in the first slide are given the declaration of class="first", those in the second have the declaration class="second".

```
<?xml version = "1.0"  encoding="ISO-8859-1" ?>
<slides>
<slide>
<title>Content Management Systems (CMS)</title>
<topiclist>
<topic class="first">What must a CMS be able to do?</
topic>
<topic class="first">Who should use a CMS? </topic>
</topiclist>
</slide>
<slide>
<title>Motive for the use of a CMS </title>
<topiclist>
<topic class="second">A large amount of content has to be
dealt with </topic>
<topic class="second">Different groups of people work
together on the same documents</topic>
</topiclist>
</slide>
</slides>
```

The corresponding style sheet contains the following rules:

slide17.css
```
slide font-family:sans-serif;}
title{display:block;
                  font-size:120%; font-weight:bold}
topic{display:block;}
.first{color:red;}
.second{color:green;}
```

Element-independent class declarations
By entering .classname, all elements whose class attribute has the value classname are selected. In the example, this makes it possible to differentiate the display of the <topic> elements so that they are displayed in red on the first slide and in green in the second (however, this cannot be seen in a black and white reproduction).

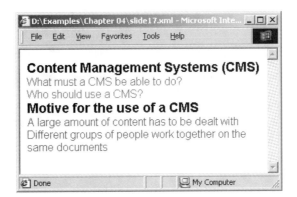

Figure 4.19 Selection of elements via a class declaration

The declaration of a value for `class` can also be combined with the declaration of a tag i.e. using an element declaration. This makes a further differentiation possible: the same attribute values can be interpreted differently depending on the element in which they are found. To demonstrate this, we give different class values for the `<title>` elements in the XML file; the corresponding lines of which then look as follows:

```
...
<title class="first">Content Management Systems
(CMS)</title>
...
<title class="second">Motive for the use of a CMS
</title>
...
```

When displaying the file structured in this way, the rules that have been used up till now should be kept for the `<topic>` elements; in the case of the `<title>` elements, the background will be green or red. The style sheet contains the following declarations:

slide17.css
```
slide{font-family:sans-serif;}
title{display:block;
                font-size:120%; font-weight:bold}
title.first{background-color:green}
title.second{background-color:red}
topic{display:block;}
topic.first{color:red;}
topic.second{color:green;}
```

The resultant display looks as follows:

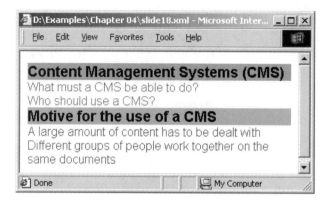

Figure 4.20   slide18.xml

4.3.2   ID

The ID attribute is used to access individual elements: Using this attribute, any arbitrary element can be assigned an identifier, which makes it possible for it to be addressed explicitly. This identifier (the value of the ID attribute) must be unambiguous, and can therefore only appear once in the document. The method of addressing elements individually offered by the attribute is somewhat contradictory to the concept of application-neutral data management. Application-neutral data management assumes the existence of homogeneous elements whose identity is to be visualized by a corresponding homogeneous presentation, separated from other groups of homogeneous elements. In practice, however, there is an obvious necessity for individualization, for the specific presentation of elements which only appear once, which the ID attribute caters for.

4.3.3   Pseudo elements and pseudo classes

The use of XML and CSS together leads to a consequent distinction between content-related structures on the one hand, and their presentation on the other. This separation leads to a characteristic reduction of presentation options: rules for the presentation of a document can only ever be formulated on the basis of the logical structures, i.e. the elements (nested if necessary) or rather their attributes.

The presentation of information
The presentation of a structured document in concrete form, such as on a Web site, cannot, however, be carried out according to the requirements of document structure alone. On the one hand, it has to be oriented towards the visual habits of human readers which are moulded by the traditions of typography; on the other hand, it has to offer controls with which the specific possibilities offered by the electronic medium for linking and navigating within the display can be used and modified.

Logical structure vs. typographical tradition
These typographical traditions include the special display of the initial letters on the first line of a paragraph: In printing, it is usual to display this part of a paragraph in another or a larger font than the rest of the paragraph. When displaying a struc-

tured element with CSS, however, the initial letter or the first line of a paragraph cannot be addressed using the tree or container structures via the element or attribute names or values that have been discussed previously. The first line is of a size which is variable and completely independent from the element, and among other things, is influenced by the current width of the browser window and the font features that have been set.

Furthermore, reading habits and layout traditions require the first element of several that are the same to be treated in a different way (with regard to distance or indentation) from subsequent elements in the layout. The differentiation that is required could be achieved by providing an appropriate `class` attribute, however, this would have the disadvantage that information regarding the layout of the document would be introduced into the markup. This can be avoided if there is a mechanism available that can evaluate relative structures in the layout and can establish that an element is the first of several elements that are the same; in doing so, CSS encroaches on the sphere of operations of XSL.

Finally, it is not possible to vary how links are displayed as a result of user activities (mouse-clicks etc.) using the selection tools that we have been discussing up to now: An element, i.e. its attributes, does not change if the mouse pointer is run over it or clicks on it.

Pseudo elements and pseudo classes were defined in order to avoid the restraints that result from the use of a markup that is not oriented to layout but merely to logical structures. They are concessions of the "pure theory" of the application-independent data markup to reality, in which the different concepts of the structuring and presentation of text or information have to be compatible with each other. Since they solve problems that arise in different areas, they are somewhat non-uniform.

Pseudo elements, along with a selecting element name, describe a part of the content of the element which cannot be described using a tree or container model and, if necessary, are constructed in the same way as a rule (`:first-letter`, `:first-line`, `:before`, `:after`). Pseudo classes describe elements either in relation to their relative position in the document (`:first-child`) or by using features that vary according to the user activities (`:link`, `:visited`, `:hover`, `:active`, `:focus`).

4.3.4 Pseudo elements

Pseudo elements describe properties that each element can have. These elements can be used to address and then formulate parts of the content that refer to the layout of or supplement the content of an arbitrary element. In CSS1 the `first-letter` and `first-line` pseudo elements are defined, which describe the first letter or first line, respectively, of an element that is displayed – in the latter case, of course, as a variable part of the whole content, depending on the width of the browser window. Pseudo elements are written down after the element to which they refer, separated from it by a colon.

```
topic:first-letter {font-size:120%}
title:first-line   {background-color:yellow}
```

The first rule determines that the first letter of each <topic> element must be larger than the others. The second rule sets a yellow background for the first line of each <title> element.

In CSS2, two further pseudo elements were defined: before and after. These make it possible to supplement the content of an element. Using the notation ELEMENT:before or ELEMENT:after, the name of the element whose content will be supplemented is indicated, as well as where in this element this will take place. The content of the addition is declared using the content property, and its value can be a string, a URL, or one of the following constants: open-quote, close-quote, no-open-quote, no-close-quote. These constants are used to control the form and existence of quotation marks. Furthermore, a reference to the value of an attribute can also be given, or a counter for automatic numbering. At this point we will only deal briefly with the two last-mentioned possibilities, which make it possible to generate content dynamically. They are presented in more detail in Section 4.6 (*Generated content*).

```
title:before   {content: "Title: "}
slide:after    {content: "End of the unit"}
```

The first rule determines that the string "Title" is to be inserted in front of every <title> element; the second rule inserts the string "End of the unit" at the end of every <slide> element.

Unlike pseudo classes, pseudo elements must only be written directly after the subject of a selector.

4.3.5 Pseudo classes

Whilst a class declaration describes the attribute value of an element to be selected, the pseudo classes (apart from :first-child) declare the status of an element to be selected with regard to mouse events. In CSS1 the :link, :visited and :active pseudo classes are defined. In CSS2, these were augmented with :hover and :focus, and the area within which :active is valid was extended. The first three pseudo classes mentioned make it possible to affect all properties of the element declared as a link (not only its color), i.e. they can be made to change depending on the status of the link (e.g. whether or not it has been visited). Furthermore, using :hover, :focus and :active the appearance of elements, not necessarily links, can be changed depending on their status. When the mouse passes over an element, :hover takes effect, whilst :focus – no more surprisingly – selects the element that has the focus, i.e. accepts input. At the moment when it is clicked on, an element, also belongs to the :active pseudo class.

4.3.6 Attributes

In theory – or rather according to the CSS2 specification – selecting elements for which the display rules are to apply can – as has already been mentioned – be controlled using arbitrary attributes or their values. The possibilities that open up as a result go beyond the evaluation of the class and ID attributes.

A selector that accesses attributes and their values is made up of two parts. The declaration of the element in question is followed by the description of the attribute in square brackets, which we want to illustrate using the example of the slide. In the process, we start with the status attribute, which will be given in the <slide> elements, i.e. the elements that frame each individual slide. The following rules demonstrate four different ways of accessing the status attribute and its value. On the one hand, its mere existence can be queried – independently from the value of the attribute. When the value is queried, a distinction is made between attributes that only have one value and those which have a list of values.

```
slide[status]          {font-family:monospace}
slide[status="new"]    {font-family:monospace}
slide[status~="new"]   {font-family:monospace}
slide[status|="new"]   {font-family:monospace}
```

The first rule specifies all <slide> elements that have a status attribute. This kind of selection criterion could be used meaningfully if the status attribute is first entered at the completion of a specific phase during the course of the construction of the slide. The second rule tests all <slide> elements that have a status attribute, and selects those whose attribute has the value "new". Unlike in the case of the following two rules, "new" cannot be one of several attribute values that are given. The third rule, on the other hand, selects the slides in which "new" is present in a list of attribute values, and whose components are separated from one another using white space. If the hyphen is used as a separator instead, the fourth rule takes effect. In other words, the third and fourth rules allow the evaluation of attribute declarations with several parts or sections. The first rule includes both the following two tags, but the second, on the other hand, includes only the second:

```
<slide status="old">
<slide status="new">
```

The tag <slide status="new kopp"> is matched by the third rule; if on the other hand the attribute status is assigned subvalues which are strung together using hyphens (<slide status="old-kopp-checked">), the fourth rule comes into effect.

4.4 Inheritance and cascade

The display features of elements can be specified in CSS by means of declarations on various levels. In addition to the features that are assigned to an element directly through style sheets, there are also the presentation features of its parent elements, which (apart from the non-inheriting background properties) each element takes on by means of inheritance.

The concurrence of inherited and specific properties may lead to a situation where there is conflict. This is resolved in favour of the specific declaration.

In addition to the passing on of properties through inheritance, there are three more hierarchical levels on which presentation features are defined and then passed on in a so-called "cascading" fashion. First, the declarations that are found in an external style sheet integrated via a LINK may also be entered directly in the head of the document (and therefore with higher priority); second, there is the possibility of incorporating further style sheets using an import instruction. These have a lower priority than all those which have been mentioned previously because of this mechanism. Last, there is also the possibility of setting display properties directly in the tag using a STYLE attribute. These have the highest priority (cf. Section 4.7).

These competing mechanisms, in particular the STYLE attribute in the tag, contribute to the incompatible requirements for, on the one hand, uniformity in the presentation and, on the other, differentiation. As you can using the ID selector, it is also possible to use the STYLE attribute to specifically address one of several homogeneous elements and customize the way in which it is displayed. In practice, these mechanisms can however only be used meaningfully if the number of "individuals" generated in this way remains manageable for the programmer or the designer. Otherwise, the advantages of the automatic generation of presentations disappear. Likewise, the person who is looking at a page does not gain anything if orientation is made more difficult by lots of different designs.

4.5 Measurements and units of measurement

Areas, distances, margins and font sizes are defined by the declaration of measurements. According to the CSS specifications, values that have no unit of measurement should be ignored – so long as the value is not a factor which can be interpreted without a unit of measurement (e.g. line-height). For absolute declarations, the decimal units of measurements cm, mm, as well as inches (in) and traditional printers' units such as pt (point = 1/72 in) and pc (pica = 1/6 in) can be used.

For relative measurements, in addition to percentages, the units em and ex are available, as well as keywords that are used for the font-size property, for example. The unit em reflects the height of the font that is being used. If it is used in measurement declarations that do not refer to fonts (e.g. padding declarations), the height of the font is based on that of the corresponding element through inheritance – even if this element does not even have any textual content.

In contrast to em, ex indicates the height of the letter "x" in a concrete font. Like the em, this unit is thus not an absolute value, but depends on the font.

The unit of pixels (px) refers to the smallest picture element that can be shown on the screen. For printing, which in general has a higher resolution than the on-screen display (in a printout there are more pixels than there are in the same area on a screen), the pixels are multiplied accordingly by the browser.

Despite the stipulation of the CSS specification given above, in practice, measurement declarations without units not ignored by most browsers, but are instead interpreted as pixel specifications.

4.6 Generated content

At first glance, the insertion of dynamically generated contents appears to go beyond the definition of presentation features and thus the objectives of CSS. On closer inspection, it turns out that there are parts of the text that can be used in a similar way to the layout to express the internal structure of documents, and therefore cannot be counted as content. In addition to the list symbols in the narrow sense (bullet / rhombus / circle – to name just a few) there are of course list enumerations. Like list symbols, these are always implicitly available, but are not simply static. In fact, they have to be successively incremented and, if necessary, have to be able to change if additions are made to the content. Just like the definition of specific quotation marks (which vary from language to language) these functionalities are mentioned here, but are not discussed in great detail. However, the insertion of static and dynamically generated strings using CSS will be presented here briefly.

4.6.1 Inserting strings

The `content` property, with which content can be inserted in front of or after an element, was mentioned in Section 4.3.4 in connection with pseudo elements. A selector, which has the form `ELEMENT:before` or `ELEMENT:after`, respectively, specifies the element and, within this element, the position at which the content is to be inserted. The content is declared using the `content` property, whose value is a string enclosed by quotation marks.

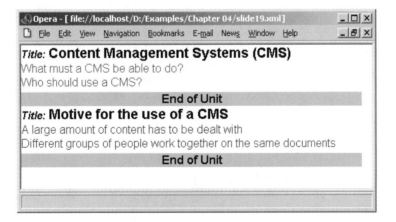

Figure 4.21 slide19.xml in Opera4.

slide19.css

```
    . . .
title:before {content: "Title: "; font-style:italic;
                font-size:80%;}
slide:after  {content: "End of Unit"; display:block;
                margin-top:5; font-weight:bold;
            background-color:lightskyblue; text-align:center}
```

The first rule specifies that the string `"Title:"` should be inserted before each `<title>` element. It also specifies that it should appear in italics at a font size of 80%; the second rule inserts the string `"End of Unit"` at the end of each `<slide>` element. This string is set as bold and is set against a blue background. Using this mechanism, static text, i.e. text that stays the same and whose wording is known when the style sheet is written, can be inserted into a document, or rather into a particular element. The mechanism described in the following section goes considerably further, and makes it possible for attribute values to be inserted into the presentation.

4.6.2 Inserting attribute values

As well as permitting the selection of elements through the existence and values of arbitrary attributes, the extended evaluation of attributes in CSS2 opens up further areas of use. In conjunction with the `content` property, arbitrary attribute values can now be introduced into the presentation of a document. We explain this mechanism, with which documents can be dynamically generated to a limited extent, using an `author` attribute in the `<slide>` tag, which here has the value either `"knobloch"` or `"kopp"`:

slide20.xml

```
<?xml version="1.0" encoding = "ISO-8859-1"
  standalone="yes"?>
<?xml-stylesheet type="text/css" href="slide19.css" ?>
<slides>
<slide author="knobloch">
<title>Content Management Systems (CMS)</title>
<topiclist>
<topic>What must a CMS be able to do?</topic>
<topic>Who should use a CMS?</topic>
</topiclist>
</slide>

<slide author="kopp">
<title>Motive for the use of a CMS</title>
<topiclist>
<topic>A large amount of content has to be managed
</topic>
```

```
<topic>Different groups of people work together on the
documents</topic>
</topiclist>
</slide>
</slides>
```

The referenced style sheet has the following content:

slide20.css

```
slide{font-family:sans-serif; display:block;
                border-size:1; border-style:solid;
                border-color:gray; margin-left: 10;
                padding-left:10; margin-top: 20}
title{display:block;
                font-size:120%; font-weight:bold}
topic  {display:block;}
topiclist{display:block}
slide:after{content: "Responsible:" attr(author);
                display:block;
                font-style:italic;
                margin-top: 10; text-align:left}
```

In Opera 5.0 this is displayed as follows

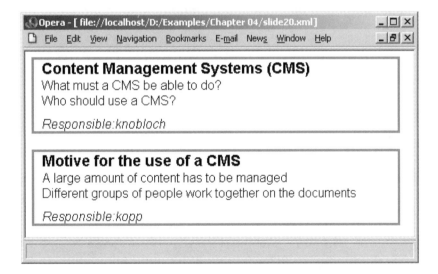

Figure 4.22 slide20.xml in Opera 4. The details about the author shown by the browser were generated from an attribute value using a style sheet

4.7   Style declarations in the tag

It has already been mentioned on various occasions that style properties can not only be written in an external style sheet, but also directly in the tag. This procedure will usually lead to redundancies, since many occurrences of the same tag will have identical style information, and thus the source code becomes unnecessarily long. Nevertheless, the manipulation of style information in tags, circumstances permitting, can be useful if the different occurrences of the same element are to be displayed differently – without the ID selector and appropriate global adjustments to the style sheet being used to do so.

In order to illustrate this, using the following style sheet we will first specify global presentation rules for the whole set of slides: Usually, the font family Verdana should be used. The <title> elements will be displayed larger, in bold, and in yellow.

slide21.css
```
slides{font-family:verdana}
title{display:block; color:yellow;
                font-size:120%; font-weight:bold}
topic{display:block}
```

As in all the previous examples, this style sheet is referenced from by an XML document. In addition, in some opening tags of this document, there are also STYLE attributes, with which presentation rules are formulated – partly as a supplement to and partly in competition with the declarations in the style sheet: The <title> elements contain other color declarations, and likewise each <topic> element is characterized as a list-item. The last of these is displayed in blue.

slide21.xml
```
<?xml version = "1.0" encoding ="ISO-8859-1"
  standalone="yes"?>
<?xml-stylesheet type="text/css" href="c5_7.css" ?>
<slides>


...


<slide>
<title style="color:red">Content Management Systems
(CMS) </title>
<topiclist>
<topic style="display:list-item">What must a CMS be able
 to do? </topic>
<topic style="display:list-item">Who should use a CMS?
</topic>
</topiclist>
</slide>

<slide>
```

```
<title style="color:green">Motive for the use of a CMS<
title>
<topiclist>
<topic style="display:list-item">A large amount of
content has to be dealt with</topic>
<topic style="display:list-item; color:blue">Different
groups of people work together on the documents</topic>
</topiclist>
</slide>

    . . .

</slides>
```

Figure 4.23 shows that (because of the priority rules of the cascade) if there is a conflict, the declarations in the tag have higher priority than those in the style sheet. The `<title>` elements and the last `<topic>` element are displayed in the specified colors, every `<topic>` element is reproduced as a `list-item`.

For further slides, which are neither given in the source code nor in the reproduction of the browser here, the globally valid (and graphically less meaningful) declarations of the style sheet would however be effective.

A possible use for this mixed strategy would be the automatic generation of XML files, in which – depending on the content of certain elements – local style declarations are inserted in the tags. We are thus touching on the problems of the transformation and modification of XML data, which is dealt with in the following chapters using much more powerful mechanisms.

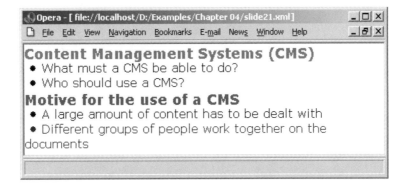

Figure 4.23 Style declarations in a style sheet and in the tag

5

XSL

This chapter provides an overview of the three topic areas that the WWW Consortium describes under the name of eXtensible Style Language (XSL). Following a schematic overview of the process of a transformation, we will explain how to use the tools with which the examples of this book were created.

Topic areas of XSL   XSL was planned as a style language, that is, as a formatting language for XML. During the definition of XSL, the experiences that were gained from Cascading Style Sheets for HTML came in very useful, as did those from the very powerful Transformation language DSSSL (a formatting language for SGML).

During the development of XSL, it was found that three complex tasks had to be taken care of in the definition of the layout language.

XPath • The task of developing a notation for the identification of parts of documents was solved by the XPath specification [XPATH]. The recommendation of the WWW consortium for XPath describes an addressing schema, which, along with its own document model, has become accepted in other parts of the XML specification family (XPointer, XML Query Language). Within XSL it serves as a sublanguage for the transformation language XSLT.

XSLT • Syntax and semantics were defined as control instructions for a universal XML transformation program in the WWW consortium Recommendation of a transformation language for XML [XSLT]. This transformation program is called an XSLT processor. XSLT thus has the function of a script language. The control files which contain XSLT code, are usually described in the literature under the name of style sheets.

Formatting Objects • According to the beliefs of the WWW Consortium, an appropriate use of the combination of XPath and XSLT is to create documents that contain formatting instructions. The third part of the XSL specification [XSL] describes the so-called Formatting Objects (FO). Formatting Objects are tags which control a formatting process.

The combination of XPath and XSLT can also be used independently of XSL. This combination is frequently used for the creation of HTML pages. However, XSLT and XPath are also being increasingly used to convert the structure of available data into other structures. Strictly speaking, XSLT has nothing to do with formatting, i.e. with style. The name was arrived at because the WWW consortium wanted to develop a substitute for Cascading Style Sheets and DSSSL.

5.1 XPath

Navigation in the document using XPath

XPath expressions are used to navigate through the source document. A parser reads the elements of an XML document in the order in which the document is constructed. This ordering of the elements in a document is called document order. The XPath working group of the WWW Consortium defined an interpretation of an XML document, which abstracts from the document and offers optional access to parts of the document.

A program that implements the XPath specification such as, for example, an XSLT processor, builds up a representation in the form of a hierarchical structure made up of nodes when it is reading in an XML source document. This document model is very similar to, but not identical to, the DOM. All subsequent procedures consequently do not work on the document itself, but on this abstraction of the source document, which is often referred to as the source tree or the input tree.

XPath expressions

In order to ensure free access to all parts of this tree, XPath defines expressions which make it possible to address subtrees, elements, or attributes. For this purpose, XPath uses path expressions, which have a similar appearance to path specifications in file systems:

```
/slide/topiclist/topic[2]
```

This XPath expression describes, for example, the second <topic> element within the <topiclist>. In the following document, the element thus described is shown in bold.

```
<?xml version="1.0" encoding="ISO-8859-1" ?>
<slide>
    <title>Content Management Systems (CMS)</title>
    <topiclist>
        <topic>What must a CMS be able to do?</topic>
        <topic>Who should use a CMS?</topic>
    </topiclist>
</slide>
```

For the description of the input tree, XPath defines its own system of names. These names are reflected in the XPath functions and will be briefly explained at this point.

Node types

XPath represents the elements and attributes of an XML document in nodes. These nodes are broken down into different types which are shown in the following list:.

• Root node

- Element node

- Text node

- Attribute node

- Namespace node

- Processing instruction node

- Comment node

Evidently, even comments are of interest. When creating an XML file, comments are normally only entered for the human editor. It is perhaps surprising that they should be the explicit object of mechanical processing by style sheets. The same applies to processing instructions. They too are not actually relevant for potential formatting. An important use of XSLT is, however, the generation of XML files from XML files that already exist, like copying of sub-documents. For this purpose, the addressability of these seemingly unimportant elements is necessary.

Node descriptions   In order to describe the current location within the input tree, we talk about the *current node*. For the moment, we set <topiclist> as the current node.

In accordance with the XPath naming convention, we talk about a *parent node* and *child node* to describe hierarchical *ancestors* or *descendants*.

The current node is always understood to be part of a set of nodes that were described via a selection. This list is called the *current node list*. The current node <topiclist> is part of the list of child elements of <slide>.

Nodes that are on the same hierarchical level are *siblings*. In the sequence of processing, there is a distinction between *preceding siblings* and *following siblings*.

When going through an XML document, the current node property shifts through the nodes of the tree that represent the XML document, starting from the root element of the input document. This movement throughout the tree can be influenced by XSLT instructions.

We understand that various working groups of the WWW Consortium had to solve similar problems when describing parts of documents. When creating a query language for XML (Extensible Query Language, XQL) and during the specification of how hyperlinks can refer to XML documents and parts of documents, the question arose of how to name the location of an element or a group of elements – or, to put things more technically – how they can be addressed. Because of these connections, outcomes from the work on XQL and XLink/XPointer have flowed into the XPath specification. On the other hand, the XPath notation is used for the description of the targets of links in XPointer notation. An XPointer expression consists of a URI+XPath expression.

Nevertheless, XPath is not a complete query language. The retrieval of parts of documents does not only take place on the level of elements and attributes. A full text search, for example with dummy symbols in terms of regular expressions, is cannot be expressed as an XPath expression.

For the construction of an output structure for formatting or other kinds of further processing, the existing capabilities of XPath do, however, offer a wide range of functions. In the next chapter, only simple XPath expressions will be used to begin with.

5.2   XSLT

Processing logic using XSLT

Whilst XPath is used for navigation in XML input documents, XSLT describes the sequence in which the source document is traversed, and how to control the frequency with which this is done. The aim of repeating output sequences or outputting modified input data repeatedly makes control structures such as loops, conditional processing, sorting possibilities etc. necessary. These functions are established in the specification of "XSL Transformations (XSLT)" [XSLT]. XSLT transforms XML into XML or into an XML fragment. The task of an XSLT transformation is to create an output data stream (output tree or result tree) from an XML document which contains information for a downstream formatter or other downstream processes. A structure that contains information for formatters is called a formatting tree. The sequence and the number of elements in this formatting tree can differ greatly from the input document. In practice, owing to the lack of a formatter, this use as a preliminary stage for a formatting process is currently not the main area of use for XSLT processors. For the creation of HTML, only the general result tree is used.

The XSLT Recommendation was adopted in November 1999

With the help of XSLT control structures, it is possible to use XPath expressions that are repeated or controlled by template rules, and thus address parts of the source document. Sections or elements of the source document can be "retrieved" as often as desired and can be output at different points of the formatting tree. The keywords sorting, repetition, selection and addition of new contents indicate the possibilities of XSLT.

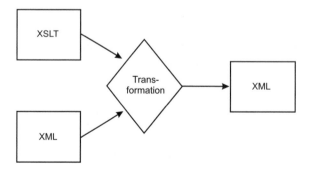

Figure 5.1 Transformation for output in browsers

XHTML documents are special. HTML was defined as XHTML, i.e. as an XML application, at the start of 2000. At present, XHTML is nothing more than HTML 4.0.

written in XML-conforming notation. Further development of HTML by the WWW Consortium will occur on this basis. The initials HTML and XHTML are therefore used without any distinction in the following.

The outcome of an XSLT transformation can be XHTML. This form of transformation produces a result that can be displayed immediately by current browsers. Since the output result is another XML document, in this case it needs no further processing. In all other cases, the output has to be processed further for it to be displayed. The rendering by the browser is the further processing of the X(HT)ML document. Within the transformation, CSS code can also be generated in the HTML document. Above all, in the case of Web pages that are modified frequently, this can mean a rationalization, by not writing such pages, but changing a content container (XML) into HTML using a transformation.

Output of XML fragments   A wide range of XSLT applications arises from the possibility of outputting an XML fragment. A fragment simply means a sequence that would represent well-formed XML as long as there was an enclosing element present. Because of this, text-based formats of any shape can be created. These could be shell scripts or batch files, as well as code for interpreted programming languages such as, for example, Perl, PHP or even SQL instructions. The output data in these cases is not in a form that can be displayed or printed directly. Using XSLT, one is not therefore restricted to the production of end-user documents.

For all the aforementioned applications, it is common for the use of XSLT to reduce the time taken for maintenance of content. The XML source file only contains relatively few tags, and these organize the content. Through the use of a transformation script, the contents for the respective use-context are generated. When changes are made to the contents of the source document, names remain consistent. Because of this, the complexity of the output document can be decoupled from people that only want to maintain the contents. To some extent, this applies to control files for formatters. Files containing Postscript code or Rich Text are normally compiled by appropriate programs and are not written manually. XSLT processors are to do the same for Formatting Objects.

5.3 XSL and Formatting Objects

In the narrow sense of the word, formatting is the third problem area that is dealt with by the XSL specification [XSL].

By means of a transformation, format control instructions – so-called Formatting Objects (FO) – can be inserted into the formatting tree. The specification of formatting is therefore often described using XSL:FO. The abbreviation XSL is also used for the description of Formatting Objects.

The the XSL:FO Recommendation defines elements and attributes that include many of the familiar constructs from Cascading Style Sheets and in some places extends them. The FO elements and attributes in the formatting tree are changed into a final file format by a further process, namely the formatting process.

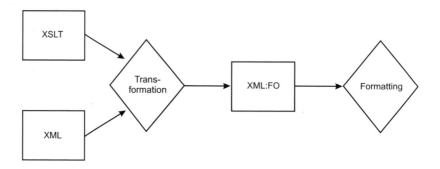

Figure 5.2 Transformation into a tree structure using Formatting Objects

The result of the transformation does not have an output medium or a specific file format. The downstream formatting program is therefore given a data stream as input, which only contains information regarding the page size, fonts, colors, etc. From this information, a formatting program for PDF creates PDF files. Another formatting program, for example for RTF, only creates RTF files. And so on.

An XSL:FO processor is a specialized program that recognizes the FO file structure and converts this into its specialized document format. As a rule, a formatter only recognizes its own document format as legal input. The data is only bound together into a document format by this last step of the formatting. All the preliminary steps are open to other ways of processing, further transformations and further forms of presentation.

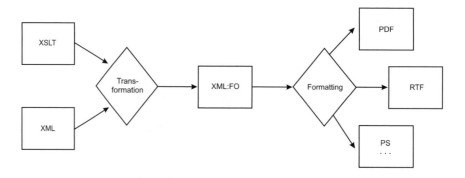

Figure 5.3 Conversion of an FO document into a special output format

Only the future will show whether the software industry is ready to make formatters available for their file formats. The sub-project FOP (Formatting Objects for PDF) of the xml.apache project is working on a formatter for PDF, i.e. on a program that changes a formatting tree into a PDF document. It is the intention of FOP to provide a full implementation of the basic conformance level of the XSL:FO standard, but at the time of writing, it still has some limitation. So far, there have only been very few commercial systems.

Because of this, we only have a rough picture of XSL: With the help of XPath expressions, XSLT extracts data from the source document and outputs it in a modified form. The modified output is a tree structure in the form of XHTML documents or XML fragments, which are processed in other ways. Alternatively, the output can be an XML document in which formatting instructions are generated. In this case, a formatting program processes the content to a specific format.

The control instructions for this process are saved in style sheets, which, due to their power, should more appropriately be called transformation scripts.

The topics of XSLT and XPath will be introduced in more detail in the next chapter. But first, let's say a few words about how an XSLT processor processes XML source data and XSL style sheets.

5.4 The process of a transformation

In an XSLT transformation, an XSLT processor processes an XML input file (better called an input data stream) with the help of an XSL style sheet file, which is used as a control file.

You could imagine the function of an XSLT processor like that of a zip fastener. A new strand of information is put together out of two XML documents, the content file and the style sheet. This synthesis then contains information from both sources as a new entity. Since the output can conform to the specification of XML, it can be used as a source for further transformations.

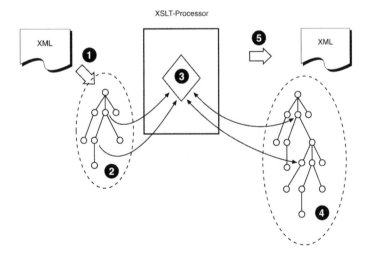

Figure 5.4 The process of an XSLT transformation

During an XSLT transformation, the files that are being processed go through four states. Figure 5.4 attempts to illustrate these. The source of the control instructions, the XSLT style sheet, is not taken into account.

- First, the input data is in the form of an XML file (or of a query result).

- The input data is deserialize (1) and represented in main memory in the form of a tree. The XSLT processor works with this input tree (2) and not with the file.

- The outcome of the transformation process (3) is also kept in a tree structure in memory. This is described as an output tree (4). The XSLT processor creates this structure, but also uses it for further processing. Some XSLT instructions use parts of the result tree (result tree fragments).

- The output tree is serialized into an output target, normally in an output file (5). Depending on the character of the processor, this may also support manipulations when writing to the file. For example, the XSLT specification allows an XSLT processor to change namespace specifications when writing to the file.

The processing of an XSLT transformation uses the input tree, the result tree and the output target. The different XSLT instructions affect these components in different ways. This is the topic of the next chapter.

Assignment of
style sheets to
XML documents
The connection between the XML file and the XSL style sheet is declared using a processing instruction. This is no different from the integration of a CSS file.

```
<?xml-stylesheet type="text/xml" href="example.xsl" ?>
```

An XSLT processor is a program that is able to interpret the XSLT and XPath keywords, instructions, and functions in style sheets. The processor itself does not offer an API, but is simply an application program that works with a parser or the API's parser. As a rule, XSLT processors have interfaces that allow a call from application programs. For the examples in the book, we use the command line call of the XSLT processor Xalan.

For this reason, the example transformations in this book deal with batch processes or Shell scripts. Compared to an integration of the processor into an application such as, for example, a browser, this method unfortunately stands out because of its poor execution times. It does, however, have the advantages of being easier to comprehend and reproduce: what works on the command line level, can also be used quite easily in the program environment. The location of the execution is thus neither fixed to the server nor to the client (browser). Execution from command lines is therefore very well-suited for testing style sheets.

Web design with XML basically means the definition of XSLT scripts which determine the assignment of HTML tags, CSS selectors, formatting objects, or other markup to the elements of the source tree. What can be found in the style sheet?

Content of
XSLT style sheets
A style sheet contains the transformation instructions and the description of which instruction is assigned to which element of the source file. Transformation

rules and assignments are described using XSLT and XPath. An XSLT script contains a number of templates and, within these, instructions define the details of the processing.

```
<xsl:template match="slide">
   <!-- instructions, output-elements...-->
   <xsl:for-each .....>
     <!-- even more instructions, output-elements... -->
     ...
   </xsl:for-each>
</xsl:template>
....
```

Assignment of processing templates by pattern recognition

Through the definition of a pattern in a template's definition, such as, for example `<xsl:template match="slide">`, the template can be assigned to an element of the XML document.

If, during processing, the XSLT processor runs into the relevant pattern that corresponds to the current node of the input tree, the instructions within the template are used on this node. Its content is evaluated, the instructions executed, and the results output. A short example will illustrate this.

```
<?xml version="1.0" encoding="ISO-8859-1"?>
<slide>
    <title>Content Management Systems (CMS)</title>
    <topiclist>
      <topic>What must a CMS be able to do?</topic>
      <topic>Who should use a CMS?</topic>
    </topiclist>
</slide>
```

Our simple slide is to be converted into an HTML document. The rules that are used for this can be found in the following style sheet. The elements in this example that you are still not familiar with will be explained in Chapters 7 and 8. For the time being, only pay attention to the definition of the templates on the lines in bold.

Figure 5.5 Transformation of a simple slides document

```
<?xml version="1.0" encoding="ISO-8859-1"?>
<xsl:stylesheet version="1.0"
      xmlns:xsl="http://www.w3.org/1999/XSL/Transform">

<xsl:template match="slide">
    <html>
        <head><TITLE>First demo</TITLE></head>
        <body ><xsl:apply-templates /></body >
    </html>
</xsl:template>

<xsl:template match="topiclist">
```

```
       <ul><xsl:apply-templates /></ul>
    </xsl:template>

    <xsl:template match="topic">
       <li><xsl:value-of select="." /></li>
    </xsl:template>
    <xsl:template match="title">
       <h2><xsl:value-of select="." /></h2>
    </xsl:template>
  </xsl:stylesheet>
```

In each template HTML markup is defined, which is output if the element described in the pattern is met. Within a template, it is defined whether HTML tags are immediately output or whether the work will be delegated to further templates. The latter is achieved with the help of the `match="xyz"` attribute within a `<xsl:template ...>` element and the `<xsl:apply-templates...>` instruction. In the case of this rule-driven way of activating individual templates, we talk about template rules. It is also possible to call a template directly.

The cooperation between the XML parser and the XSLT processor

When going through the source document, the XSLT processor uses the XML parser. If this returns an element that is equivalent to a `match` expression, the instructions of the corresponding template – that is, whatever appears between `<xsl:template>` and `</xsl:template>` – are applied. Each template can contain markup and data that is copied from the source document into the new document. A single template cannot, as a rule, work through the transformation instructions for all elements of an XML document. Using the XSLT instruction `<apply-templates>` the XSLT processor can therefore be told that further templates will be looked for, which contain a `match` expression that suits the current element more accurately. For example, in a document, the `<topic>` element could appear as the child of `<topiclist>` and as the child of a `<paragraph>` element. In this case, there will probably be several templates that allow for the `<topic>` element in its context. There are more details about this in the next chapter. First, the following section will introduce the installation and use of the tools.

5.5 Tools and aids

All examples were created using version Xalan 1.2D02 and Xerces 1.1.3

At this point, a few tips are offered regarding the definition of a work environment which make it possible to reproduce the examples in practice. The Xerces parser and the XSLT processor Xalan from xml.apache.org are used as the basic tools. These tools are freely available. Download Xerces and Xalan and take note of the terms of the licensing agreement.

The tools we have mentioned are used in their Java versions. Make sure that you have installed a Java runtime environment (available at java.sun.com) on your computer. In a command line environment, it should be guaranteed that the Java VM is available by calling `java` or `jre` (java runtime environment). This can be es-

Unpacking using jar

tablished easily by entering `java -version`. The call should create a message which looks something like `java version "1.2.2"`.

Unpack the most recent version of the Xerces parser and of the XSLT processor Xalan into a directory of your choice with the instructions:

```
jar -xvf xalan_0_19_2.jar
```

The unpacking process normally creates a subdirectory. If not, do this beforehand. Using the option `-t` in the call

```
jar -tvf xalan_0_19_2.jar
```

you can obtain an insight into the structure that the unpacking process has created. Amongst other things, the unpacking process produces a file called `xalan.jar`. This is a program library that contains an XSLT processor. Newer versions of Xalan are normally also offered as a ZIP files. In this case, the file will need to be unpacked using a decompression program.

CLASSPATH entries

In order to use Xalan, a `CLASSPATH` variable has to be defined. Under the Windows versions, you can use the `set` command in a DOS window to manipulate the `CLASSPATH`. If Xalan was unpacked under `E:\xml` and `xalan.jar` was saved there

```
SET CLASSPATH=E:\xml\xalan.jar;
```

achieves the desired effect. A similar method is used for all other tools (Xerces, Formatting Objects for PDF FOP). A `CLASSPATH` to Xerces is also necessary even if 'only' the XSLT process Xalan is being worked with, since an XSLT processor always uses a parser to read through the input document. When using a Java VM older than version 1.2.x, another `CLASSPATH` entry to `classes.zip` is also required.

The call of Xalan from the command line to process the XML file `my.xml` using the associated transformation script in `my.xsl`:

```
java org.apache.xalan.xslt.Process -v -xsl my.xsl
-in my.xml -out my.html
```

The result is written in `my.html`. Of course it is tiresome to have to type this kind of thing every time. Therefore a batch file (or under Unix/Linux a Shell script of course) should be created for this. As an example, we will use a DOS/Windows batch file. (Unix/Linux users do not get an explicit example for a Shell script, but they should know whether they need to use `EXPORT` or `SETENV` or whatever else.) On this occasion, we also temporarily set `CLASSPATH` so that we do not have to adapt the whole system to possibly changing libraries.

```
set savedCLASSPATH=%CLASSPATH%
set CLASSPATH=xerces.jar;xalan.jar;%CLASSPATH%
java org.apache.xalan.xslt.Process %4 %5 %6
-v -xsl %2 -in %1 -out %3
dir %3
```

```
@echo off
set CLASSPATH=%savedCLASSPATH%
```

The environment variable `savedCLASSPATH` records the present path, after which the entry is saved in the necessary libraries which, in the above configuration, are found in the current directory. The call of the processor is carried out using values that are submitted to the batch files as parameters (`%1 %2...`), where, for reasons of personal preference, the first parameter during the call is the XML file, and the second is the XSL file. Finally, the outcome of the transformation process is shown, and the `CLASSPATH` variable is set back to its original value. Therefore the call of the previous example can be shortened to the following more readable line:

```
transform my.xml my.xsl my.html
```

You may have noticed that Xalan also accepts other parameters (`%4 %5 %6` in the batch file) in front of the file details. Calling the processor without parameters causes it to notify the user of other existing control parameters.

```
java org.apache.xalan.xslt.Process
```

The most important value is `-PARAM`. With this, is it possible to pass a value to the style sheet. In the W3C specification of XSLT it was stipulated that this has to be possible. It was however left up to each manufacturer of an XSLT processor as to how they wanted to realize this. Not all XSLT processors currently support this possibility, and, those who do, possibly do it in different ways from others.

Standards and specialities You can use other Java-based parsers and processors in similar ways. All XSLT processor are relatively new programs. This means that the degree to which they adhere to the XSLT recommendation can be quite different. The same style sheets can therefore create different results from the same data. It is expected that the differences will quickly be eliminated as XSLT matures. On the whole, the Java-based programs have the lead when it comes to fulfilling the standards, because, as a rule, they have been developed for the longest period of time. However, programs written in C, Perl and Python are becoming increasingly available.

An important exception is the XSLT processor from Microsoft, which was used in Internet Explorer 5.x (IE5.x). This processor stands out because of its very short execution times. Internet Explorer 5.0 is, however, based on the status of the XSLT design from December 1998. It can therefore quite rightly be praised as being a pioneering implementation. Unfortunately, the changes that were made during the time between this design and the Recommendation in November 1999 are serious. The optimal possibility of testing style sheets would be to simply have them processed by the browser and to have the results displayed. This is possible with IE5.x, however, currently only on the basis of the design of 1998. Anyone installing the updates and the MSXML3.DLL from the year 2000 is already close to the XSLT recommendation of the WWW Consortium, but there are still discrepancies. Anyone who chooses this possibility and develops style sheets that work in IE5.x must take into account that this does not use the full specification and can be subject to migration costs for porting to other systems. In an Intranet environment in which the use of a particular browser can be prescribed, such a decision may nevertheless be sensible.

Because of this, the building and test environment described above is defined for processing style sheets. The examples that are used in the following chapters will be introduced in this environment.

6

Transformations using XSLT

This chapter introduces the basic properties and mechanisms of transformations using XSLT. The elements of XSLT are described by means of their use in a running example. A separate presentation of the elements and declarations can be found in the reference section "*Language elements of XSLT*", starting on page 179.

Templates: central elements of XSLT

XSLT transformation instructions are written as well-formed XML documents and are normally saved in files. These documents contain a fixed vocabulary of XSLT instructions. XSLT is therefore a markup language based on XML. Processing patterns, which are collectively described as templates, are established in this markup language. The following is a simple example of a template for processing the `<topic>` element:

```
<xsl:template match="topic">
    <i><xsl:value-of select="." /></i>
</xsl:template>
```

Templates describe how the elements of the XML input document are processed. This takes place within the template element. Everything that is written between the start and the end tag of the template is henceforth described as a template body, or instruction body. The example above specifies that the text of the `<topic>` element is to appear in italics. The direct output of the HTML tag `<i>..</i>` is called a literal result element because it was not generated from computation by the XSLT processor, but was entered in the style sheet as a character string.

In the conceptual framework of XSLT, we do not talk about elements, attributes, comments or processing instructions, rather these are grouped under the general description of *nodes*.

There are different ways of assigning templates and their processing instructions to these nodes. The most common way is to specify *patterns*. These are entered as a `match` attribute in the start tag of the template. When going through the source tree, the nodes that are found are compared to the pattern. If a corresponding pattern is found for the current node, then the instructions of the template body are executed. The processing of a single template merely produces one part of the intended output structure. It can therefore delegate further processing steps to other templates.

6.1 Structure of an XSLT style sheet

An XSLT style sheet has a normal XML prologue, a document element (`<xsl:stylesheet>`) and is built up as a hierarchy of child nodes.

<xsl:stylesheet>
<xsl:transform>
The name `<xsl:stylesheet>` is prescribed for the root element of the document, which is also called a style sheet element. The expression `<xsl:transform>` can also be used. Both names are normative, i.e. their appearance signals to the XSLT processor that this is a transformation script.

Furthermore, the declaration of an attribute indicating the XSLT version is also prescribed. At the moment, this is limited to `version="1.0"` since as yet there are no newer versions available.

All further XSLT instructions are written within the style sheet element. They are subject to a partially standardized hierarchy, whose structure is documented in a DTD. This can be found in the appendix of the XSLT specification. Although XSLT can be written using a DTD, XSLT processors do not process any of the information from a DTD. The resolution of entity references, validation and similar tasks are still the task of the parser alone, which is used by the XSLT processor.

Namespace declarations are used for the differentiation between markup with which XSLT instructions are marked, and tags which have other functions. An XSLT document follows the recommendations of the WWW Consortium with regards to namespaces. These are described in the document "XML Namespaces" [XMLNS].

6.1.1 The XSLT namespace

In order to ensure that the XSLT elements are unique, a separate namespace was defined for the transformation language. In principle, each name tag in an XSLT style sheet belongs to its own namespace.

Ensure
unambiguity
An XSLT processor must be capable of using namespaces in order to recognize XSLT instructions and to differentiate between the markup of other namespaces. Since the output of an XSLT transformation contains new markup (e.g. HTML, XML, WML), which, for example, may be coded directly in the style sheet as a literal element, the use of namespaces within XSLT is important. Namespaces make it possible to mix tag names within the file and still differentiate between those that are to be used as the instruction for the XSLT processor and those that merely have to be written in the output data stream.

The `<title>` markup element can be used as an example here. People with academic titles such as Dr., Prof. or similar, have often written books that likewise have titles. In order to keep the different types of titles apart from each other, in XML documents tag names are given a prefix which makes `<person:title>` distinguishable from `<book:title>`. Since XML documents are transported over the WWW, these prefixes are, however, not unique enough. The concept of the namespace therefore determines that the respective prefix may only appear as a representative of a definite unique character string. Since domain names are unique on the WWW, it was suggested that a URI be used as a marker for a namespace.

http://www.w3.org/1999/XSL/Transform was established as the URI of the namespace for XSLT. The specification explicitly points out that the date in this identificator (URI) does not give any information regarding the version. The version number is only indicated by means of the version attribute. The following style sheet shows the basic structure and the use of namespaces.

```
<?xml version="1.0" encoding="ISO-8859-1"?>
<xsl:stylesheet
            version="1.0"
            xmlns:xsl="http://www.w3.org/1999/XSL/
Transform">
      <xsl:template match="slide">
            <html><head><TITLE>First Demo</TITLE></head>
                  <body>
                        <xsl:apply-templates />
                  </body>
            </html>
      </xsl:template>
</xsl:stylesheet>
```

Figure 6.1 Style sheets and namespaces

The XSLT namespace is explicitly declared in the attribute beginning xmlns (xml namespace). The xsl after the colon allows the XSLT namespace to be shortened to xsl. In contrast to the namespace URI itself, the prefix can be allocated freely. In order to make it easier to read, the prefix xsl is normally used. In the previous example, all XSLT instructions could be recognized by the namespace prefix xsl:. However, the processing of this style sheet also produces markup, which does not originate from the XSLT namespace. In this case, HTML markup elements are output. This second namespace is not explicitly defined. In this case, this is the default namespace to which all tags that are declared without a prefix are assigned. In the above example, these are the HTML markup elements.

XSLT instructions are only recognized as control instructions by the XSLT processor in the style sheet itself. XSLT instructions that may appear in the XML input file are not be executed. The purpose of this restriction is understandable. It has to be possible to generate style sheet "B" from style sheet "A" by means of an XSLT transformation, since XSLT style sheets deal with XML documents.

Once again, it should be pointed out that the identification of the namespace does not have to be a URL which is a declaration of an existing resource. The fact that an HTML page actually appears during the attempt to resolve the XSLT namespace URI in a browser, may add to the confusion. However, it is merely a case of using an identification –the very same URI – that is unique on the WWW for every namespace declaration which then ensures the uniqueness of the elements that belong to its namespace.

6.1.1 First level elements

<xsl:stylesheet>
Reference
page 183
In accordance with the XSLT Specification, only certain elements are allowed to be used as a direct descendant of `<xsl:stylesheet>`. The elements in this group are described as top-level elements. The name top-level is not meant to indicate their importance, but instead merely describes their permitted location within the document hierarchy. Many top-level elements may also be written in the template body of XSLT instructions that are not top-level elements. For example, a `<xsl:variable>` element can be used at top-level position but also within a `<xsl:template>` element. A normal instruction such as `<xsl:apply-templates>` must not however be written at the top-level position. This distinction plays a part in the notation of elements in the XSLT style sheet. The position of language elements is therefore also discussed in the reference section "Language elements of XSLT" page 179, in which a language element is described as a top-level element or as an instruction.

<xsl:variable>
Reference
page 194

<xsl:import>
Reference
page 184
The order of elements in the style sheet is not important, with the exception of `<xsl:import>`, which, if used, has to come first. The identifiers will be introduced in the next section on the basis on how they are used. In practice, the `<xsl:template>` element is the most frequently used element.

The XSLT specification gives an example of the use of the top-level elements, which does not however take into account the frequency of their use. It simply shows how these elements have to be coded.

```xml
<?xml version="1.0" encoding="ISO-8859-1"?>
<xsl:stylesheet
      version="1.0"
      xmlns:xsl="http://www.w3.org/1999/XSL/Transform">

      <xsl:import href="..." />
   <xsl:include href="..." />
      <xsl:strip-space elements="..." />
      <xsl:preserve-space elements="..." />
      <xsl:output method="..."/>
      <xsl:key name="..." match="..." use="..." />
      <xsl:decimal-format name="..." />
      <xsl:namespace-alias
      stylesheet-prefix="..." result-prefix="..." />

      <xsl:attribute-set name="...">
            ...
      </xsl:attribute-set>

      <xsl:variable name="...">...</xsl:variable>
      <xsl:param name="...">...</xsl:param>
      <xsl:template match="..."> ... </xsl:template>
      <xsl:template name="..."> ... </xsl:template>
</xsl:stylesheet>
```

Figure 6.2　Code example for top-level elements

The ellipses mark the places where values have to be entered by the person writing the style sheet. These values contain names of elements of the source file, search patterns (XPath expressions), other XSLT instructions, or possibly also literal elements that are added to the output data (literal result elements). These are character strings that are not part of defined instructions. You will find HTML markup elements in the listing "*Style sheets and namespaces*", page 93.

As well as top-level elements, there are also other XSLT instructions that are written within a template (`<xsl:template>`).

Templates as a representative of a later event
All XSLT instructions are dummies for the result of the calculation that the XSLT processor generates as a consequence of these instructions. If, within a template, another instruction is branched to, and thus delegated detailed work, this instruction is processed first. This is done using the XSLT instruction `<xsl:apply-templates ...>`, which is not one of the top-level elements. If this instruction is also branched, the process goes on to the next instruction. This continues in a recursive sequence of delegations until an instruction is reached that only produces literal elements. This happens if a terminal node in the input tree is reached, or if the value is selected using the `<xsl:value-of>` instruction. In both cases, the recursive process is ended and the result of the calculation is used instead of the XSLT expression.

6.2 Style sheet processing

The different XSLT instructions are now introduced by means of examples of how they are used. To demonstrate the behavior of XSLT scripts, a simple HTML document will be generated. In order to do so, the examples use the slide documents that we are already familiar with. In the process, these source documents will be changed as little as possible. The following version of the first slide document is used as the starting point.

```
<?xml version="1.0" encoding="ISO-8859-1"?>
<?xml-stylesheet type="text/xsl" href="slide.xsl" ?>
<slide id="1"          date of creation="12.04.2000"
                       authors="Knobloch &amp; Kopp">
      <title>Content Management Systems (CMS)</title>
      <topiclist>
           <topic>What must a CMS be able to do?</topic>
           <topic>Who should use a CMS?</topic>
      </topiclist>
</slide>
```

Figure 6.3 slide.xml

id()
Reference page 209
A DTD is not used for this version of `slide.xml`. As a rule, an XSLT processor does not refer to the information in a DTD. The only exceptions to this are the data type ID and the `id()` function of XPath. For the current example, it is not necessary for

the parser to validate or resolve entities or entity references, with the exception of the predefined entities.

In the second line, a style sheet was declared in the processing instruction. The type attribute now has the value "text/xsl", since we are not attaching a CSS style sheet to the XML document, but an XSL style sheet. The connection of style sheets by means of processing instructions is used by application programs such as browsers, for example. When using the command line call, this processing instruction is ignored. It is therefore no longer given in the following examples, since the style sheets are not linked statically to the XML document, but are instead entered during the call of the XSLT processor.

The <slide> element has been supplemented with three attributes. The attribute for identification is used with numerical values, as it will also be subsequently. Textual values would also be allowed. Various forms of style sheet will now be used with this document.

6.2.1 Processing templates

<xsl:template>
Reference
page 180

Templates are a central concept in the processing of XSLT style sheets. The match attribute of the <xsl:template> instruction determines for which nodes or for which sets of nodes this template contains processing rules. The first template in the following style sheet refers to the root node of the document, the <slide> element.

```
<xsl:template match="slide">...</xsl:template>
```

As soon as the <slide> element is met, and thus becomes the current node, the XSLT processor activates the instructions within <xsl:template> and replaces the block with the result of the computation.

The basic structure of an HTML file is built up in the first template of our first style sheet.

```
<html>
  <head>
      <title>...</title>
  </head>
  <body>...</body>
</html>
```

The same structure, only incorporated into the XSLT template, looks as follows:

```
<xsl:template match="slide">
    <html><head><TITLE>First demo</TITLE></head>
      <body >
          <xsl:apply-templates select="topiclist" />
      </body >
    </html>
</xsl:template>
```

After the template for `<slide>` has been activated, the appropriate HTML tags are output as processing instructions, including a title that was coded in the style sheet.

The possibility of coding character strings or references etc. in the style sheet can be used to take on some of the functions of entities that otherwise require a DTD. It is thus possible to postpone the decision of whether information should be input into the basic document and whether it should be saved there as an element or as an attribute. For example, a copyright note can be incorporated into a transformation without any problems, since a protection law only becomes effective when the document is used. An entity declaration in a DTD is not necessary for this.

<xsl:apply-templates>
Reference
page 181

You must take into account that, as an XML file, an XSLT style sheet distinguishes between upper and lower case text. It is possible to use `<html>` and `<TITLE>` in a document. The closing tags must however be written in the same way as the opening tags. The HTML parser in the browser that reads the result document does not take into account that the style sheet is not processed if there is no consistency here.

Processing of a
selection

Within the `<xsl:template match="...">` instruction, and therefore in the template body, a template can also contain instructions that delegate further processing to other templates in the style sheet.

```
<xsl:apply-templates select="topiclist" />
```

With the empty `<xsl:apply-templates>` element, the XSLT processor is asked to search for and make use of other templates. In the above expression, this request is described in more detail. The current node is the `<slide>` element. The `select` attribute is used to branch explicitly to the `<topiclist>` child node. This also means that the `<title>` element is not selected. In order to allow all child nodes to be processed, the instruction can be used without an attribute.

Processing all
child elements

```
<xsl:apply-templates />
```

With this instruction, templates for all child nodes of the current node would be searched for. The `<xsl:apply-templates>` instruction processes all child elements of the current node, unless just one subset is selected by means of a `select` expression. After the processing, the process returns to the point after that at which it entered the recursion and then continues from there onwards. This form is used for the further processing of the `<topiclist>` element.

```
<xsl:template match="topiclist">
  <ul>
    <xsl:apply-templates />
  </ul>
</xsl:template>
```

When this template was entered and consequently processed, the `<topiclist>` became the current node. It is known that this element only has homogenous child elements., and it is therefore not necessary to define an explicit selection of the `<topic>` nodes. Before the delegation of the processing to the template for

<topic>, an unordered list is opened using <ul>. After <xsl:apply-templates> has been processed, this list is closed again. The <xsl:apply-templates> instruction will be replaced by the appropriate <li> tags and their content. The last template, which is still missing, will be displayed in conjunction with the whole style sheet in the following.

```
<?xml version="1.0" encoding="ISO-8859-1"?>
<xsl:stylesheet version="1.0"
            xmlns:xsl="http://www.w3.org/1999/XSL/
Transform">
<xsl:template match="slide">
        <html><head><TITLE>First demo</TITLE></head>
                <body>
                                        <xsl:apply-templates
select="topiclist" />
                </body>
        </html>
</xsl:template>

<xsl:template match="topiclist">
  <ul><xsl:apply-templates /></ul>
</xsl:template>

<xsl:template match="topic">
        <li><xsl:value-of select="." /></li>
</xsl:template>

</xsl:stylesheet>
```

Figure 6.4   slide1.xml

<xsl:value-of>
Reference
page 185 The <xsl:value-of> instruction that is introduced here calculates and returns the value of the current node. By doing so, it terminates the recursive processing at this point, since no further delegations to templates that may exist are necessary. The select attribute limits the selection to the value of the current node. This is signaled by the single dot.

The advantage of recursive, rule-driven processing is that a separate template can be defined for each node of the input document. As will be shown, this assignment can also be controlled more rigorously. Different templates can be used, depending on additional requirements on the same nodes.

The control of the passage through the document therefore does not have to be determined during the writing of the style sheet. The XSLT processor finds suitable templates for any further processing steps for the current node. Each time a template body is entered, a new context is built up, in which the processing of the instructions takes place.

<xsl:call-template>
Reference
page 182
In contrast to this method of processing, in which the "current node" property shifts, `<xsl:call-template>` creates another possibility, that of directly activating particular templates without changing the context.

We initiate the transformation using the following command:

```
transform slide.xml slide1.xsl slide.hmtl
```

The result, as shown in Figure 6.5, still looks a little scanty, because we have not yet shown the content of the `<title>` element anywhere.

We add the title of the slide as an HTML tag by making two small changes. First, we make sure that the root element does not specifically branch to the `<topiclist>` element by simply leaving out the `select` attribute in the first template, and as a result of this allowing the template to be used for all child elements of `<slide>`.

Figure 6.5   Result of transformation slide1.xsl

```
...
<xsl:template match="slide">
    <html><head><TITLE>First demo</TITLE></head>
      <body>
            <xsl:apply-templates />
      </body>
    </html>
</xsl:template>
...
<xsl:template match="title">
    <h2><xsl:value-of select="." /> </h2>
</xsl:template>
    ...
```

The sequence of the `<xsl:template>` blocks is not important, since the processing sequence is controlled via the `select` and `match` attributes. For this reason, we place the template for the display of the slide's title somewhere in the list of previous `<xsl:template...>` entries.

A further change to the style sheet has the effect that the title of the slide does not only appear in the body of the HTML file, but also in the window heading of the browser. The `<TITLE>` element in the document head is also filled with the value of the title element.

```
<TITLE><xsl:value-of select="title" /></TITLE>
```

The current node inside the first template of our style sheet is the `<slide>` element of the document. The `<xsl:value-of>` instruction selects the `<title>` child element and is replaced by its value.

So far, we have only used the elements of the source document. The `id` attribute of the input document can however also be displayed in the title of the browser. Once again, the generation of the HTML markup element `<TITLE>` is therefore amended and the number in the `id` attribute is displayed along with a character string. The reference to an attribute is signaled by the @ symbol.

```
. .
<TITLE>slide No.:
    <xsl:value-of select="@id" />-
    <xsl:value-of select="title" />
</TITLE>
. . .
```

The result of the transformation with `slide2.xsl` looks somewhat more useful.

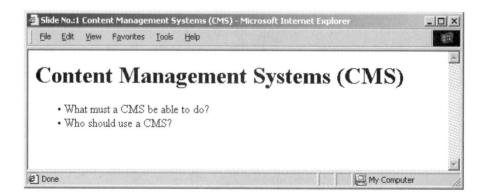

Figure 6.6   Result of transformation slide2.xsl

Both `<xsl:value-of>` instructions, which now constitute the window heading, access nodes that have a hierarchical child relationship to `<slide>`. However, these are two different types of nodes: one is an element and one is an attribute.

This is important for navigation – and thus for XPath expressions. In order to be able to access the different entities, the node types must be distinguished explicitly. For attributes, this is done using the @ symbol. This shows that the perception of XSLT or XPath deviates from that of pure document structuring. First and foremost, an XML document is seen from the stand point of traversing a document tree.

The previous example has shown that the omission or addition of a template can lead to parts of the document being visible or invisible. The <title> element was used twice: once as part of the window heading, and once as the title of the document. It is also possible to manipulate the sequence in the output document. The replacement of the <xsl:apply-templates> instruction without attributes by two instructions with explicit child element names moves the heading to the end of the topic list.

Excerpt from
slide3.xsl

```
... <xsl:template match="slide">
      <html>
        <head><TITLE>slide N0.:1 Confused</TITLE></head>
        <body >
            <xsl:apply-templates  select="topiclist" />
            <xsl:apply-templates  select="title" />
        </body >
      </html>
    </xsl:template>
```

In doing so, the templates for the individual elements remain unchanged from the previous example.

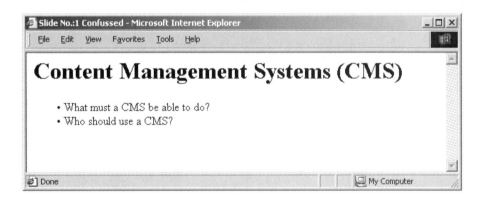

Figure 6.7 Result of the transformation slide3.xsl

The example shows that the sequence of the output can be freely manipulated, whilst the layout instructions for the individual elements are retained.

The reverse of this is however more interesting. An element is to appear several times in an output document and is to be displayed differently each time. In order to do this, it is possible to mark the template definitions with the help of another attribute. The mode attribute makes it possible to mark a hierarchy of templates with regard to how they are used.

Excerpt from
slide4.xsl

```
. . .
<xsl:template match="title">
  <h2><xsl:value-of select="." /></h2>
</xsl:template>

<xsl:template match="title" mode="footer line" >
    <font size="-1"><i>
       <xsl:value-of select="." />
    </i></font>
</xsl:template>
. . .
```

The first template for the <title> element is shown again in the first block and has not been changed. The second block contains the template with the additional attribute mode="footer line". The value of the <title> element is to be displayed in a smaller font size and in italics. The output of the title element by means of an <xsl:value-of select="." /> instruction is identical to the instruction that generates the title.

For demonstration purposes, we pack even more information into the footer line. In our example, the slide number that comes from the id attribute of the slide itself will be shown, and a copyright note copied as fixed text. As a result, the template is extended by two lines.

Excerpt from
slide4.xsl

```
. . .
<xsl:template match="title" mode="footer line" >
    <font size="-1"><i>
       Slide <xsl:value-of select="../@id" /> -
       <xsl:value-of select="." />
       &#xA9; Knobloch &amp; Kopp, January 2000
    </i></font>
</xsl:template>
. . .
```

It is easy to understand how the names of the authors and the date can be used here. But how can the id attribute of the document element be accessed? We will look more closely at the appropriate XPath expression:

```
<xsl:value-of select="../@id" />
```

The current node is the <title> element. The access to the id attribute can therefore be achieved using a relative path declaration. As is the case in many file systems, ".." describes the parent element. Therefore, the slide number can be accessed using "../@id".

As a result, the appearance of the footer line is defined. However, its position in the output document is not yet fixed. The HTML output format does not grant a lot of freedom in the control of positioning.

XSLT and CSS   It is quite sensible at this point to define a style sheet so that Cascading Style Sheet instructions can be incorporated into the HTML output during the transformation. This can be done using the method with which HTML markup is generated. Even when used together with XSLT, Cascading Style Sheets make free positioning possible and, in the case of extensive documents, make the code more legible.

We do not wish to make the examples too complex, and so we will not go into the use of Cascading Style Sheets at this point, but will look at simple positioning by defining a single-column table.

The structure of the table and the assignment of content to the lines of the table are all taken care of by the starter template. There is space for the `<title>` element, the content of the `<topiclist>` and the footer lines in a cell of a table.

Excerpt from
slide4.xsl

```
. . .
<xsl:template match="slide">
<html>
    <head><TITLE>...</TITLE></head>
  <body >
     <table>
     <tr><td>
          <xsl:apply-templates select="title" />
     </td></tr>
     <tr><td>
<xsl:apply-templates select="topiclist" />
     </td></tr>
     <tr><td align="bottom">
          <xsl:apply-templates select="title"
                               mode="footer line" />
     </td></tr>
     </table>
  </body >
</html>
</xsl:template>
. . .
```

In order to activate the template for the footer line, `<xsl:apply-templates>` is likewise called with the corresponding mode attribute. The result of the transformation shows that the XSLT processor differentiates between the templates.

The modal call of templates is used primarily in the creation of navigation structures and tables of contents which are looked at in more detail in a later section "Creating internal links", page 131.

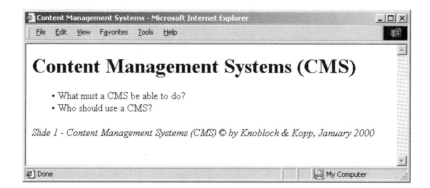

Figure 6.8   Result of a transformation: slide4.xsl

A summary of template processing

The call of templates by means of the `mode` attribute is not the only way of enforcing formatting. This can also be achieved by using the `<xsl:call-template>` instruction. To complete this first section on the processing of templates, the process will be reiterated.

- An XSLT document is made up of templates that contain processing instructions for nodes of the XML document.

- These processing instructions can output values from the source document and output generated text. In addition, it is also possible to delegate further processing to other templates. In the output document, the instructions of the XSLT style sheet are replaced by the results of their computations.

- When working through a source document (or input tree), the XSLT processor activates the templates whose match expression is equivalent to the current node. With the help of the `mode` attribute, it is possible to differentiate between various templates for a node and to use these selectively for different purposes.

- If a template delegates further processing to another template, the name of the node concerned does not have to be known. The XSLT processor has to look into the inventory of the existing templates to find one which matches the current node as closely as possible, and then activate it. This is done using `<xsl:apply-templates />`.

- This process is continued recursively through all activated templates until a node is reached that does not contain any further child nodes, or until the value of a node is calculated and returned within a template using the instruction `<xsl:value-of />`.

- The use of a named template can also be enforced in the transformation script using an `<xsl:call-template>` instruction. As a result, the current node is retained and the template body of the called template is processed in its context.

6.2.2 Built-in templates

What happens if the XSLT processor was asked to look for further templates but there are no other suitable ones available? For this kind of scenario, the WWW Consortium has defined default template processing (Built-in template rules [XSLT], §5.8).

Built-in rules   An XSLT processor should behave as though the following templates were present in all style sheets, so that recursive processing of further templates is not interrupted. This would be the case if there was no template available for a node that forms an intermediate stage in the document hierarchy.

For the processing of root nodes and all element nodes, the first of the following templates applies. Here, the asterisk is an XPath 'wildcard' which stands for arbitrary element nodes, the slash for the root node. Using this template, the recursion is continued via the enclosed `<xsl:apply-templates />` instruction.

```
<xsl:template match="*|/">
   <xsl:apply-templates />
</xsl:template>
```

Attribute nodes and text nodes (the textual values of element nodes) are included by a different template. The `"text()"` function is used to mark arbitrary text nodes, and `"@*"` to mark arbitrary attribute nodes. In these cases, only the value of the node is copied into the target document. Since both types of node must not have any child elements (see *Types of document nodes*, page 107), the recursion can be stopped here.

```
<xsl:template match="text()|@*">
   <xsl:value-of select="." />
</xsl:template>
```

Absolutely nothing happens if a processing instruction or a comment appears.

```
<xsl:template match="processing-instruction() |
                     comment()" />
```

In this case, no action is carried out. Further processing of the recursion is unnecessary since neither node type has any child elements. As a result, any output in the target document is not the default, but can be generated using separate definitions.

The following minimal style sheet uses these "built-in templates" to display the content of the `<topiclist>` element.

minimal.xsl
```
<?xml version="1.0" encoding="ISO-8859-1"?>
<xsl:stylesheet version="1.0"
        xmlns:xsl="http://www.w3.org/1999/XSL/Transform">
```

```
<xsl:template match="slide">
<html>
    <head><TITLE>Minimal</TITLE></head>
    <body><xsl:apply-templates /></body >
</html>
</xsl:template>

</xsl:stylesheet>
```

The transformation produces a legible representation, if needs be.

The HTML document shown here was not produced using the XSLT processor of IE5. This implementation does not have built-in templates. The minimal style sheet would have not produced any visible results with the XSLT processor from IE5. Anyone producing style sheets for IE5 can take remedial action by including explicit declarations of the templates mentioned above.

These default templates can be overwritten by the user's own definitions. This interacts with the priority rules which come into effect if parts of the XSLT document are inserted in the style sheet using `<xsl:import>`. XSLT processors treat the default templates as if they were available in the style sheet as per an import instruction. This mechanism is discussed in a later section "The modularization of style sheets", page 121. The possibility of overwriting the default definitions is used in the next style sheet to show how the processor works through the input document and creates a document model that corresponds to the descriptions in XPath. The default templates also use XPath notation in their match expressions. We should therefore now look at the structure and use of XPath expressions.

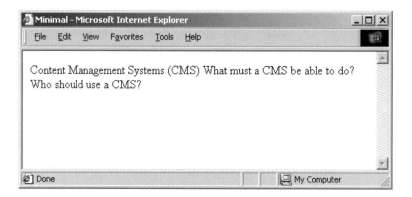

Figure 6.9   Result of the transformation minimal.xsl

XPath

The definition of XPath describes a navigation language that owes its name to the fact that the notation of its expressions follows path specifications. Its construction is similar to that of URLs. This chapter introduces the basic definitions of XPath that are used in XSLT.

Addressing parts of documents

The overriding aim of XPath is to make parts of an XML document addressable. XPath is not an independent language, but a sublanguage that is used in other languages such as XSLT or XPointer for writing expressions. An implementation of XPath is therefore only possible within such a "carrier language". XPath uses a syntax that does not conform to XML.

7.1 Types of document node

As has already been said, XPath describes XML documents with the help of a document model that is different from the perspective of textual structuring. It is similar, but not identical, to the Document Object Model (DOM).

An XML document is seen as a tree structure consisting of nodes that are connected to one another. The different parts of an XML document such as elements and attributes, comments or processing instructions, are merely represented as different node types.

At the start of the processing, these nodes are created as representatives of objects of the input document. Operations and functions that are defined in XPath work with this representation, and therefore do not work directly on the source document. The properties of the different node types play an important part in the access to these nodes. The different types and their properties are listed in the following.

Table 7.1
Node types in
XPath

- **Root Node**
  The root node is the starting point of the document tree and therefore this is a node that only appears once. It is not identical to the element node which contain all other elements of the document (the document element). The `<slide>` element in the example document is in fact just a child node of the root, for instance. The root has no expanded name and only the document element and all processing instructions or comments that appear before or after the document

element are written down as child nodes. The root has no counterpart in the source document, but is in fact a generated point of entry to the document representation.

- **Element Nodes**
  Each element of the document is represented by an element node. An element node has a name by which it may be referred to in XPath expressions (its "callable name") that corresponds to the tag name in the document. The value of an element node consists of the concatenated values of all text nodes that are descendants of the element.
  The child nodes of an element node can be other element nodes or text nodes. Other possible child nodes are comments and processing instructions.
  Each element node can have an assigned set of attribute nodes associated with it.

- **Attribute Nodes**
  Attribute nodes are not treated like child nodes, even though the Specification describes the associated element nodes as parent nodes. This has the effect that attributes and namespace nodes are not included in the processing of all the child nodes of an element invoked by `<xsl:apply-templates/>`. An attribute node is created for each attribute of the source document. The callable name of an attribute node is the name of the attribute, its value is the attribute value. Attribute nodes cannot contain any further child nodes.

- **Text Nodes**
  Text nodes are created for all character strings in the document that do not belong to the markup of the document. Text nodes do not have callable names, and their value is the character string (`PCDATA`), for which they were created. Text nodes cannot contain any further child nodes.

- **Comment Nodes**
  A comment node does not have a callable name, and no child elements. The value of a comment node is the text of the comment.

- **Processing Instruction Nodes**
  The node representation of a processing instruction has a callable name. This is the name of the application, and is written down after the opening delimiter `<?`. The value of the node is the text that comes after the name and the blank space. The closing delimiter (`?>`) is not part of the value of the node.
  The XML declaration `<?xml version="1.0"?>` is not a processing instruction and therefore does not have any counterpart in the tree.

- **Namespace Nodes**
  An element node has a namespace node for each namespace prefix within the element. The callable name of a namespace node is the declared prefix, and the value of the node is the URI of the namespace. As in the case of attribute nodes, the associated element is described as a parent element, but the namespace node is not described as the child of the element.

A central concept of XPath is the *expression*. The evaluation of an XPath expression produces the following fixed set of value types:

- character strings (`string`),

- boolean values (`boolean`),

- numerical values (`number`)

- an ordered set of nodes from the input tree (`node-set`)

- a result fragment of the output tree (`result tree fragment`)

Frequently, the "value" of an expression is referred to. What this includes depends in turn on the node types that are used in the expression. The above list of node types therefore indicates what the value of a node consists of, or how it is calculated when expressions are analyzed.

The following style sheet illustrates how XPath interprets the structure of a document. The script produces an HTML file showing how the location (the current node) moves during the processing of the input document.

In order to enter the root node, the selection expression in the first template is set to "/".

```
<xsl:template match="/">
```

In this template, the descriptions are set as headings. The name of the current node is output with the HTML heading level 3. In order to make the angle brackets around the name visible in the output, these are written in the coding as a standard entity reference. The XPath function `name()` returns the callable name of a node, as long as it has one. This happens for element nodes.

Extract from
xpath0.xsl

```
. . .
<h3>current node
    &lt; <xsl:value-of select="name()" />&gt;
</h3>
<xsl:apply-templates />
. . .
```

With `<xsl:apply-templates>`, the processing of all child nodes of the root node is activated. The default settings for all element nodes are overwritten with the following template.

```
. . .
<xsl:template match="*">
<h3>current node
        &lt; <xsl:value-of select="name()" />&gt;
```

```
</h3>
<ul>
      <xsl:apply-templates select="*|@*|text()" />
</ul>
</xsl:template>
...
```

The output of the node name is identical to the processing in the previous template. After a list has been opened, the processing is delegated to the templates for further child nodes. The selection is limited to element nodes, attribute nodes and text nodes. When meeting a child node that is of the node type element, the template therefore calls itself again. If attribute or text nodes appear, the following template comes into effect, which just produces the name and value of the node as a list item.

```
<xsl:template match="@*|text()">
   <li>
      <xsl:value-of select="name()" />
      <xsl:text> </xsl:text>
      <xsl:value-of select="." />
   </li>

</xsl:template>
```

The `<xsl:text>` element is merely used to retain the blank space between the two `<xsl:value-of>` instructions.

Since the processing sequence in the style sheet was not interfered with, the document will be worked through in document order.

In fact, XPath defines the rule that the root node may only have one child. Contrary to this definition, XSLT nevertheless allows the root node to have text child elements in the output tree structure. Obviously, this is not implemented in the same way in all implementations of XSLT processors. However, this should not cause any problems if it is ensured that selections in the area of the root node are worded explicitly. Figure 7.1 shows the processing sequence as a result of a transformation. You can also see that the attribute nodes are processed before the others.

The manipulation of the processing sequence or the selection of specific nodes can be controlled using XPath expressions that operate on this node hierarchy.

The evaluation of expressions always takes place in a context. This consists of the context node (almost always identical to the current node), the current position (context position) within a set of nodes, and their number, which is likewise always available (context size). Within an evaluation context, a variable, a function library, and definitions for the namespace are also useful.

Location paths have a prominent meaning within XPath expressions and are described in the following.

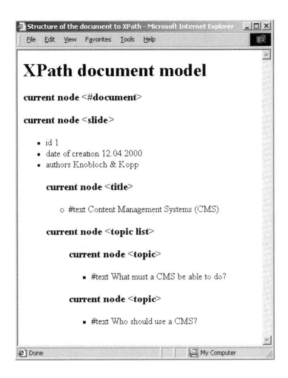

Figure 7.1 Result of transformation xpath0.xsl

7.2 Location paths

Location paths show the path through the document hierarchy to the location of one or several nodes. This kind of expression describes the selection of a set of nodes

- starting with the context node as a relative declaration or

- in an absolute path declaration starting from the root node beginning with an initial slash.

The evaluation of the expression produces the specified set of nodes and replaces the expression with the result of its calculation.

In order to describe the location path, a syntax was defined that was supplemented with an abbreviated syntax because of how verbose it was. However, because the verbose syntax uses meaningful names, it will be used in some of our examples.

How is this kind of path constructed? A location path consists of several location steps, separated from each other by slashes. In turn, the location steps consist of a so-called axis identifier and a node test separated by two colons. In abstract terms, a relative location path can look as follows:

```
axis-identifier::node-test/axis-identifier::node-test
```

A node test consists of

- either simply the name of the node, for example `title`,

- or a type description with the help of the following node tests:
  `text()` identifies text nodes,
  `comment()` identifies comment nodes,
  `processing-instruction()` identifies PIs,
  `node()` selects all nodes, independent of their type.

An axis identifier is, for example, `child::`. A location step such as `child::node()` thus selects all child nodes of the current element. The current element now depends on what the outcome of the evaluation of the preceding location steps is. The following location path contains three location steps:

```
/child::slides/child::slide/child::node()
```

Starting from the root node, in the first step the child nodes called `slides` are selected. In our example, there is only one of these. In the second step, the child nodes of `slides` called `slide` are selected, and in the third step, all child nodes of `slide` are selected, regardless of their type.

The axis identifier can be used to divide the tree-structured nodes. The XPath Specification gives names to different parts of the tree.

7.3　Document axes

Thirteen axes are listed in the Specification.

- The `self` axis only contains the context node.

- The `child` axis contains the child nodes of the current node.

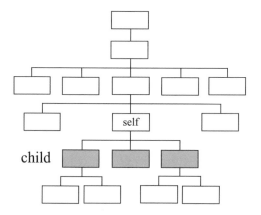

- The descendant axis contains all descendants of the current node: its child and grandchild nodes. This axis does not contain any attributes or namespace nodes.

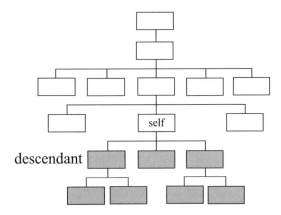

- The parent axis contain the parent node of the current node, provided it has one

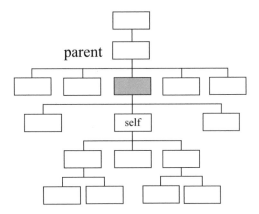

- The ancestor axis contains all ancestors of the current node up to the root node.

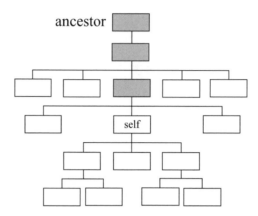

- The following-sibling axis contains the sibling nodes that follow in the document order sequence. In the case of attribute or namespace nodes, this axis is empty.

- The preceding-sibling axis is the same as the following-sibling axis, but goes in the opposite direction

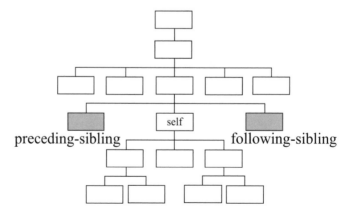

- The preceding axis contains all nodes of the document that come before the current node in the processing sequence, but are not ancestors of the current node. This does not include any attribute or namespace nodes.

- The `following` axis contains all nodes of the document that come after the current node in the processing sequence, but are not descendants of the current node. Again, this does not include attribute and namespace nodes.

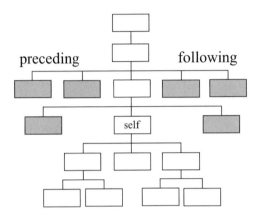

- The `attribute` axis contains all attributes of the context node. Since only element nodes contain attributes, this axis only exists in the case of element nodes.

- The `namespace` axis contains all namespace nodes of the context node. This axis also only exists if the context node is an element node.

- The `descendant-or-self` axis contains the context node and all its descendants.

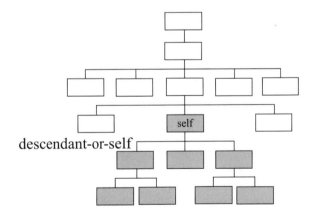

- The `ancestor-or-self` axis contains the context node and all its ancestors including the root node, unless the current node is itself the root.

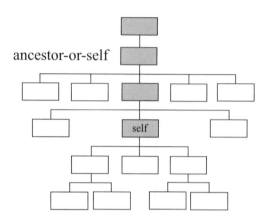

The `preceding`, `following`, `ancestor` and `descendant` axes, together with the context node (`self`) contain all nodes of the document, without them overlapping each other.

7.4 Predicates and full location paths

Another element that is still missing from the notation of a full location path, comprises the so-called predicates. They are written as boolean expressions in square brackets and describe further limitations in the selection of nodes. They are appended directly to the node tests.

```
child::topiclist/child::topic[position()=1]
```

This example restricts the selection of the <topic> elements to the first element. Path declarations can become long and complex. For this reason, it is possible to use an abbreviated notation. When abbreviated, the above expression looks as follows:

```
topiclist/topic[1]
```

In most cases, this abbreviated syntax is used.

In addition to the function of navigation, which is of prime importance, XPath also has a number of other functions that make it possible to carry out simple manipulations on character strings or to check the existence of nodes.

XPath location paths in verbose syntax

The following examples illustrate this. They are subsequently processed in a style sheet.

- `descendant-or-self::title`
  Finds <title> elements in the current node and all its descendants.

- `attribute::*`
  Finds all attributes of the current node.

- `attribute::creationdate`
  Finds the "creationdate" attribute of the current node.

- `child::*`
  Finds all child elements of the current node.

- `child::topiclist`
  Finds all child elements called "topiclist".

- `child::topiclist/child::topic[position()=last()]`
  Finds the last `<topic>` element node that is child node of `<topiclist>`.

- `child::topiclist/child::topic[position()=1]`
  Finds the first `<topic>` element node.

- `child::topiclist/preceding-sibling::*`
  Finds all elements of the `preceding-sibling` axis of `<topiclist>`.

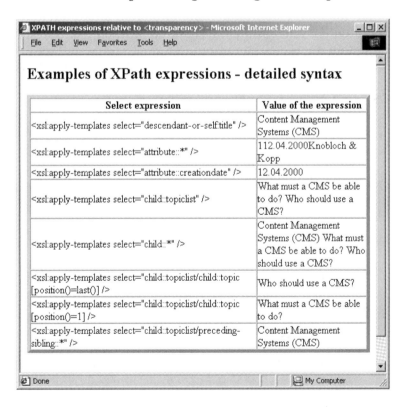

Figure 7.2 Result of transformation xpath1.xsl

You can try out these examples practically in a style sheet. The style sheet that produces an HTML representation of the expressions and their calculation only uses a single template to construct a table. The left column displays the full XSLT instruction with the location path, and the right column displays the result of the calculation. The result of the transformation is shown in the browser in Figure 7.2.

All location paths are given relative to the current node here. In the following, only fragments of the style sheet are reproduced, since it has a very simple structure.

Excerpt from
xpath1.xsl

```
...
<xsl:template match="slide">
 <html><head><TITLE>XPATH expressions...</TITLE></head>
   <body>
   ...
      <table border="1" cellpadding="4" >
      ...
      </table>
   </body>
 </html>
</xsl:template>
```

All instructions for the display of the location path and the results are located within the table definition as table rows. In order to prevent its execution by the XSLT processor, the XSLT instruction in the first table cell has to be written in a CDATA section. The instruction to be interpreted is given in the second table cell, which is replaced by the result of the calculation.

Another possibility
would be to use an
<xsl:text> element

```
...
<tr>
   <td>
     <![CDATA[
     <xsl:apply-templates select="attribute::*" />
     ]]>
   </td>
   <td><xsl:apply-templates select="attribute::*"/></td>
</tr>...
```

This stylesheet does not contain any further templates for layout instructions, since this work is the task of the built-in templates.

7.5 Abbreviated notation

XPath defines an abbreviated notation for expressions that are used frequently. For example, if a location step does not specify any document axis, it is assumed that the child axis (child::) is being referred to. Thus

```
/child::slides/child::slide
```

can be abbreviated to

```
/slides/slide
```

The following abbreviations for XPath expressions are allowed:

Examples of abbreviated notation

Full syntax	Abbreviated syntax
`attribute::`	@
`self::node()`	.
`parent::node()`	..
`/descendant-or-self::node()/`	//
`[position() = 3]`	[3]

As a rule, this abbreviated notation will be used in the examples of code that are used in this book from now on. Sometimes, the detailed notation is easier to understand and in some cases cannot be abbreviated. Since a mixture of both forms of notation is possible, this should not cause any problems.

8

Other XSLT language elements

Now that we have looked at XPath, we will go back to the processing of style sheets. Until now we have only used templates that were able to create output directly or delegate the detailed work to other templates. The more complex the structure of the input files, the larger the number of templates that have to be defined for the desired output structure. Because of this, style sheets may become quite long and confusing. For this purpose, the XSLT Specification offers two instructions that make it possible to divide style sheets up into segments. This division also aims to make processing instructions easier to use, of course.

8.1 The modularization of style sheets

<xsl:import>,
<xsl:include>
Reference
page 184

The `<xsl:import>` and `<xsl:include>` XSLT instructions make it possible to incorporate the content of style sheet files in the current style sheet. Both instructions are top-level elements of XSLT, which means that they can only appear as direct child elements of `<xsl:stylesheet>`.

To illustrate these instructions, we go back to the creation of the footer line from the previous example. In order to make things simpler, and so that we can use them again, we reduce the footer line to the copyright note and the authors. For the time being, the title of the slide will still also be included, to show that the integration has the same effect as the notation of the corresponding template in the style sheet itself.

At the moment, the template shown below is the only one in the external style sheet.

general.xsl

```
<?xml version="1.0" encoding="ISO-8859-1"?>
<xsl:stylesheet
    version="1.0"
    xmlns:xsl="http://www.w3.org/1999/XSL/Transform">

<xsl:template match="title" mode="footer line" >
    <font size="-1"><i>
    <xsl:value-of select="." />
```

```
        &#xA9; Knobloch &amp; Kopp, January 2000
      </i></font>
    </xsl:template>
  </xsl:stylesheet>
```

The definition of the template for processing the footer line has been removed from the calling style sheet. The incorporation of the external style sheet now takes place using the `<xsl:include>` instruction.

```
  <xsl:include href="general.xsl" />
```

The instruction reads in the external file `general.xsl`. The reference to the external file is in this case a relative specification, i.e., the external file is searched for in the same directory as the one in which the style sheet is. Absolute path specifications are likewise possible.

The processing of this instruction causes the child elements of `<xsl:stylesheet>` from the file `general.xsl` to be used instead of the `<xsl:include>` instruction, as if they had appeared in its place.

An error occurs if a style sheet incorporates itself. In the case of a direct incorporation of another style sheet, the source of the error is soon obvious. However, since it is possible to deploy inclusion over several file levels, these errors can creep in without being noticed.

Another possibility which can be used for integration is to use the `<xsl:import>` instruction. This works in the same way as inclusion.

```
  <xsl:import href="general.xsl" />
```

However, the definitions in the external file do not have the same priority as those in the calling file. If there is an internal template with an identical match expression, then this overwrites the definition in the external style sheet. An import instruction must be written as the first child element of `<xsl:stylesheet>`. It must also appear before any include instructions that may be present. The import instruction is the only top-level element whose position in the style sheet is fixed.

"Excerpts from xpath0.xsl", page 109

The priority mechanism has already been used in the chapter on XPath in order to overwrite the built-in template in the example `xpath0.xsl`. The built-in templates are treated by the XSLT processor as if they were imported from an external file into the first position in the XSLT document.

If multi-level imports are to be used, there has to be some careful planning. The priority rules for cascaded imports are illustrated in the specification using the following example.

Style sheet A imports style sheets B and C. File B imports style sheet D; C in turn imports a further style sheet E. The sequence of imports in this case is D, B, E, C, A.

For the aim of merely making templates reusable, the include instruction is adequate. In the `general.xsl` style sheet so far there have only been templates for the footer lines. The title of the slide was therefore kept in the footer line to demonstrate that, even in the case of included templates, full access to the node hierarchy is possible.

For contents that should have a certain degree of independence from the concrete document, this access is not necessary. For a more practical version of a style sheet, which is to be used as a library, or pool, of templates, footer lines are therefore exempt from direct connection with the `<title>` element of the source document. As a result, the activation of the template no longer needs to be controlled via the occurrence of the `<title>` node.

Named templates
Reference
page 182

To force the call of a template, the `<xsl:call-template>` instruction is available. This uses a `name` attribute to specify the template to be called, which must therefore have a name. The activation of the template from the calling style sheet only changes slightly:

```
<xsl:call-template name="footer line" />
```

The start of the template then looks like the following:

```
<xsl:template name="footer line"> ...
```

The most important difference from templates that are called using `<xsl:apply-templates>` is that, during the entry to a named template, the context does not shift. This means that the current node remains the same and can be used directly in the template body.

Inserting a graphic
and CSS

In order to finally put a bit of life into the text-heavy result of the transformation, we also define another template for one graphic that is to appear in the upper half of the title of the slide, and another that generates a single CSS definition in our HTML document so that the table moves away from the left margin. In the main style sheet `slide6.xsl` we have one `include` instruction and three `<xsl:call-template>` calls, which access the referenced file `pool.xsl`.

Excerpt from
slide6.xsl

```
...
<xsl:include href="pool.xsl" />
<xsl:template match="slide">
    <html>
    <head><TITLE>Content Management Systems </TITLE>
    </head>
        <xsl:call-template name="wd-css" />
    <body >
        <xsl:call-template name="wd-logo" />
        <table>
            <tr><td>
            <xsl:apply-templates  select="title" />
            </td></tr>
            <tr><td>
            <xsl:apply-templates select="topiclist" />
            </td></tr>
            <tr><td align="bottom">
```

```
        <xsl:call-template name="footer line" />
      </td></tr>
    </table>
  </body >
  </html>
</xsl:template>
 . . .
```

Of course, an <xsl:call-template> call can also reference an internal named template. The file with the template pool contains the three named templates, which do not require any access to the nodes of the input document. All three templates simply create elements for the output.

```
pool.xsl
<?xml version="1.0" encoding="ISO-8859-1"?>
<xsl:stylesheet version="1.0"
      xmlns:xsl="http://www.w3.org/1999/XSL/Transform">

<xsl:template name="footer line" >
  <font size="-1"><i>
         &#xA9; Knobloch &amp; Kopp, January 2000
  </i></font>
</xsl:template>

<xsl:template name="wd-logo" >
  <img src="web-design.gif" border="0" width="436"
       height="85" alt="Web design with XML logo" />
</xsl:template>

<xsl:template name="wd-css" >
    <style type="text/css">
       table { margin-left:30px; margin-top:30px;}
    </style>
</xsl:template>
</xsl:stylesheet>
```

These three templates demonstrate that it is possible, with little effort, to intersperse repeated objects in the HTML output. The above example used CSS, but it could of course also be JavaScript or PHP, ASP tags or SSI instructions.

To conclude this section, the result of the transformation will be shown in the browser.

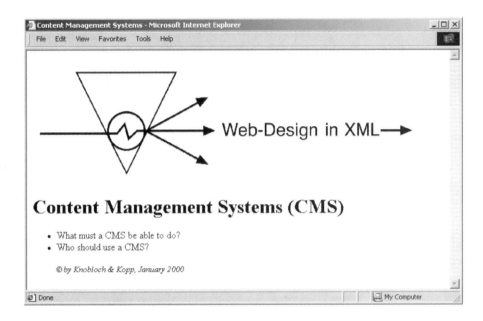

Figure 8.1 Result of the transformation slide 6.xsl

8.2 Direct control of processing

For further examples, and in order to show further elements from XSLT, we will now modify the source file. All the slides of the collection are now grouped together in one file, and this file is given another enclosing `<slides>` tag. Appropriately, the source file is called `slides.xml`. In outline, the structure looks as follows:

Summary of the individual files

```
...
<slides>
    <slide id="xxx" status="active"> ... </slide>
    <slide id="xxy" status="active"> ... </slide>
    <slide id="xxz" status="unfinished"> ... </slide>
    <slide id="xyz" status="active"> ... </slide>
</slides>
```

The structure within the `<slide>` element remains unchanged from the previous examples.

The `id` attribute should contain a prefix that is suitable for indicating the content of the slide in a file name, for example `id="overview"`. As a result, the slides no longer contain numerical labels.

The `"status"` attribute is used as a simple way of including a slide in the transformation or excluding it during the creation process. This label can be used to exclude slides with too much detail if the lecture is to be reused for a different audience.

The control of the processing in previous style sheets mainly used the `<xsl:apply-templates>` mechanism to ensure the assignment of templates to parts of the document. An `<xsl:apply-templates>` instruction does not determine which template is processed next. This mechanism makes it possible to specify processing steps in the form of templates without controlling or knowing the whole processing chain. The activation of the templates in this case is the task of the XSLT processor. We have already met an enforced activation of templates with `<xsl:call-template ...>`.

<xsl:for-each />
Reference
page 197

For cases when it is not clear to the developer of the style sheet how the (sub)structure of the input document looks, the `<xsl:for-each>` instruction is available. Using this instruction, what happens with each node that meets the select expression can be defined directly in the template body.

In order to explain this, we use this instruction on the `slides.xml` file. First, a list of all of the slide titles needs to be created. The titles will be formatted using the HTML tag `<h2>`. The current node is `<slides>`. The instruction thus reads:

```
<xsl:for-each select="slide">
    <h2><xsl:value-of select="title" /></h2>
</xsl:for-each>
```

In contrast to `<xsl:apply-templates>` the select expression no longer needs a separate template that then determines how the title of the slide is to be output.

In order to select only slides in which the the `status` attribute is set to `active`, the select expression needs to be changed slightly.

```
<xsl:for-each select="slide[@status='active']" >
    <h2><xsl:value-of select="title" /></h2>
</xsl:for-each>
```

The test expression within the square brackets checks whether the `status` attribute is identical to the character string `"active"`. Since this testing expression appears inside the quotation marks of the select expression, a single quotation mark must be used to delimit the character string that is to be tested.

The `<xsl:for-each>` variant without the test to see whether the slide is active produces five heading entries; without it, four entries are produced, which are restricted to active slides.

<xsl:number... />
Reference
page 200

Control over the numbering of the slides will now also be left to the style sheet to take care of. `<xsl:number .../>` provides XSLT with a powerful and complex instruction for creating enumerations in the output document. The instruction has a whole collection of attributes, which will only be discussed briefly here. In a first extension, we use an `<xsl:for-each>` expression, in which a cardinal number will be inserted within the heading. This is done using the instruction `<xsl:number format="1." />`.

<xsl:text>...
</xsl:text>
Reference
page 190

In order to create blank space between the number and the heading, the `<xsl:text>` instruction is used, which works in a similar way to a CDATA section. In the example, it contains a blank space, which will not be suppressed.

```
<xsl:for-each select="slide[@status='active']" >
    <h2>
        <xsl:number format="1." />
        <xsl:text> </xsl:text>
        <xsl:value-of select="title" />
    </h2>

</xsl:for-each>
```

This instruction does only produce the headings of active slides in the output document. The numbering, however, is not as we want it to be.

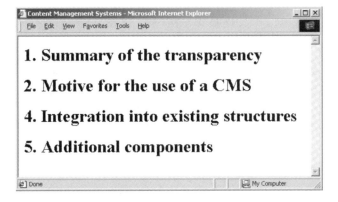

Figure 8.2 Result of transformation from slides1.xsl. With slides2.xsl, the gap in the numbering is avoided.

If `<xsl:number ..>` is used without any further modifier, the value of the counter is calculated from the position of the node in the source document. In the source document, the inactive third slide is available, but it is not in the output document. What should be shown is the current position in the set of selected nodes, which will be the context position in the the result tree. The value of the counter can be manipulated using the `value` attribute. A running enumeration from 1 to 4 is achieved by generating the value using the `position()` function.

```
<xsl:number value="position()" format="1." />
```

This XPath function is not oriented to the input document, but to the fragment of the result tree generated by means of the select expression of the `<xsl:for-each>` instruction.

Conditional processing <xsl:if> Reference page 196

A different version of the list of headings will be used as an example for conditional processing: In order to get an overview of the status of the slides, we will look at them all in turn. In the case of active slides, as before, the title will be output. In the others, there will simply be an indication that they still need to be processed.

The body of the `<xsl:for-each>` loop therefore basically consists of two `<xsl:if>` instructions. Since there is no equivalent to the `if-else` constructs in other programming languages, each different case has to be written with its own `if` instruction. The first instruction therefore tests for the existence of the value `'active'` in the `status` attribute, and the second explicitly for its non-existence. The `not()` function will be used for this purpose.

Excerpt from slides3.xsl; example of <xsl:if>

```
. . .
<xsl:for-each select="slide" >
    <xsl:if test="@status='active' " >
        <h2>
        <xsl:number value="position()"  format="1." />
        <xsl:text> </xsl:text>
        <xsl:value-of select="title" />
        </h2>
    </xsl:if>
    <xsl:if test="not(@status='active')" >
        <h2>
        slide <xsl:number value="position()" format="1"/>
        <xsl:text> is still missing!</xsl:text>
        </h2>
    </xsl:if>
</xsl:for-each>
. . .
```

In the same way, conditional processing can also be defined using the `<xsl:choose>` instruction. The instruction consists of an arbitrary number of `<xsl:when>` elements. Using the `<xsl:otherwise>` element, it is possible to define a default case that is processed if none of the explicit conditions are evaluated as true. The following shows the preceding code segment rewritten using `<xsl:choose>`.

Excerpt from slides4.xsl; example of <xsl:choose> Reference page 197

```
. . .
<xsl:for-each select="slide" >
    <xsl:choose>
        <xsl:when test="@status='active' " >
            <h2>
            <xsl:number value="position()" format="1." />
            <xsl:text> </xsl:text>
            <xsl:value-of select="title" />
        </h2>
    </xsl:when>
    <xsl:otherwise >
        <h2>slide
            <xsl:number value="position()" format="1" />
            <xsl:text> is still missing!</xsl:text>
```

```
    </h2>
   </xsl:otherwise>
  </xsl:choose>
 </xsl:for-each>
  ...
```

Both variants produce an identical output:

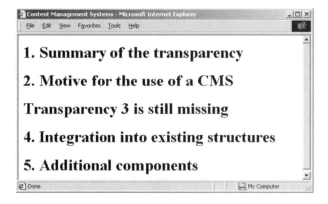

The language elements of XSLT and XPath we have introduced so far are used in the next chapter to create navigation structures.

The question of the context of the current node is very important. Using examples, we will explain what the terms "current context", "current node" and "current node list" mean respectively.

Creating navigation structures

In this chapter, the slides example will be expanded into a collection of navigable HTML files in several stages. In the first stage, internal links will be created, which make it possible to navigate within a document containing all the slides.

The second stage is the division of the source document into individual HTML files. After this, these individual files will be linked to each other using a navigation system. In order to enrich the presentation, an increasing number of CSS definitions are worked into the pages. A final example will show how a whole site can be generated from XML sources.

9.1 Creating internal links

Construction of HTML hyperlinks

A traditional and simple navigation structure within a HTML document is created using anchor elements. In this context, an `<a href="....">` element always refers to an `<a name="....">` element. In a classic navigation structure, the `<a href="....">` elements are put into a small list at the start of the HTML file to give an overview of the content. They take on the form of hyperlinks referring to following sections of the file.

In order to create these links, the transformation script has to go through the collection of slides in two passes.

- In the first pass, the texts for the overview of the content have to be extracted and processed.

- In the second, the content sections have to be formatted and marked as link targets.

The multiple passes through a source document can be done in various ways. In the following example, an `<xsl:for-each>` instruction is used, and for the second, an `<xsl:apply-templates>` instruction is used. In both instructions, the selection is limited to slide entries whose `status` attribute is `"active"`.

The expression `select="slide[@status='active']"` takes care of this in the first template, which places the current node on the `<slide>` document element. The expression specifies the `child` axis of slides. The name of the child node acts as a level selector, and the `[@status='active']` comparison expression is used as the predicate. The HTML body is formed using this fragment.

Excerpt from slides1_1.xsl; creation of the HTML body section

```
    . . .
  <body>
      <h2>Overview of contents</h2>
      <xsl:for-each select="slide[@status='active']">
        <p>
            <xsl:number value="position()" format="1" />
            <xsl:text> </xsl:text>
            <xsl:value-of select="title" />
        </p>
      </xsl:for-each>
      <hr></hr>
      <xsl:apply-templates
      select="slide[@status='active']"/>
  </body>
    . . .
```

First we create a simple overview of the content in the form of a list of the headings of the slides. This happens within the `<xsl:for-each>` loop.

Methodical advice This process can be standardized as a rule of thumb for the development of style sheets:

First, our style sheet is written so that it creates only the information that we want to be turned into links later on. We therefore start off by just defining the selection of the content, then we check that it is correct, and later add the formatting instructions. We therefore look at how to make HTML links out of the character strings that are obtained in this way later on. This greatly reduces the complexity of the style sheet, and we can be sure that our selection mechanisms are defined correctly.

But now back to our example: The current node list within the `<xsl:for-each>` loop consists of all the active slides of the document. The `position()` function, which supplies numbers for the `value` attribute, then indicates the position of the node that is currently being visited within the list of active slides. If the `value` attribute is not provided, the position within the source document is automatically used as a value. In that case, the inactive slides would also be counted, which would mean that there would be gaps in the numbering. In the first pass, only the heading in default font and the running number would be created.

The second pass produces the same current node list. Processing is delegated to another template by means of the `<xsl:apply-templates>` instruction, and this template does the actual work. The processing of this template, which is shown in the following, takes place within the current node list, that is, within the active slides. After this, the node that is being processed has a position within a list, even if the template head suggests that only one specific slide is being processed. The context within this template is the context of the `slide[@status='active']"` selection expression. In this context, the `position()` function works within the `<xsl:number>` instruction as expected. The processing of the title of the slide takes place there and then. The processing of other slide elements is delegated to another template. It is only after doing this that the current context is left. In this kind of template, the instruction for the numbering would have to look different.

Excerpt from slides1_1.xsl; Creation of the content of the slide

```
. . .
<xsl:template match="slide">
    <xsl:call-template name="wd-logo"/>
    <p><table>
    <tr>
      <td><h2>
      <xsl:number value="position()"  format="1."/>
      <xsl:value-of select="title"/>
      </h2></td>
    </tr>
    <tr><td>
            <xsl:apply-templates select="topiclist"/>
    </td></tr>
    <tr><td align="bottom">
            <xsl:call-template name="footer" />
    </td></tr>
    </table></p><hr></hr>
</xsl:template>
. . .
```

The only things missing now are the start of the style sheet and the templates for `<topiclist>` and `<topic>`. With this structure, first an overview of the content, as yet without any links, and then all the contents of the slide are written into the HTML file.

The creation of links can now be inserted into this structure relatively easily. In the first step, the table of contents is marked with a name anchor. This takes place within the heading, directly in front of the `<xsl:for-each>` instruction:

Excerpt from slides1_2.xsl; creation of the name anchor for the overview of the content

```
. . .
<body>
  <h2><a name="content"></a>Overview of contents</h2>
  <xsl:for-each select="slide[@status='active']">
  . . .
```

Since no variables or calculated contents are to be output here, the anchor point for the start of the file can immediately be "hard-coded". Accordingly, at the end of the content of each slide, an upward link to the start of the file is generated.

Excerpt from slides1_2.xsl; creation of the reference to the start of the file

```
. . .
<td align="bottom">
```

```
<a    href="#content"    alt="back    to    contents">[back    to
contents]</a>
<xsl:call-template name="footer line" />
</td>
. . .
```

The creation of these links can be carried out using HTML markup only. In the next version of our transformation, the `href` and `name` attributes have to be filled by selection expressions. All titles of slides have to appear in the table of contents as a `href` attribute and in the second pass as a `name` attribute. The appropriate `<xsl:attribute>` instruction allows the attributes of output elements to be named and to be filled with values. In this particular case, the instruction is written as a child element within an arbitrary output element. The anchor element is the current output element. The above instruction for creating links to the table of contents would be created using the `<xsl:attribute>` instruction in the following way:

```
<a>
    <xsl:attribute name="href">#content</xsl:attribute>
    <xsl:attribute name="alt">back to contents
    </xsl:attribute>
    [back to contents]
</a>
```

In the same way, `<person born="yes" age="45" />` can be generated from

```
<person>
    <xsl:attribute name="born">yes</xsl:attribute>
    <xsl:attribute name="age">45</xsl:attribute>
</person>
```

This laborious method makes more sense if there is no fixed value within the `<xsl:attribute>` instructions. The list of links in the overview of the content is established in the `<for-each>` loop as follows:

Excerpt from slides1_3.xsl; creation of the overview of the content as a list of links

```
. . .
<a>
        <xsl:attribute name="href">
                #<xsl:value-of select="title"/>
            </xsl:attribute>
            <xsl:value-of select="title"/>
</a>
```

Before the call of the template for the logo, the corresponding name anchor is inserted within the template for `<slide>`.

```
. . .
<xsl:template match="slide">
    <a>
        <xsl:attribute name="name">
            <xsl:value-of select="title"/>
        </xsl:attribute>
    </a>
    <xsl:call-template name="wd-logo"/>
. . .
```

The collection of data and the purpose of this document are not particularly suitable for this kind of structuring. It is however easily conceivable for chapters or sections to be given instead of the individual <slide> elements, in which case it makes sense to construct this kind of navigation.

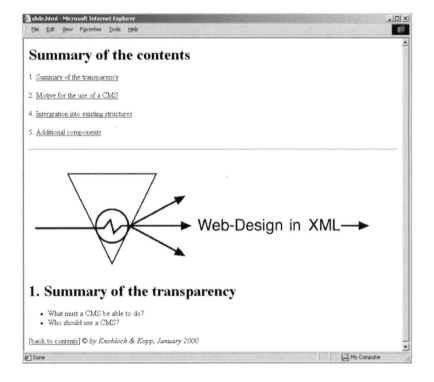

Figure 9.1 Result of transformation slides1_3.xsl

The framework of this simple link structure is a reminder that two parts are required for a link to a segment of an HTML document. The link target has to be marked using a name anchor. Therefore, for the creation of hyperlinks that do not refer back to the start of the file, write access to the document is necessary. Files that are structured in XML, on the other hand, allow access to parts of the document without the target document having to be changed. This access is defined using XPath expressions. XPath, is thus a basis for XPointer. A central idea of this development was to make it possible to define links in external and remote documents without having to change them.

9.2   Creating segments

A slide presentation that is produced in HTML requires a different design from a longer document with sequential text. The aim of this section is therefore to use the collection of slides as a source of XML for individual slide files. The style sheets that make it possible to create a set of HTML files must therefore meet two requirements:

1. The style sheet has to be able to select an individual slide from the set.

2. A style sheet has to be created that controls the production of all slides from the source file.

The selection of a particular slide is not especially difficult. If we use the style sheets that are available, it is sufficient to formulate the central select expression accordingly. As an example, the slide with the id 'addition' will be evaluated. As before, there is the additional requirement that the slide has the status 'active'. The HTML body of our example consists of an expression that selects the appropriate slide and delegates it to the template for `<slide>` elements:

```
...
<body>
    <xsl:apply-templates
    select="slide[@ident='addition'and@status='active']">
</body>
    ...
```

This XPath expression produces a single node as a result set, which together with its descendant nodes is processed by the called template. Within the template for `<slide>`, the current node list simply consists of one node: the current node or the context node. This causes some problems within the template for `<slide>`. Before we go into this, the select expression is first equipped with some more flexibility. It makes no sense defining a separate style sheet for each slide. For this kind of application, parameter values can be used. A parameter value is a value that can be placed in a variable within the style sheet.

<xsl:param>
<xsl:variable>
The XSLT specification deals with the two top-level elements, variables and parameters, in one section. Variables are names that can be connected to a value. As top-level elements, they declare a global variable, which is valid in all child elements of the style sheet, i.e. for example in all `<xsl:template ...>` templates. They can, however, also be used within a template – or within other elements. When used as a non-top-level element, they have local scope. The scope of a local variable covers

all descendants of the elements in which they were declared, and all elements that are on the `following-sibling` axis. The scope of the variable VAR is shown in grey in the following illustration.

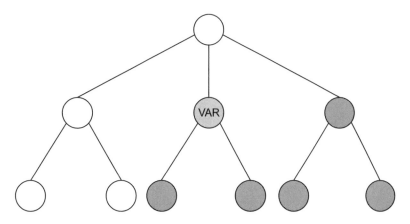

Figure 9.2 Scope of a local variable

The value of variables and parameters can be any object created by an expression. The simple difference between `<xsl:variable>` and `<xsl:param>` is that an `<xsl:param>` element is assigned a kind of default value during its declaration. When the style sheet is activated, this parameter value is overwritten by any value that is passed as a parameter. In contrast to variables in traditional programming languages, `<xsl:variable>` elements are equivalent to constants, since once assigned, their value can no longer be changed.

Document-driven processing   This property, which at first sight seems strange, is associated with the consideration that the processing of a style sheet should not be application-driven, but document-driven. The instructions `<xsl:apply-templates>` and `<xsl:for-each>` nevertheless show that XSLT allows – and even mixes – both forms of processing. The former corresponds to the document-driven approach, the latter to the approach of procedural programming. When developing XSLT style sheets, it is often difficult to think and code in the sense of the document-driven approach. For this reason, some XSLT processors offer proprietary extensions that deviate from the definition of XSLT in the way that they treat variables. For example, the XT and Saxon processors allow variable values to be set freely and to be subsequently overwritten.

According to the XSLT definition, variables and parameters must have a `name` attribute. As well as this, there can be a `select` attribute, which makes it possible to assign values by means of an expression.

```
<xsl:variable name="capital" select="'London'" />
```

Character strings as variable values   Here the variable `capital` is assigned the character string `'London'` as its value. Please note the single quotation marks within the `select` attribute. An attribute value of an XML element has to be enclosed by quotation marks. From the additional single quotation marks, the XSLT processor can tell that this is a character string. If there are no internal single quotation marks, the expression is evaluated as a node set, i.e. the following expression would be interpreted in a totally different way.

```
<xsl:variable name="capital" select="London" />
```

Here, the variable would have as a value the set of all nodes that are child elements of the current node and the <London> element. In practice, this kind of assignment frequently generates variables that have an empty character string as a value, since the value of an empty node set is evaluated as an empty character string.

Alternatively, the assignment of values can also be carried out by means of a direct declaration of a value within the element.

```
<xsl:variable name="capital">London</xsl:variable>
```

This expression is the same as the one on page 137, and assigns the character string "London" to the variable capital. The following list gives a summary of the rules for variables:

- If the element <xsl:variable> is empty, a select attribute should be present. The expression in the select attribute produces a node set or a character string. If the expression of the select attribute is enclosed by single quotation marks, the expression is interpreted as a character string and assigned.

- If the select attribute is empty as well as the value of the <xsl:variable> element, the variable contains the value of an empty character string.

- If there is no select attribute and the value is set, this is assigned to the variable.

Use of parameters as selection criteria Within the current style sheet we define a parameter that we call 'param_id'. Its initial value is the character string 'nothing'. If a variable or a parameter is to be referenced, so that its value can be used in the script, a '$' symbol must be put in front of the name.

```
<xsl:stylesheet version="1.0"
    xmlns:xsl="http://www.w3.org/1999/XSL/Transform">
<xsl:include href="pool.xsl"/>
<xsl:param name="param_id" select="'nothing'"/>

<xsl:template match="slides">
    <html>
    <head><TITLE>Selection with parameter</TITLE></head>
    <xsl:call-template name="wd-css"/>
    <body>
        <xsl:apply-templates
          select="slide[@ident=$param_id and
```

```
                                          @status='active']"/>
        </body>
        </html>
    </xsl:template>
    . . .
```

Passing parameters on the command line

If no parameter is passed when this style sheet is activated, $param\_id$ contains the value 'nothing', otherwise, it contains the value that was entered. With the XSLT processor Xalan, which is used here, the submission of a value begins with the -PARAM flag. Since several parameters can be passed, the name to which the value entered is to be passed in the style sheet also has to be given. On the command line level, a call with parameter passing looks as follows:

```
transform slides.xml slides2_2.xsl addition.html
-PARAM param_id="'addition'"
```

With this call, the character string 'addition' is associated with the variable 'param_id' within the style sheet. The resultant file contains a meaningful name, which harmonizes with the parameter. It is also useful to provide file names with calculable names or subnames such as, for example, slide_1.html, slide_2.html or similar. But more about this later.

The passing of parameters is described in the XSLT Specification. The manner in which this is done is up to the manufacturers of XSLT processors. The form of call shown above may possibly work differently or even not at all with other processors.

Context-dependent evaluation of expressions

We will now consider the aforementioned effects of the selection of a single node on the template that processes the <slide> nodes again. In the previous example, a number was output before the title within this template. The position() function was used to do this. If the template is simply taken on, this function now produces an unwanted result, since the position of the current node within the current node list is always one because this list only consists of this node.

It would be easiest to do without this number. However, when solving this problem, a few difficulties have emerged. Since a possible solution is connected to the use of variables, we will keep the numbering.

The problem of determining the position of nodes that appear when selecting them individually can be solved in several ways. We use the method "ask the parent element" here. What is needed therefore is a template that contains its own node and all its sibling nodes as the current node list. The following instruction first addresses the element nodes, and from there on, all child elements whose status attribute is set to active.

```
<xsl:for-each select="../*[@status='active']" >
```

Before entering this loop, an identification of the current node has to be saved. This is done in a variable. This variable can then be used inside the loop to query every node that is processed, in order to find out whether it is the node whose position is being searched for.

Template for determining the position of a node within its sibling nodes.

```
<xsl:template name="node-position" >
    <xsl:variable name="act-id" select="generate-id(.)"/>

    <xsl:for-each select="../*[@status='active']">
        <xsl:if test="generate-id(.)=$act-id" >
            <xsl:value-of select="position()" />
        </xsl:if>
    </xsl:for-each>
</xsl:template>
```

generate-id()   A variable called act-id is put in front of the loop. It contains as a value a unique identification that is produced from the current node – and thus from the node whose position is to be determined – by the function generate-id(). This function produces a unique code from the input parameter. In the example, the current node is used as a parameter, which is indicated by the dot (using abbreviated XPath syntax). The value of a node depends on the node type. In our case, this is an element node, i.e. its value consists of the concatenated textual content of the descendant-or-self axis. The practical thing about the generate id() function is that the value produced is not random, but instead, a value that can be repeatedly calculated if the function is given the identical input value. It is exactly this that is used inside the loop. An identification is likewise created for each of the sibling nodes using generate-id(). This is compared with the identification that was put in the variable in front of the loop. If the identifications are identical, the condition in the <xsl:if> test becomes true and the position() function can return the position number.

This template is still not flexible enough. The selection expression within the <xsl:for-each> loop is tailored to elements that have a status attribute. In order to make the determination of the position more independent from this, we use a possibility that we have not yet discussed in order to be able to pass parameters to templates.

To do this, a parameter is defined within the template, which carries the name 'src' for a search expression.

```
<xsl:param name="src" />
```

The template is saved in the template pool pool.xsl and is called from the calling style sheet using <xsl:call-template>. Within the <xsl:call-template> instruction, a child element is defined that signals the passing of parameters and also passes parameters and values. Because of this, the code segment from the calling style sheet that creates the title of the slide has grown:

Excerpt from slide2_2.xsl. Call of the template for the calculation of the position of nodes

```
...
<h2>
    <xsl:variable name="pos">
        <xsl:call-template name="node-position" >
            <xsl:with-param name="src"
```

```
                        select="../*[@status='active'] " />
        </xsl:call-template>
    </xsl:variable>

    <xsl:number value="$pos" format="1."/>
    <xsl:text> </xsl:text>
    <xsl:value-of select="title"/>
</h2>
    ...
```

The whole of the select expression is placed in the variable 'src' and passed to the template. The result of the <call-template> call is assigned to the variable 'pos' in the calling style sheet. It is then used to control the position() function.

Template for the determination of the node position with control through template parameters

```
    ...
    <xsl:template name="node-position" >
        <xsl:param name="src" />
        <xsl:variable name="act-id" select="generate-id(.)"/>
        <xsl:for-each select="$src">
            <xsl:if test="generate-id(.)=$act-id" >
                <xsl:value-of select="position()" />
            </xsl:if>
        </xsl:for-each>
    </xsl:template>
```

This solution to the problem is a little laborious, but does have the advantage that the interaction between the XSLT and XPath instructions can be seen clearly. A simpler solution for the determination of positioning can be achieved using the count() XPath function on a document axis. This kind of solution will be introduced in the following section "*Structure of a hierarchical navigation*", page 147.

Result of a transformation: Batch file

This example does not show the final step of the automated generation of all slides from the source file. A second style sheet produces the appropriate batch file or a shell script for Unix environments. During the pass through the source file, a line with a command line call is created for each <slide> element. The attribute ident from the slide is used as the parameter that is passed to our previous style sheet and also as the source for the name of the HTML file.

slides-maker.xsl

```
    <?xml version="1.0" encoding="ISO-8859-1"?>
    <xsl:stylesheet version="1.0"
            xmlns:xsl="http://www.w3.org/1999/XSL/Transform">

    <xsl:template match="slides">
    @ECHO OFF
    <xsl:for-each select="slide[@status='active']">
        call transform slides.xml slides2_2.xsl
```

```
        <xsl:value-of select="@ident"/>.html
        -PARAM param_id="'<xsl:value-of select="@ident"/>'"
   </xsl:for-each>
   </xsl:template>

   </xsl:stylesheet>
```

The central segment of this short style sheet consists of the `<xsl:for-each>` loop in which the calls for the transformation process are generated. The restriction of only selecting active slides for the processing also ensures that only calls for the production of individual files are generated, and that they also make sense. Someone having to type in all the command lines could easily run the risk of producing a call for a page that is not active.

The line within the `<xsl:for-each>` instruction is only used for display purposes here. In the style sheet file, there should be no line break at this point! In this line, literal elements and XSLT instructions are mixed up with each other. In the previous examples, HTML markup elements and XSLT instructions were normally mixed. Therefore, we will now provide a brief explanation of how these lines are processed. First, the two `<xsl:value-of select....>` instructions are evaluated. They are then replaced by the result of the calculation. The following line is therefore output for the slide with the `ident` attribute `'addition'`:

Output of a command line command

```
call transform slides.xml slides2_2.xsl addition.html
            -PARAM param_id="'addition'"
```

Later, the `call` keyword will require the command line interpreter, so that after the execution of `transform`, the processing can continue with the next line. The parameters of `transform` include – as already described – the input document, style sheet and the output document. When passing the expression

```
-PARAM param_id="'addition'"
```

from the command line to the XSLT processor, the outer quotation marks are removed from `"'addition'"`. In the template, this then appears as `'addition'`. This is used in the select expression of `slides2_2.xsl` to select the desired slide. The call of the 'maker' style sheet through

```
transform slides.xml slides-maker.xsl make-all.bat
```

generates a batch file that contains all the calls. By using `make-all` in the command line, all slides are created. The slides are still not connected to each other at this point. Each one stands alone, and a presentation would only be possible by typing the URL into the browser. The construction of a navigation structure is therefore the topic of the next section.

Other output targets

In this example, it will become clear that with all transformations you must think about what the target system does with the data that is produced. When creating a batch file, the target system is the command line interpreter of the operating system. When outputting in HTML, the target system is a browser. If ASP, PHP or Cold-Fusion markup are generated, or if JSP pages are created, the target systems are programming language interpreters that run in the context of a Web server. The forms of processing of the respective target systems have to be taken into account and must therefore be known.

9.3 Creating sequential navigation structures

The aim of the next modification of the style sheet which creates a single slide, is to generate hyperlinks to the next and the previous slide. The specifications of 'next' and 'previous' refer to the sequence in the input document. There is another condition, which makes things a little more difficult, that also has to be taken into account. A slide whose status attribute is not the same as the previous or the next slide has to be omitted.

The selection of the slide for which an HTML file is to be created is the same as in the previous example. During the execution of the template that controls the output of the slide, we first find out the position of the current slide within its siblings with the help of the pos variable. In order to do this, we use the callable node-position template from pool.xsl. The parameterization of this template is also the same as in the previous example. The variable is initialized using the following instructions:

Excerpt from slides3_1.xsl; storing the position of the current node in a variable

```
. . .
<xsl:template match="slide">
<xsl:variable name="pos">
    <xsl:call-template name="node-position" >
        <xsl:with-param name="kp"
                select="../*[@status='active'] " />
    </xsl:call-template>
</xsl:variable>
. . .
```

Within the template for <slide>, the position of the slide is now available using $pos. Since calculations are also possible in XPath expressions, an expression such as $pos+1 or $pos-1 can be used to calculate the next or the previous position. If <slide> is the current node, the subsequent node can be addressed using this expression.

```
<xsl:value-of select="../*[$pos + 1]" />
```

The location path is evaluated from left to right. First of all, the parent axis is switched to. This is the first location step. From here on, all child nodes that are element nodes are selected. Using the predicate [$pos+1], this selection is limited to the node that has the calculated position.

With this expression, however, the complete value of the node is returned. This is not the intention. For access to the adjacent node, only a hyperlink to the HTML file should be created, which refers to the appropriate slide. Therefore, only the value of the ident attribute is searched for. As a result, after the predicate one more step is declared:

```
<xsl:value-of select="../*[$pos + 1]/@ident" />
```

The expression is still not complete. By choice, we have disregarded the status attribute of the neighboring node. This present selection does not prevent us from addressing an inactive slide. Therefore, the inactive slides have also to be excluded here to begin with. The position of the next node then has to be calculated from the remaining set of nodes. The complete expression is as follows:

```
<xsl:value-of
select="../*[@status='active'][$pos + 1]/@ident" />
```

Using this information, we can now create the HTML hyperlink.

Excerpt from slides3_1.xsl, creation of a hyperlink to the previous slide

```
. . .
<xsl:if test="not($pos=1)" >
<a>
    <xsl:attribute name="href">
    <xsl:value-of
    select="../*[@status='active'][$pos-1]/@ident" />
                                        .html
    </xsl:attribute>
    [previous slide]
</a>
</xsl:if>
. . .
```

Two further safeguards against inconsistent hyperlinks can be put in place. First, the current position is checked to make sure it is not the first. If it is, there can be no link to the previous slide. This safeguard can be added to the above example using the <xsl:if> instruction.

Secondly, there has to be a test to see whether or not the current position is the last position. If this is the case, there can be no link to a subsequent slide as one does not exist. To check whether the last position has been reached, the generate-id() function is used again. The block for the creation of the link to the next slide is as follows:

Excerpt from slides3_1.xsl; Checking whether the current node is the last position

```
. . .
<!-- Test whether last position has been reached -->
<xsl:if test="not(generate-id(.)=
        generate-id(../*[@status='active'][last()]) )" >
    <a>
    <xsl:attribute name="href">
    <xsl:value-of
```

```
           select="../*[@status='active'][$pos+1]/@ident"/>
                                                  .html
       </xsl:attribute>
       [next slide]
       </a>
    </xsl:if>
    ...
```

The `generate-id()` function creates an identical code for identical nodes. This code can be used for comparison purposes.

In order to position the hyperlinks on the left margin of the slide, we extend the HTML table which contains the content of the slide by one column. The present table has space for the contents of the slide in the right hand column. The following shows some excerpts from the template for `<slide>` for controlling the construction of the page within the table.

Excerpt from slides3_1.xsl; structure of the table for positioning the elements on the page

```
...
<table><tr>
<td><!-- Table cell for positioning the navigation -->
   <xsl:if test="not($pos = 1)">
    <a><xsl:attribute name="href">
    <xsl:value-of
    select="../*[@status='active'][$pos-1]/@ident"/>
                                      .html
    </xsl:attribute>[previous slide]</a><br/>
    </xsl:if>
    <xsl:if test="not( generate-id(.)   =
      generate-id(../*[@status='active'][last()]))">
    <a>
     <xsl:attribute name="href">
     <xsl:value-of
     select="../*[@status='active'][$pos+1]/@ident"/>
                                      .html
     </xsl:attribute>
     [next slide]
     </a>
    <br/>
   </xsl:if>
</td>
<td>
<!-- embedded table for the content of the slide -->
<table>
<tr><td>
    <h2>
      <xsl:number value="$pos" format="1."/>
```

```
        <xsl:value-of select="title"/>
      </h2>
</td></tr>
<tr><td><xsl:apply-templates select="topiclist"/>
</td></tr>
...
</table><!-- End of the embedded table -->
</td></tr>
</table>
```

Breaking the source file up into segments can be carried out without changing the logic from the previous example. Only the names of the files that are to be called have to be adapted. The result of this transformation will now be shown again.

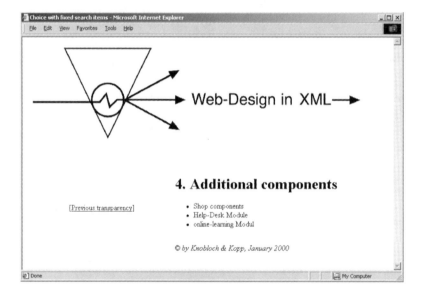

Figure 9.3 Higher, but constant effort

Result of a transformation slides3_1.xsl The effort that was required in the previous examples for the small number of slides is of course not necessarily proportionate to the number of documents in question. After all, the production of the set of slides is independent of how many slides there are. And even if there is an increasing amount of input data, the amount of effort does not increase. The navigation elements adapt themselves to the start and the end of the sequence.

It has probably become clear that not only was content from the source document displayed in some way, but that the structure of the file was also used as a source of information, e.g. in order to create a navigation structure.

To conclude this section, it would be a good exercise to create a summary page which lists all slide titles of the slide document as hyperlinks. To do this, a separate style sheet can be created. Within each slide, a link to the summary document then has to be generated. This can be done by modifying `slides3_1.xsl` slightly.

Since we have now discussed many of the basic XSLT instructions and a few techniques, in the next section a whole site will be produced in the form of a hierarchically ordered set of pages.

9.4 Structure of a hierarchical navigation

In this section, the navigation for a Web site, that is, a whole collection of Web pages which are grouped together because of their content, is to be created using style sheets. For this purpose, we temporarily leave our slides example, and construct some different document structures. Since we have already got to know all the necessary elements and functions of XSLT and XPath, the focus of this section lies on the question of document modelling.

9.4.1 Conceptual formulation and the structure of documents

Requirements for appearance and navigation

Our example site will make it possible for users to navigate through the whole inventory of the site with the help of clickable menu items. No frames will be used. Each HTML page must therefore contain all the links that are necessary for navigation. The following example shows a page from the site.

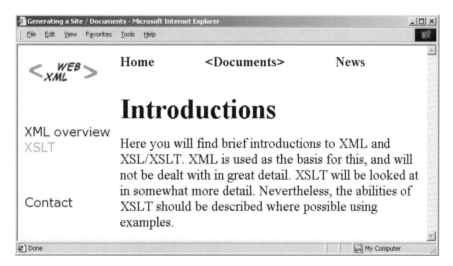

In the main menu, the topic "Documents" was clicked on, which is indicated by angle brackets. In the left column, the sub-items "XML overview" and "XSLT" are visible. A click on the menu item "Home" or "News" would make other subtopics visible in the navigation area of the left column. The overview document on the topic of 'documents' is shown in the content area of the window.

Requirements for
the style sheet
The style sheet for the creation of pages must therefore take care of the following:

1. The selection of all elements that are needed for the creation of links to the page shown.

2. The selection of the content that is to be shown.

3. The consolidation of navigation structure and content in an HTML file.

In order to meet these requirements, we will first develop the structure of the site. You can find the entire style sheet for this printed in the appendix. We will develop it step by step here.

As a hierarchy of pages, a Web solution is highly XML-friendly right from the moment the problem is defined. Hierarchical orderings are easy to map in XML. Thus the first version of our structure description can look as follows:

```xml
<?xml version="1.0" encoding="ISO-8859-1"?>
<site title="Generation of a site ">
  <page id="home" title="Home" src="home.xml">
    <page id="us" title="Us on ourselves"
                          src="defcont.xml"/>
    <page id="people" title="People"
                          src="defcont.xml"/>
    <page id="projects" title="Projects"
                          src="defcont.xml"/>
  </page>
  <page id="documents" title="Documents"
                            src="intr.xml">
    <page id="xml" title="XML overview"
                          src="defcont.xml"/>
    <page id="xslt" title="XSLT" src="xslef.xml"/>
  </page>
    <page id="news" title="News"
                          src="defcont.xml">
    <page id="news" title="News from W3C"
                          src="defcont.xml"/>
    <page id="events" title="XML Events"
                          src="defcont.xml"/>
  </page>
</site>
```

The site consists of three main topics (Home, Documents, and News), for each of which there are subtopics. They are represented by nested <page> elements. To make things simpler, the hierarchy only has two layers, however a deeper hierarchy is easy to create. The title attributes should be displayed as links which branch to the appropriate pages in the HTML files, which are yet to be created. The page area is divided up as shown in Figure 9.4.

The content of the page is saved in separate files that can be found via the entry in the `src` attribute. Since the connection to the content files is not established through entity references, there is no check to see whether these files even exist. This is rather convenient, at least during the development of a site structure, since reminders are not constantly sent by the parser regarding missing content and the processing aborted. The references to the content files can be opened during a transformation with the help of the XSLT function `document()`. This has another advantage over the solution that uses entity references. Entity references are always resolved by the parser, i.e., all content files are read and integrated into the document. For the creation of an HTML page, however, only a subset of `<page>` elements is used, and only a single content file. The choice as to which content file must be opened depends on which page is needed, and should therefore be selected by the style sheet. Above all, if the Web site does not contain just a few pages, but hundreds, it is best to leave out static entity references, since the whole extent does not have to be loaded in the main memory.

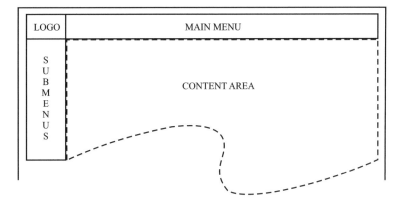

Figure 9.4 Schematic structure of a page

The identification of the desired page using the `src` attribute also offers the possibility of logically separating the creation of navigation elements from the construction of the display of the content.

Requirements on the navigation   The style sheet therefore must distinguish between two cases:

- **Click on a `<page>` element at the first level:** all elements of this level have to be visible, as do all child elements of the selected element. The selected element must be marked so that it is obvious what has been clicked on.

- **Click on a `<page>` element at the second level:** all sibling elements of this level have to be visible. The selected element has to be marked so that it is obvious what was selected. Likewise, the parent element of the selected element must also be marked so that is still obvious where the page belongs. Furthermore, the parent element and all its siblings, but not its child elements, have to be visible.

9.4.2 Production of a page

First, we create a transformation that produces a single page. It is given a parameter value, which allows the style sheet to determine which page was requested. It must then produce the elements of the above cases, depending on the kind of menu item selected. As a parameter we use the id attribute of the <page> element. We will look first at a few definitions (top-level elements) of the style sheet to be created, which we need for the creation of navigation structures.

```
<xsl:output method="html" version="1.0"
                         encoding="UTF-8" />
<xsl:include href="content.xsl" />
<xsl:variable name="menu-width">140</xsl:variable>
<xsl:param name="selpar" select="'home'"/>
```

We will set the output method to "html". We put the templates for the presentation of the content area in a completely separate style sheet (content.xsl). This is incorporated using the <xsl:include> instruction.

This style sheet is not discussed here. Anyone can find out how these content files are put together themselves – the style sheet merely needs to interpret the tags that are used in appropriate ways. The content files of the example in question use the <content> element as a document root.

In the next step, a global dummy variable is declared for the width of menu entries (menu-width), as is as the parameter value (selpar).

The navigation elements and the content area are positioned using HTML tables. The attributes of the table definition should not be written explicitly in the <table> tag each time. For this reason, we use <xsl:attribute-set> for the definition of margins and distances in an attribute set with the name "navtable-atts".

```
<!-- Attribute set for navigation tables -->
<xsl:attribute-set name="navtable-atts">
   <xsl:attribute name="border">0</xsl:attribute>
   <xsl:attribute name="cellspacing">0</xsl:attribute>
   <xsl:attribute name="cellpadding">4</xsl:attribute>
</xsl:attribute-set>
<xsl:attribute-set name="navtable-atts-down"
   use-attribute-sets="navtable-atts">
   <xsl:attributename="class">down_menu</xsl:attribute>
   <xsl:attribute name="width">140</xsl:attribute>
</xsl:attribute-set>
```

An extension of `navtable-atts` (`navtable-atts-down`) is created specially for the left column, which reuses the definitions. This attribute set contains a `class` entry with which the CSS formatting details are controlled.

With this code, the pre-definitions are taken care of and the first phase of the template processing can begin:

First an HTML document head and the link to the CSS style sheet are created in the template body of `<xsl:template match="site">`. The table structures are formed within the `<body>` element, and are used for the incorporation of the navigation and content areas. In the following code examples, these HTML oriented topics are left out and are indicated by ellipses.

The complete style sheet can be found in the appendix. Here we will concentrate on the construction of the HTML links as a way of navigating. The central processing logic of the style sheet is shown in the following section. In some places this has been shortened:

Creating main menus

Creating submenus in the left margin column

Copying content from a file

```
...
<xsl:template match="site">
....
<body>
<!-- (1) Creating menu level 1-->
<table xsl:use-attribute-sets="navtable-atts">
<tr>
    <td width="{$menu-width}"><img src="logo.gif" /></td>
    <xsl:apply-templates select="page" mode="top_toc"/>
</tr>
<!-- (2) Creating left menu margin columns -->
<tr>
    <td width="{$menu-width}" valign="top">
        <table use-attribute-sets="navtable-atts-down">
                <xsl:apply-templates
                    select="//page[@id=$selpar]"
                    mode="down_toc"/>
        </table>
    </td>
<!-- (3) Copy content from file -->
    <td valign="top" colspan="{$content-span}">
    <xsl:apply-templates
        select="document($content-file)"
        mode="cont_base"/>
    </td>
</tr>
</table>
</body>
...
```

In this example, the framing table is defined. The logo is placed in its first cell. Using `<xsl:apply-templates>`, all `<page>` elements that are direct descendants of `<site>` are selected. This selection, shown by the `mode` attribute, is used to create the top table of contents (`top_toc`: top table of contents). The first line of the table is thus filled with the logo and the main menu.

Within the second `<tr>` entry, a further table is created in the first cell (`<td>`) for positioning the downward running submenu. In the associated `<xsl:apply-templates>` element, a single `<page>` element is selected, which contains the page that is to be shown. Translated into an XPath expression, this means that a `<page>` element is searched for whose `id` attribute is equivalent to the parameter value (`select="//page[@id=$selpar]"`).

The second cell of the second table row is filled with the actual content. With the help of the `document()` function, the content file is opened and the entire input tree of the second XML file is included in the processing using `<xsl:apply-templates>`. In the example, the file name and the width of the table cell are specified using a variable. How these variables are given values will be discussed later in this section.

Here is another summary of the processing structure that is defined by the first template in this style sheet.

1. Creation of the logo and main menu in the first row of the table.

2. Creation of a submenu for the selected main menu entry in the first cell of the second row.

3. Creation of the content in the second cell of the second row by incorporating a further XML source document.

What do the details of these three steps look like? The beginning of the creation of the main menu is simple:

```
<!-- Template for the main menu -->
<xsl:template match="page" mode="top_toc">
    <td>
        <div class="right_menu">
            <xsl:call-template name="create-link-mark"/>
        </div>
    </td>
</xsl:template>
```

Delegation of detailed work to callable templates

Only one table cell is created for each of the `<page>` elements and a `class` selector is set for the CSS commands here. The actual creation of a link is delegated to a named template (`create-link-mark`). This template has the task of creating an `<a href>` entry. In addition to this, it will mark the text of the entry if the `<page>` element of the input document that has just been processed is identical to that whose page content is to be shown. The text will also be marked if the current node is a parent node of the selected page.

```
<xsl:template name="create-link-mark">
    <a>
        <xsl:attribute name="href">
            <xsl:value-of select="@id"/>.html
        </xsl:attribute>
        <xsl:if test="@id=$selpar or page[@id=$selpar]">
            <img src="open.gif" border="0"/>
        </xsl:if>
        <xsl:value-of select="@title"/>
        <xsl:if test="@id=$selpar or page[@id=$selpar]">
            <img src="close.gif" border="0"/>
        </xsl:if>
    </a>
</xsl:template>
```

The href attribute of the link is filled using the <xsl:attribute> instruction because the value has to be calculated using XSLT instructions. The file name to which the link is to refer is formed from the id of the respective <page> element, with ".html" appended as an extension.

The test to see whether the text is to be marked by open.gif and close.gif is carried out using the expression

```
<xsl:if test="@id=$selpar or page[@id=$selpar]">
```

If the current node is equivalent to the requested page (@id=$selpar) or if the current node is a parent element of the page (page[@id=$selpar]), the graphic is incorporated into the text of the link. This is carried out once before the selection of the text from the title attribute and once afterwards. Thus the main menu is written.

Something that is a bit more difficult is the creation of the submenu. To remind you, once again here is the beginning of the template for the creation of the submenu.

```
<xsl:apply-templates
                select="//page[@id=$selpar]"
                mode="down_toc"/>
```

A single element node is selected here. During entry into the template

```
<xsl:template match="page" mode="down_toc">
```

the current context only contains a single node, not a set, as is the case when the main menu is created. This means, however, that within this template it is not obvious which menu hierarchy was addressed, whether it was an element of the main menu or a child element of a menu item that was selected previously from the main selection. The position of the hierarchy in which the selected page is, has therefore to be determined within the template. This can be achieved though a combination of the count() function and the ancestor axis. The expression

```
<xsl:value-of select="count(ancestor::node())"/>
```

calculates the number of nodes in the set of ancestors of the current node. These ancestors of course include the root node and the document node, that is, the `<site>` element node. Therefore, for the first menu level, two is returned as the number of ancestors. In the following template, the result of the calculation is saved temporarily in the `level` variable and is then used in an `<xsl:choose>` expression for further conditional processing.

```
<xsl:template match="page" mode="down_toc">
<!-- Establish level -->
   <xsl:variable name="level">
     <xsl:value-of select="count(ancestor::node())"/>
   </xsl:variable>
   <xsl:choose>
<!-- Main menu element -->
   <xsl:when test="$level = 2">
       <xsl:for-each select="page">
           <xsl:call-template name="down_toc"/>
       </xsl:for-each>
   </xsl:when>
<!-- Sub menu element -->
     <xsl:when test="$level = 3">
       <xsl:for-each select="../page">
           <xsl:call-template name="down_toc"/>
       </xsl:for-each>
     </xsl:when>
   </xsl:choose>
</xsl:template>
```

If the current node is part of the main menu, only the child elements need to be output in the submenu. This is initiated using the `<xsl:for-each select="page">` instruction. The `"down_toc"` template that is called as a result of this only creates one HTML table row and calls the `"create-link-mark"` template shown earlier to create the links. If the current node belongs to the submenu, then all sibling elements of the current node are selected using

```
<xsl:for-each select="../page">
```

and for each of these, `create-link-mark` is called. As a result, the menus are defined.

Capability of style sheets to be transferred to deeper hierarchies

It does not require any more effort to analyze even deeper hierarchies in this way. The central coordinating point for this is the `<xsl:choose>` expression in the previous template. It just needs to be supplemented with more `<xsl:when>` elements. Other templates can be branched to, which then contain the logic for the presentation of further submenu layers.

The last step of our style sheet produces the actual content from the external file, and puts this into the second table cell of the second row. As a reminder, here is the call again:

Integrating the content of the page

```
<td valign="top" colspan="{$content-span}">
    <xsl:apply-templates
        select="document($content-file)"
        mode="cont_base"/>
</td>
```

Attribute-Value template "Names and conventions", page 179

Sensibly, the presentation of the content is as wide as the menu items of the main menu. The number of columns over which the width of the content area can stretch is given in the variable "content-span". It is used as a attribute-value-template within the <td> tag.

How can we determine how many menu items the main menu has? Once again, the count() function can be used in conjunction with a suitable XPath expression. The following instructions have to be placed in the style sheet as top level elements in order to make the above call possible.

```
<xsl:variable name="content-span">
    <xsl:value-of select="count(site/page)"/>
</xsl:variable>
<xsl:variable name="content-file">
  <xsl:value-of select="//page[@id=$selpar]/@src"/>
</xsl:variable>
```

The name of the content file is saved in a further global variable (content-file). This is done by selecting the src attribute of the page, which corresponds to the parameter value.

The complete style sheet can be found in the appendix. It contains a few more lines than were discussed here. However, these simply consist of instructions and variables for controlling distances or positions, which do not need any further explanation.

9.4.3 Creating a site

The example shown starts off with a call of the style sheet with a call parameter. For the creation of an entire site, as shown in the example of the previous section, another style sheet can be created that creates the batch processing file, which calls all parameter combinations one after the other. This method is slow, but has the advantage of being independent of the special functions of any particular XSLT processor. According to the standard, when an XSLT style sheet is processed, each time it is gone through, a file is produced.

XSLT extension elements

Many XSLT processors, however, contain extensions that allow several output documents to be written during a transformation. This is done with the help of a so-called 'extension element'. The Xalan processor implements an extension element <xalan:write>, and Saxon the <saxon:output> element. An example of this can be found in the reference section. The production of several HTML pages is a lot faster using these extension elements than it is using a parameterized command line call. Furthermore, the declaration of a parameter value is dropped, since a further preliminary pass through the source document is able to read all `<page>` elements and to write a file for each of these. This solution is well-suited to a production environment involved in the batch publishing of HTML pages.

This ability to create several output files will be included in the next version of XSLT, version 2.0, as a requirement of XSLT processors.

Dynamic creation of pages, dynamic publishing

For reasons of system-independence, this solution is not looked at in detail in this book. The documentation of the particular processors does, however, make it easy to adjust style sheets accordingly. Another reason why the slow version was selected in this book is that the method of passing parameters to XSLT style sheets can also be used in dynamic publishing environments.

An XSLT transformation that is carried out as a process in the context of a Web server (CGI, servlet or ASP) can be used by passing a style sheet parameter in order to create the appropriate page on request. In the style sheet example that was introduced, only the creation of the links needs to be modified. Instead of having the `<a href>` elements refer to different HTML files, they need to refer to the name of the structure file. The `@id` attribute then has to be provided as a parameter of the HTTP request. A possible request to such a dynamic system would then look as follows:

```
http://www.xyz.de/site.xml?selpar=home
```

Within `site.xml`, there then needs to be a default connection to the style sheet by means of a processing instruction.

The way in which style sheets are used in publishing environments such as, for example, Apache Cocoon cannot be shown here for reasons of with space. If XML is revolutionizing the Web, then this is probably being done by the use of these server-side techniques. This opens up a massive potential of uses for XSL. Or, in the words of the developers of Apache Cocoon: "We have just scratched the surface".

In the following chapter, we return to our slide example in order to produce another form of Web documents: PDF. In the process, the third part of the XSL Specification will be used: Formatting Objects.

XSL Formatting Objects

This chapter introduces the XSL formatting language and its formatting objects. The previous example document will be used as the starting point. Since an XSL formatting document has an independent structure, we will explain the structure first as though the formatting objects had been written "by hand". In order to obtain the anticipated result, a style sheet will then be produced which generates this kind of formatting document from the XML source file.

In order to make the effect of the formatting instructions clear, the result of the transformation will then be transformed into a PDF document using a formatting program.

10.1 Aims and status of XSL

XSL as a format-neutral control language

With XSL, the WWW Consortium defines a language for the description of documents that are to be used to control a formatter, but not a concrete formatter for a special output device or format. In a similar way to that in which an XSLT script can be seen as a control file for an XSLT processor, you can also imagine an XSL document as a control document for formatters.

The XML elements that constitute the XSL formatting language are called formatting objects. This language allows specifications of pagination, layout, typography, lines, blocks, footnotes, etc. to be made.

Formatting Objects and properties

Formatting objects are elements such as `<fo:simple-page-master>`, `<fo:flow>` or `<fo:block>`.

In the XSL Specification [XSL] more than 50 of these formatting objects are described, and for each of these elements there is a large number of default and special attributes. These attributes of the formatting objects – altogether approximately 200 of them – are called properties. The names of these attributes are derived from the notation of Cascading Style Sheets. A CSS rule, for example, can read as follows:

```
fo:block {font-family: Arial, Verdana, serif}
```

The equivalent in XSL – written using the formatting object `<fo:block>` – looks very similar:

```
<fo:block font-family="Arial, Verdana, serif">
```

The depth of detail of the formatting objects, which were also intended for use in printing, goes beyond that of Cascading Style Sheets. This is why not all attributes come from the CSS notation.

Creating FO documents

In the jargon, an XML document that contains FO declarations is also called a formatting tree. Of course, in principle, it is possible to write this kind of document manually using an editor, or in the future to have it created by an application program that supports FO. However, the obvious way is to create an FO document by means of a transformation. To do this, the defined document structure of FO documents must be adhered to.

Construction of FO documents

The XSL document model is more like the normal perception of a document than all the other models that have been described so far. It consists of a sequence of pages described by means of a definition of their layout and of the page sequence. This kind of document cannot be used directly by a human reader, since there are still no browsers or viewers available. In a further processing step, an FO document is therefore converted into a consumable document. This last conversion is the formatting in the literal sense. A formatting program changes the FO document into a form that has a particular file format. This also means that a single FO document can be transformed into different file formats with the help of different formatters.

Formatting Objects for PDF FOP

Until now, there have only been very few formatters that can cope with FO documents. In the following examples, the formatter FOP (Formatting Objects for PDF) will be used, whose development was initiated by J. Tauber. Since FOP was submitted to the XML Apache project, it has been developed further and can now be downloaded from xml.apache.org. As might be expected, the program is of an experimental nature and does not yet implement everything that is described in the draft of XSL.

The following examples are likewise merely supported by what was implemented of the XSL draft within FOP. At this point, no attempt will be made to describe the formatting objects fully – even those that are used in the examples. Because of the extent of the standard document, a book dedicated to the detailed presentation of formatting objects would have to be written.

The configuration and use of FOP will be looked at in the following section *"Setting up Formatting Objects for PDF (FOP)"*, page 175.

Other formatters are advertised – partly on a commercial basis – such as for example, a formatter for Rich Text format ((RTF), which has become very important as an import format for a very large number of standard office programs.

10.2 The structure of FO documents

The FO namespace

A namespace was established by the WWW Consortium for formatting documents. The URI for this is:

```
http://www.w3.org/1999/XSL/Format
```

Normally, fo is used as the prefix for this namespace. Although other prefixes are feasible, most style sheet authors use fo:, which makes the documents concerned more comprehensible. The enclosing bracket, the root element of an FO document, forms the formatting object `<fo:root>`.

Division of the FO documents: `<fo:layout-master-set>` and `<fo:page-sequence>`

Within this element, an FO document can be divided into two sections.

- The first section is formed by the `<fo:layout-master-set>` element. In this section, the page types for the current document are defined and the sequence of these page types is described in *Page definition using <fo:layout-master-set>*, page 159.

- The second section is formed by a sequence of `<fo:page-sequence>` elements – see *Specifying how pages are filled using <fo:page-sequence>*, page 163. The child elements of `<fo:page-sequence>` describe in the order in which the page types that were defined in `<fo:layout-master-set>` are to be used, and what content they are to be filled with.

An FO document can only contain one `<fo:layout-master-set>`, but several `<fo:page-sequence>` sections. The following code shows the outline of an FO document.

FO fragment 1

```
<?xml version="1.0" encoding="UTF-8"?>
<fo:root xmlns:fo="http://www.w3.org/1999/XSL/Format">
   <fo:layout-master-set>
      ...
   </fo:layout-master-set>
   <fo:page-sequence>
      ...
   </fo:page-sequence>
   <fo:page-sequence>
      ...
   </fo:page-sequence>
</fo:root>
```

This fragment is simply shows the constituent blocks of an FO document. Let's now look a little more closely at the two parts.

10.2.1 Page definition using <fo:layout-master-set>

Within the `<fo:layout-master-set>` element, page definitions are determined using one or more `<fo:simple-page-master>` elements. In the following example, we will concentrate first on the definition of page geometry, and then we will deal with the sequence of page types.

Definition of the geometry of the page

The measurements and structure of pages are determined using `<fo:simple-page-master>` elements. In the following example, two page types are defined using the names `"first"` and `"rest"`.

FO fragment 2

```
<fo:layout-master-set>
    <fo:simple-page-master margin-right="2.5cm"
        margin-left="2.5cm" margin-bottom="2cm"
        margin-top="2cm" page-width="20.9cm"
        page-height="29.5cm" master-name="first">
            <fo:region-before extent="1cm"/>
            <fo:region-body margin-top="3cm"/>
            <fo:region-after extent="2cm"/>
    </fo:simple-page-master>
    <fo:simple-page-master margin-right="2.5cm"
      margin-left="2.5cm" margin-bottom="2cm"
      margin-top="2cm" page-width="20.9cm"
      page-height="29.5cm" master-name="rest">
            <fo:region-before extent="4cm"/>
            <fo:region-body margin-top="3cm"/>
            <fo:region-after extent="2cm"/>
    </fo:simple-page-master>
    <fo:page-sequence-master>
        . . . .
    </fo:page-sequence-master>
</fo:layout-master-set>
```

The measurements of the page, the margins and the top and bottom edges are specified using the large number of self-explanatory attributes of the `<fo:simple-page-master>` elements. The `master-name` attribute allows a name to be given to each of the page elements, with which this page object can be addressed within subsequent `<fo:page-sequence-master>` elements.

The two pages in the above example with the names first and rest have identical attribute sets, but differ from one another in their child elements. Within the `<fo:simple-page-master>` elements, the respective pages are described by the child elements `<fo:region-before>`, `<fo:region-body>` etc. Here, the areas into which the two pages are divided are different.

Regions of an FO document

In general, XSL understands a page as a set of rectangular areas. This box model is strongly inspired by that of Cascading Style Sheets. All the rectangular areas of an FO document can be specified with the `<fo:region-..>` child elements of `<fo:simple-page-master>`, whose names indicate their positions.

In the case of text that runs from left to right, the arrangement of the regions is as follows:

Table 10.1 The FO regions of a page

fo:region-before	Equivalent to the header line region.
fo:region-after	Equivalent to the footer line region.
fo:region-body	The column within which the content is placed.
fo:region-start	Equivalent to the left edge margin.
fo:region-end	Equivalent to the right edge margin.

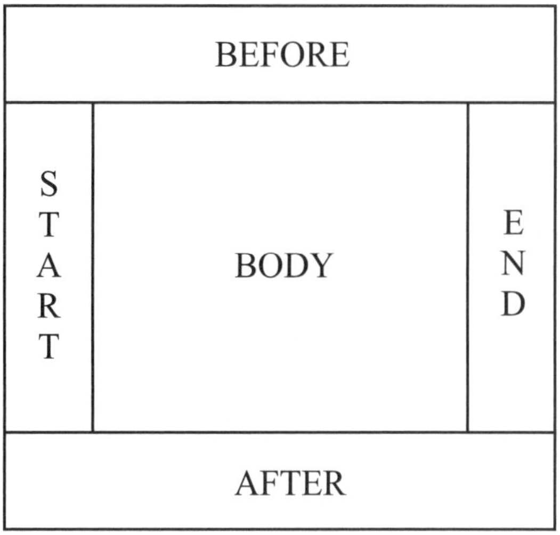

Figure 10.1 The FO regions

If the direction of the text is from right to left, the start and the end region are swapped accordingly. Figure 10.1 shows how regions are placed on a page.

The names `start`, `end`, `before` and `after` appear in many attribute names in other formatting objects. In general, they describe the positioning and alignment of regions.

If you consider an FO document as a formatting tree, then a page forms the highest level in a hierarchy of rectangular areas. A page is the region container that contains all other rectangular regions (formatting objects). The formatter differentiates between the following regions:

- Area containers can be positioned in a coordinate system and can contain further containers and other rectangular areas. In the above illustration, as an area container, the page contains five further area containers: `start`, `end`, `before`, `after` and `body`.

- Block areas are arranged sequentially inside their containers, i.e. they are not positioned using coordinates. They can contain further blocks within themselves. It is easiest to imagine block areas as sections or as list items. They flow with the amount of text that is inserted or deleted, and usually have at least one line break in front of them.

- Line areas describe lines of text within a block. Line areas can contain further subareas, such as, for example, white areas or rules. There are no corresponding formatting objects for line areas. They are calculated by the formatter according to the running and make-up of the characters.

- Inline areas are parts of a line such as, for example, an individual letter, a footnote reference, a formula or a graphic. Inline areas can also contain further subareas. Formatting objects that create an inline area are, for example, `<fo:inline-graphic>`, `<fo:page-number>` and others.

Normally, a formatting object therefore creates a separate rectangular region in which further objects can be placed. However, a directly corresponding formatting object does not exist for every region.

Defining the page sequence

The second part of the content of `<fo:layout-master-set>` is made up of the description of the sequence of the pages using the `<fo:page-sequence-master>` elements. Here we describe how often and in what sequence page types are to be used when inserting content. When flowing content into the regions in a page, the formatting program must calculate how much content can be accommodated in it. If a page is filled according to its own geometry, the formatter has to know which regions are still available for further content. These region definitions can be called using the previously mentioned `<fo:simple-page-master>` element, which defines the sequence of their availability within the `<fo:page-sequence-master>` element. For the above example we will define two page sequences:

- A start page, which is to appear just once, and

- A continuation page, which will be used for the rest of the content.

In the following, the code section is supplemented with the specification of the page sequence. The geometry attributes and elements are elided and will be indicated by ellipses in order to make the example more readable.

FO fragment 3

```
<fo:layout-master-set>
    <fo:simple-page-master ... master-name="first">
            . . .
    </fo:simple-page-master>
    <fo:simple-page-master master-name="rest">
            . . .
     </fo:simple-page-master>
    <fo:page-sequence-master master-name="startpage">
      <fo:single-page-master-reference
                        master-name="first" />
    </fo:page-sequence-master>
    <fo:page-sequence-master master-name="the_rest">
      <fo:repeatable-page-master-reference
                        master-name="rest" />
    </fo:page-sequence-master>
</fo:layout-master-set>
```

Each `<fo:page-sequence-master>` element has to have a `master-name` attribute, whose value has to be unique within the document. One or more `<page-master-reference>` elements can be named as child elements. There are three forms in which this can be done:

1. `<fo:single-page-master-reference>`
2. `<fo:repeatable-page-master-reference>`
3. `<fo:repeatable-page-master-alternatives>`

We only use the first two simple forms. Both have a `master-name` attribute, which can refer to the page geometries described in the `<fo:simple-page-master>` elements. In contrast to the `<fo:single-page-master-reference>` element, `<fo:repeatable-page-master-reference>` also has a `maximum-repeat` attribute that determines the maximum number of times that the page can be repeated during the formatting.

We will now leave this schematic outline to one side and look at how to fill pages with content.

10.2.2 Specifying how pages are filled using <fo:page-sequence>

The second part of an FO document consists of one or more `<fo:page-sequence>` elements. These determine how the previously defined page types are to be used when filling the pages with content. Using the `master-name` attribute, the formatter is told which `<fo:page-sequence>` definition is to be used inside the `<fo:page-sequence>` element.

The content of pages within each `<fo:page-sequence>` is based on further elements. Which bit of content is to be distributed to which region is controlled using two further formatting objects.

- `<fo:static-content>` is used to position content that has to be repeated on every page. This content could be, for example, header and footer lines.

• `<fo:flow>` is used to describe the flowing text which can be spread out over one or more pages, depending on its length.

Within these elements, the distribution and positioning of the contents is specified, using a further subdivision into smaller rectangular regions, the `<fo:block>` elements. For example, any text or other blocks can appear within an `<fo:block>` element. If a region, for example the body region, is filled up with block elements, these are flowed onto the next page.

Even in the case of a simple document such as a letter, the title page and the continuation pages are formed in different ways. On the second page of a letter there is no need to have an area for the address. When a new page is made up at the end of page 1, the same page type therefore must not be reactivated. This exact sequence was conveyed to the formatter within `<fo:page-sequence-master>`.

Before we take a closer look at the elements of `<fo:page-sequence>`, the following fragment will show the extended rough framework of our FO document again.

FO fragment 4

```
<?xml version="1.0" encoding="UTF-8"?>
<fo:root xmlns:fo="http://www.w3.org/1999/XSL/Format">
<fo:layout-master-set>
    <fo:simple-page-master ... master-name="first">
        ...
    </fo:simple-page-master>
    <fo:simple-page-master master-name="rest">
        ...
    </fo:simple-page-master>
    <fo:page-sequence-master master-name="startpage">
        <fo:single-page-master-reference
                        master-name="first" />
    </fo:page-sequence-master>
    <fo:page-sequence-master master-name="the_rest">
        <fo:repeatable-page-master-reference
                        master-name="rest" />
    </fo:page-sequence-master>
</fo:layout-master-set>

<fo:page-sequence master-name="startpage">
  <fo:flow flow-name="xsl-body">
        ...
  </fo:flow>
</fo:page-sequence>
<fo:page-sequence master-name="the_rest">
    <fo:static-content flow-name="xsl-region-before">
    </fo:static-content>
```

```
        <fo:flow flow-name="xsl-body">
                . . .
        </fo:flow>
    </fo:page-sequence>

    </fo:root>
```

All further details in the structure of the document can now be imagined as an extension and improvement of the dotted parts of this framework.

The two formatting objects which have already been introduced `<fo:static-content>` (fixed content) and `<fo:flow>` (flowing content) are responsible for assigning content to regions of the page. The `<fo:static-content>` element is used for placing content which is repeated but which stays the same, for example, if there is to be a header line on each page or if there is to be a page number in the footer line region, as is shown in the following excerpt from an FO file.

Static content for the definition of a footer line with a page number
```
<fo:static-content flow-name="xsl-region-after">
    <fo:block text-align="center" font-size="10pt"
        font-family="serif" line-height="14pt">
        - <fo:page-number /> -
    </fo:block>
</fo:static-content>
```

Using the `flow-name="xsl-region-after"` attribute, the footer line area is addressed, the alignment and font attributes are set in the subsequent `<fo:block>`, and the page number is output within the block. Using the element `<fo:flow>`, the addressed regions are filled with content such as running text:

Flow for positioning content that has not yet been fixed
```
<fo:flow flow-name="xsl-region-body">
    <fo:block>This is the title</fo:block>
</fo:flow>
```

The above fragment places a small amount of text inside the block element in the text column of the page. In an XSLT style sheet, instead of the fixed coded text, there can be a template the result of whose calculation is some content that is not initially known. The same attributes can be used for `<fo:flow>` and `<fo:static-content>` (e.g. space-before, space-after, ...). The two elements differ from each other only in the fact that the content of a `<fo:static-content>` element cannot move to another page, whilst in the case of `<fo:flow>` this is what is wanted. The use of `<fo:static-content>` elements is optional, i.e., documents can be created without them. If they are used, however, they have to appear within the `<fo:page-sequence>` before `<fo:flow>` elements.

You now know what the skeleton of an FO document looks like. Since it does not make sense to code FO documents manually, in the following we use an XSLT transformation to create from the XML example a small booklet in which the slides can be printed out.

10.3 Creating FO documents using XSLT

The aim of this chapter is to generate from the example document an FO document that contains the following sections:

- A section with a title page or a covering page, but with no header and footer lines.

- A section with a summary of the content, and footer lines for page numbers.

- A section with three slides per page. To the right of each slide there are to be lines for notes, and a header line containing a continuous line, and a footer line containing the running page number.

For this we create an XSLT style sheet in two steps. First we create a fragment that produces the FO skeleton, and then we process the detailed instructions by placing further formatting objects in this skeleton and output content from the source document using further XSLT templates.

10.3.1 The structure of the XSLT transformation

We start to put together the style sheet by trying to create the skeleton of our FO document again, i.e. <fo:root>, <fo:layout-master-set> and the <fo:page-sequence>, which we require for the different sections. Creating this skeleton requires a long style sheet. Because of this, the file is also introduced in several sections. If you want to read the complete style sheet in one go, it is printed in Appendix B (see page 157 ff.).

To start with, we need to declare the XSL namespace for the style sheet using the prefix fo. This declaration can be found in the first bold printed line of the following element. The template that is activated for the <slides> root element of the XML document first creates the <fo:root> root element for the FO document. A namespace also needs to be defined here, which is used later when the output document is parsed. This is given in the second line printed in bold.

FO fragment 5
```
<?xml version="1.0"?>
<xsl:stylesheet version="1.0"
    xmlns:xsl="http://www.w3.org/1999/XSL/Transform"
    xmlns:fo="http://www.w3.org/1999/XSL/Format">

<xsl:template match="slides">
    <fo:root
        xmlns:fo="http://www.w3.org/1999/XSL/Format">
        ...
    </fo:root>
</xsl:template>
...
```

```
<xsl:template match="slide" >
...
</xsl:template>
...
```

The structure of the document is then written within the `<fo:root>` element, using the elements `<fo:layout-master-set>` and `<fo:page-sequence>`.

The page types that we need for our three sections are defined in the element `<fo:layout-master-set>`. At this point, the style sheet only produces declarations that are encoded, and therefore do not come directly from the source file. The declarations concerning the page size and page sequence are deliberately not part of the source document. We can therefore output the declarations within `<fo:layout-master-set>` in the XSLT style sheet as literals, in a quite similar manner to what happened in the previous FO fragments 1–4.

Since the attributes for the area dimensions of the formatting objects take up a lot of space, they have been left out in the following examples and are replaced with three dots as an ellipsis. The attributes that are essential for understanding, such as names that are used as references within the FO document, are, however, given.

In the first section (1) a page is defined for the covering page. This does not contain any areas for the header or footer line.

FO fragment 6

```
<fo:layout-master-set>
<!--(1) The section for the covering page-->
<fo:simple-page-master master-name="covering page" ...>
   <fo:region-body ... />
</fo:simple-page-master>

<!-- (2)Page type for the table of contents -->
<fo:simple-page-master master-name="toc" ... >
   <fo:region-before .../>
   <fo:region-body .../>
   <fo:region-after .../>
</fo:simple-page-master>

<!-- (3)Page type for the content of the slides and lines
-->
<fo:simple-page-master master-name="rest" ...>
   <fo:region-before .../>
   <fo:region-body .../>
   <fo:region-after .../>
   </fo:simple-page-master>

<!-- (4) Page sequence for the covering page -->
<fo:page-sequence-master master-name="leading text">
 <fo:single-page-master-reference
      master-name="covering page" />
```

```
      </fo:page-sequence-master>

   <!-- (5) Page sequence for the table of contents -->
    <fo:page-sequence-master master-name="content">
     <fo:repeatable-page-master-reference
           master-name="toc" />
    </fo:page-sequence-master>

   <!-- (6)Page sequence for the contents -->
     <fo:page-sequence-master master-name="all">
       <fo:repeatable-page-master-reference
             master-name="rest" />
       </fo:page-sequence-master>
      </fo:layout-master-set>
    <fo:page-sequence>
    ...
    </fo:page-sequence>
```

As well as the text region, the next page type (2) contains a footer line region for the page number and a header line in which a logo will appear. The third page type (3) is constructed in the same way, but text and a continuous line are to appear in its header line.

These page types and sequences are now used in the `<fo:page-sequence>` elements. The first sequence (4) creates the covering page. This part only consists of a single page that contains an `<fo:flow>` object in the body text.

FO fragment 7
Filling the
covering page

```
   <!-- (4) The section for the covering page -->
   <fo:page-sequence master-name="leading text">
        <fo:flow flow-name="xsl-body" ...>
           <!-- Contents of the covering page -->
           </fo:flow>
      </fo:page-sequence>
```

The next section of code uses the page definition for the table of contents. On this occasion, arbitrary repetitions of this page type were allowed in `<fo:layout-master-set>`. With the conciseness of our example document, the definition of a single page would be sufficient, as in the case of the covering page. Since we do not know how large our source document will become, as a precaution we will include page breaks. The contents are entered by means of two `<fo:static-content>` objects and one `<fo:flow>` object:

FO fragment 8
Filling the table
of contents

```
   <!-- (5) Section for the table of contents-->
   <fo:page-sequence master-name="content">
      <fo:static-content flow-name="xsl-region-before">
        <!-- The logo will appear here later -->
      </fo:static-content>
      <fo:static-content flow-name="xsl-region-after">
```

```
            <!-- the page number will appear here later -->
        </fo:static-content>
        <fo:flow flow-name="xsl-body" ...>
            <!-- The summary list will be put here -->
        </fo:flow>
    </fo:page-sequence>
```

The section for the content of the slides is built up in a similar way and also contains the description of a header line element for the horizontal line.

FO fragment 9
Filling the
content region

```
<!-- (6) Section for the content of slides and lines -->
<fo:page-sequence master-name="all">
        <fo:static-content flow-name="xsl-region-before">
        <!-- Header line with continuous line -->
    </fo:static-content>
    <fo:static-content flow-name="xsl-after">
        <!-- footer with page number -->
    </fo:static-content>
    <fo:flow flow-name="xsl-body" ...>
        <!-- Space for the content of the slide -->
    </fo:flow>
</fo:page-sequence>
</fo:root>
</xsl:template>
```

The document and the XSLT templates are closed at the end of the last `<fo:page-sequence>` element. The regions that we have left out in the above fragments contain calls of further XSLT templates, and the positioning of further FO elements also takes place in them. Now that the skeleton of an FO document has been created, we will turn to these details.

10.3.2 Production of the content portions

We start again with the covering page. It only contains `<fo:flow>` objects for the body of text. They contain title and subtitle texts that are written directly in the style sheet, since our source file does not contain any declarations for a covering page.

Faults in the
document model
of the slide
example

This method is problematic because we have mixed the text of the content with the description of its presentation in the code. It is exactly this that should be avoided by using XML. At this point it becomes apparent that any attempt to structure the content independently of the display medium must be thoroughly planned in advance. In the XML source document we have not specified a title-subtitle pair for a printout. Since this is missing, we must resort to this unattractive auxiliary construction. For the aim of medium-neutral data structuring and data management, during the development of document structures, we need to know the application cases, i.e. the output channels, we are going to be dealing with. The information that they carry into the output should then be taken into account. It would therefore have made sense to provide optional elements for leading text, title, print title, etc. within our slide document. The transformation could then have taken into account the appropriate elements for the respective output channel. But now back to the content of our title page:

FO fragment 10
Filling the
covering page

```
<fo:flow flow-name="xsl-body">
    <fo:block text-align="centered"
            line-height="30pt" font-size="22pt"
            space-after.optimum="22pt"
            space-before.optimum="22pt">
        Content Management Systems
    </fo:block>
    <fo:block text-align="centered"
            line-height="30pt"
            font-size="16pt"
            space-after.optimum="16pt"
            space-before.optimum="16pt">
        Slides on the problems of content management
    </fo:block>
</fo:flow>
```

Only a few attributes that are used to control sizes and alignment are new here, all of which should be quite clear. All numerical measurements that are used in attributes have to be given along with a unit of measurement. For fonts, sizes are usually specified in points (pt), and these are used here too. Other units, such as cm or px can also be used for dimensions. These units can even be mixed, hence the indication of the unit is mandatory.

The attributes space-before and space-after carry the sub-attribute optimum. Here minimum and maximum would also be possible in order to give the formatter some leeway in the calculation of page breaks. At the time of writing, the "Formatting Objects for PDF" (FOP) formatter only implements optimum, which is why there is no room for experimentation with these attributes.

Another simple content element is the page number, which is to appear in the second section of the footer line. In the <fo:static-content> element, we merely stipulate that there should be a hyphen before and after the page number:

FO fragment 11
Creating a
footer line with
page numbers

```
<fo:static-content flow-name="xsl-region-after">
    <fo:block text-align="center"
            font-size="10pt"
            font-family="serif"
            line-height="14pt">
        - <fo:page-number/> -
    </fo:block>
</fo:static-content>
```

Using the attribute initial-page-number, the start of the numbering of fo:page-number can be set.

The header line of the table of contents is to consist of a logo and a continuous line. For this purpose, two blocks are written inside the `<fo:static-content>` element:

FO fragment 12
Creating a
header line with
a logo and
continuous line

```
<fo:static-content flow-name="xsl-region-before">
   <fo:block>
      <fo:external-graphic src="file:web-design.gif"/>
   </fo:block>
   <fo:block>
      <fo:leader leader-pattern="rule" />
   </fo:block>
</fo:static-content>
```

In the first block, an external graphic is incorporated, and in the second block the fill element `<fo:leader>` is used. Both elements are only implemented in FOP rudimentarily at the moment. Thus, no size attributes are evaluated for the graphic, and in the case of the fill element, only the linear fill pattern can be used (producing a horizontal rule). Attributes can be specified in the XSL document for these elements, but are not evaluated.

So far, only fixed-coded `<fo:...>` elements have been copied into the output data stream. When creating the overview of the content, the capabilities of XSLT for outputting the content of the source file are brought into play.

FO fragment 13
Creating a table
of content with
page numbers

```
<fo:flow flow-name="xsl-region-body">
   <fo:block>
      <xsl:for-each select="slide[@status='active']">
         <fo:block>
            <xsl:number value="position()"/>
            <xsl:text> </xsl:text>
            <xsl:value-of select="title"/>
            <xsl:text> </xsl:text>
            <fo:page-number-citation>
            <xsl:attribute name="ref-id">
            <xsl:value-of
            select="generate-id(.)"/>
            </xsl:attribute>
            </fo:page-number-citation>
         </fo:block>
      </xsl:for-each>
   </fo:block>
</fo:flow>
```

The blocks that are created inside the `<xsl:for-each>` instruction use the font attributes of the surrounding FO elements. They are omitted in this fragment, as is the positioning of the two blocks inside a table. To create this overview of the content, a table had to be built as an auxiliary construction to position the title, together with page specifications. The implementation of the fill element `<fo:leader>` in FOP unfortunately does not allow any restrictions on the length of the connecting lines.

However, what happens inside the loop instruction is more important: It selects the active slides in the way that was mentioned previously, and outputs a running number and the title of the slide. Since this output takes place in a block, a carriage return is created at the end of each block.

The bold passage after the output of the title of the slide contains an element that makes it clear that XSL goes beyond Cascading Style Sheets. XSL supports the division of the document into pages and provides numbering for them. But what use is a table of contents that cannot refer to these page numbers? At the moment when the table of contents was created, the formatter had not positioned any characters of the content on the content pages. There are therefore still no content pages. The `<fo:page-number-citation>` element was designed for this case. In its `ref-id` attribute it refers to a unique identifier inside the document. Since we do not have the content yet, we do not actually have a unique identifier for this content yet. We do know, however, which node we are working on within the loop. More precisely, the XSLT processor knows this. Using the `generate-id()` function that we have already met, it is possible to produce a unique identification from a node that can also be reproduced for this node. We therefore use the `generate-id()` function as a value for the `ref-id` attribute of the `<fo:page-number-citation>` element. Later on, when outputting the content, we just have to make sure that we reuse the `generate-id()` function when we create an `<fo:block>` element for this content. The corresponding block is provided with an `id` attribute, to which the `<fo:page-number-citation>` element then refers.

The header and footer lines of the content section are defined in a similar way to those from the section for the table of contents. They are therefore not discussed in detail.

The main part of the work is the placement of the content into the `<fo:region-body>` region, the control of the page breaks after each third slide, and the creation of unique identifiers to which the `<fo:page-number-citation>` element can refer.

FO fragment 14
Creating the
content of the page
with a break after
every third slide

```
<fo:flow flow-name="xsl-region-body">
    <xsl:for-each select="slide[@status='active']">
        <fo:block break-after="page">
          <xsl:if test="position() mod 3 = 0 ">
            <xsl:attribute name="break-after">
             page
            </xsl:attribute>
          </xsl:if>
          <xsl:attribute name="id">
                <xsl:value-of select="generate-id(.)"/>
          </xsl:attribute>
```

```
      <xsl:call-template name="postable"/>
    </fo:block>
  </xsl:for-each>
</fo:flow>
```

The actual output of the slide and lines is taken care of within a named template (postable). This template is called within an <fo:block> element. A test now has to be carried out to find out whether there ought to be a page break or not. Using the position() function (from XPath) and modulo division it can be established whether the current slide is the third on the current page. If it is, a page break attribute is incorporated into the block containing the output. The instruction <fo:block break-after="page"> specifies that after the end of this block (break-after) a break of the "page" element (page) is to take place. The block is therefore first filled by the named template postable and when the block is closed, the page break is induced. The attribute break-before would accordingly induce a page break before the block is opened.

The positioning of the content is controlled in our example using a single-row table. The slide is reproduced in the left hand table cell. The layout is left up to the templates that are defined for each of the content elements. They are activated with <xsl:apply-templates> and are discussed in the following. The empty lines for notes are output in the right hand table cell by means of the named template make_empty-lines.

FO fragment 15
Positioning the
content of the slide
and the lines

```
<xsl:template name="postable">
  <fo:table space-before.optimum="32pt">
    <fo:table-column column-width="3in"/>
    <fo:table-column column-width="3in"/>
    <fo:table-body font-size="12pt">
      <fo:table-row>
        <fo:table-cell border-width="1pt"
                       border-style="solid"
                       padding="6pt" spacing="6pt">
          <xsl:apply-templates/>
        </fo:table-cell>
        <fo:table-cell padding="6pt"
                       spacing="6pt">
          <xsl:call-template
             name="make_empty_lines"/>
        </fo:table-cell>
      </fo:table-row>
    </fo:table-body>
  </fo:table>
</xsl:template>
```

With `<fo:table>` we are using another block-oriented formatting object. Making up the table out of child elements is quite similar to the way in which tables are defined in HTML. It should to be said, however, that in XSL it is not the `<fo:table>` element that is the root element of a table, but `<fo:table-and-caption>`. This deviation from the official documents can be traced back to the implementation. For each column of the table, an `<fo:table-column>` element has to be given, which specifies the extent using the usual attributes. Both columns are three inches wide. If the contents of the columns are wider than the explicit column definition, the width is automatically adapted by FOP. The specifications regarding the lines and cells are put into the `<fo:table-body>` element.

Now only the templates for the ruling and the remaining content elements of the source document are missing. The template for the `<title>` element will not be introduced here in its entirety, because only one block with font attributes will be created and the text will be output within this block. The templates for `<topiclist>` and `<topic>` are much more interesting. For the `<topiclist>` element, an `<fo:list-block>` is initiated and, in this block, the formatting of the list items is delegated to the template for `<topic>` using `<xsl:apply-templates/>`.

FO fragment 16
Formatting object
for the creation
of a list

```
<xsl:template match="topiclist">
    <fo:list-block font-size="12pt" start-indent="1cm">
        <xsl:apply-templates/>
    </fo:list-block>
</xsl:template>
```

Using the `start-indent` attribute the list is moved away from the left edge by one centimeter (left indented). The `<fo:list-block>` element is made up of `<fo:list-item>` entries. Within `<fo:list-item>`, the content of a list item (`<fo:list-item-body>`) is distinguished from previous markers (`<fo:list-item-label>`), as can be seen in the following template:

FO fragment 17
FO list elements

```
<xsl:template match="topic">
    <fo:list-item>
      <fo:list-item-label>
          <fo:block>*</fo:block>
      </fo:list-item-label>
      <fo:list-item-body>
          <fo:block>
                  <xsl:apply-templates/>
          </fo:block>
      </fo:list-item-body>
    </fo:list-item>
</xsl:template>
```

We use the asterisk as a marker, and in `<fo:list-item-body>` the content is copied in by means of the `<xsl:apply-templates>` instruction.

In the example document, this instruction produces the content of the `<topic>` element, since this does not have any further child elements.

As a result, the left column of the positioning table is filled. In the right column, the lines that are to indicate the space for notes are used, which the template `make_empty_lines` is to take care of. Only one more further named template is called in this named template. This defines the lines. In the following, only two calls are written out in full. The others are indicated by ellipses.

FO fragment 18
Creating empty
lines for notes

```
<xsl:template name="make_empty_lines">
    <xsl:call-template name="make_empty_line"/>
    <xsl:call-template name="make_empty_line"/>
    ...
</xsl:template>
<xsl:template name="make_empty_line">
    <fo:block start-indent="1cm">
        <fo:leader leader-pattern="rule"
                space-before.optimum="0.5cm"
                space-after.optimum="0.5cm"/>
    </fo:block>
</xsl:template>
```

The above template draws a line using an `<fo:leader>` element, which gets its extent from the enclosing block.

Along with some graphic elements, the structure of the document is now defined according to our target setting. The complete style sheet with the attributes of all the formatting objects that are used can be found in the appendix.

For the conversion into PDF format we require a few more adjustments.

10.3.3 Setting up Formatting Objects for PDF (FOP)

Formatting Objects for PDF is a Java application and, like our previous tools, requires a Java runtime environment. First, you should download and unpack the most up-to-date version of FOP from `xml.apache.org`. The examples in this section were developed using the version fop_0_14_0. After unpacking this, in the newly created directory, you will find the Java library `fop_0_14_0.jar` and `w3c.jar`. Change the CLASSPATH entries so that they refer to `fop_0_14_0.jar` and `w3c.jar`, or simply rename the library to `fop.jar` if this name is too long for you. Of course, the CLASSPATH entries then accordingly have to refer to `fop.jar`. The call of FOP takes place through

```
java org.apache.fop.apps.CommandLine xy.fo xy.pdf
```

The first parameter value is the name of the formatting object document to be processed, and the second parameter the output file that is to be created. Since the FO file is generated from a transformation which is produced by the following call

```
java org.apache.xalan.xslt.Process
-xsl xy.xsl -in xy.xml -out xy.fo
```

it makes sense to convert the whole process into a script. In Windows, the `.bat` file then looks as follows:

```
@ECHO OFF
java org.apache.xalan.xslt.Process %5 %6 %7 -v
                          -xsl %2 -in %1 -out %3
java org.apache.fop.apps.CommandLine %3 %4
```

Here the % markers stand for input parameters. If, for example, the script has the name `makepdf.bat`, the production of the PDF file will be activated as follows:

```
makepdf slides.xml slides2fo.xsl slides.fo slides.pdf
```

If you experiment with this environment and want to obtain concrete results, you will have to use the documentation to FOP. This will have been written into the appropriate FOP directory during the unpacking process. The most important document is "What's implemented". In this document you can find a list of the formatting objects and properties that are actually available. Details about the names of the properties, which can sometimes differ from the current standard document, can be found in the examples that are also in the FOP directory. In this directory, there is a whole number of FO example documents whose PDF representation can be seen in a parallel directory. What you find here, works.

The version of FOP that is used in the book is very different from the pre-version `fop_0_13_x`. If you have to work with the older version, you cannot use the example style sheets without changing them. Between the versions, the names of FO elements and attributes have changed, and to some extent the structure of the FO documents have as well. This is due to the fact that the version 0_14_0 follows the draft of the year 2000, however the pre-version follows that of 1999. In the example files, you will therefore find a complete style sheet called `slides_fop13.xsl`. This style sheet was developed with the pre-versions. If you are free to choose which version to work with, always use the most up-to-date version, as it will be the next one to become the future recommendation of the WC3.

If you are interested in the background and the details of the formatting objects, the current document to the working draft [XSL] and the book from Neil Bradley [BRA00] are recommended.

10.4 Summary and outlook

In this chapter, it has become clear that with the help of XSLT transformations, files can be generated from an XML data source which correspond to the formatting semantics of formatting objects. In this context, FO serves as an example for any semantics that can be written on the basis of XML. In principle, it is also possible to create markup languages such as Scalable Vector Graphics (SVG) or Synchronized Multimedia Integration Language (SMIL) in the same way. And, although all these developments are still quite new and have not been established for long, they are expected to achieve an integration of text, graphics and animation, and sounds and languages that until now has not been possible: integration on the level of the creation of these formats.

Until now, images, sounds, animations etc. were created separately using a large number of programs. The integration of these elements into a unit consisted of their being incorporated into a master document. The maintenance or further development of the contents therefore had to be carried out within a number of sources. After each change, they had to be re-consolidated into a document again.

XML technology holds out the prospect of bringing a serious change here. Whether this will actually succeed depends on a number of factors such as, for example, software companies. It is, however, also acknowledged that these possibilities of media-neutral data require a high level of effort for the modelling of source data. A decisive factor, which plays an important part in keeping the "promises" of XML is therefore whether decision makers and developers are prepared to put in this extra effort with regards to data and information modelling.

Elements of the XSLT language

The following brief description of the language elements of XSLT is limited to the documentation of the syntax and explanations. The level of detail provided in the explanations is determined by each element's use in the examples in this book. Instructions that are used rarely or not at all are only discussed briefly, but those that are used frequently are discussed in more detail. The arrangement and grouping of the elements is arbitrary. By way of introduction, some terms and conventions are explained; to some extent, these have their roots in the XSLT Specification.

A.1 Terms and conventions

- An **attribute value template** can be used to provide a value for an attribute of an XSLT element; the value is not written as a static character string, but instead as an expression, which must be written in curly brackets.
  The following line contains a static attribute value:

  ```
  <a href="test.xml">test</a>
  ```

  In contrast, the corresponding attribute value template that gets its value from the input document looks as follows:

  ```
  <a href="{@src}">test</a>
  ```

  Attribute value templates may only be used for attributes of elements which are explicitly identified in the XSLT standard as permitting them.

- **Document order** describes the sequence of the elements as they are written in the XML document. The output of an XSLT transformation can be in a different order from the document order of the input document.

- **Input/source tree, output tree**. At the start of the processing, each XSLT transformation builds up a representation of the input document that looks like a tree structure made up of nodes (XPath document model). The transformation works on this representation and not on the original document. The output is likewise structured in a tree. Accordingly, the two representations are described as an *input tree* (sometimes a *source tree*) or *output tree*.

- **Result tree fragment** describes part of the output structure. This kind of fragment is treated differently from a node set, which originates from the input tree.

- **Node set** describes a selection of nodes from the input tree. This selection is the result of the evaluation of an expression.

- **Literal result element** is an element that is written directly in the output target e.g. <h1>.

- **Qualified name** (QName) is a name that conforms to XML (e.g. title in the element <title>) with an optional declaration of a namespace prefix (e.g. <xsl:template>).

- **Template body/ instruction body** describes the content of an instruction, for example, everything that is written between the start and end tag of <xsl:template> </xsl:template>, <xsl:if> </xsl:if> etc.

- **Top-level elements** are the XSLT elements that can appear as direct child elements of <xsl:stylesheet> in an XSLT script.

- **Whitespace** describes blank space, line breaks, paragraph markers and tabs. These markers are ignored during the processing of an XML file, provided that they are not part of a character string.

A.2 Elements for the definition of templates and the control of their call

A.2.1 <xsl:template>

The output of data is controlled using the top-level element <xsl:template>. An <xsl:template> element is activated either through the comparison of nodes using a (search) pattern or through an explicit call by means of a name.

```
<xsl:template>
   name=QName
   match=pattern
   mode=QName
   priority=Number >
      <xsl:param>*</xsl:param>
      template-body
</xsl:template>
```

All attributes of `<xsl:template>` are optional. Using the `name` attribute, the template can be assigned a name. If a name is provided, the template can be activated via the `<xsl:call-template>` instruction.

However, if no name is given, a `match` attribute has to be formulated. This defines a pattern, with which the nodes of the input tree are compared. If the pattern and the nodes match, the nodes are processed via an `<xsl:apply-templates>` instruction. The `match` attribute of `<xsl:template>` must not contain any direct reference to a variable (e.g. `$selpar`). If the `match` attribute is not given, a `name` attribute must be provided. If there is both a `name` attribute and `match` attribute, the template can be activated in both ways.

For the case in which different template patterns apply to the same node, a numerical `priority` attribute can be provided, with which the priority of a template over others can be established. Another way of enforcing the use of one template over another rival template is to use the `mode` attribute. This attribute can be given during the activation of templates using `<xsl:apply-templatesmode= "xyz">`.

The processing rules for the matching node are formulated in the *template body*. A possible child element can be `<xsl:param>`, whereby a parameter value can be passed to the template. This element has to be written before any other child elements.

A.2.2 `<xsl:apply-templates>`

The `<xsl:apply-templates>` instruction selects a node set to be processed. It instructs the XSLT processor to look for a suitable template (`<xsl:template>`) for processing the node that is indicated.

```
<xsl:apply-templates select=expression mode=QName>
    <xsl:with-param>template body</xsl:with-param>
    <xsl:sort />
</xsl:apply-templates>
```

This instruction is always used in the instruction part of a template (the template body). The specification of the nodes that are to be selected for processing is carried out using the `select` attribute. Within the `select` attribute there is an XPath expression, which has a `node set` as a return value. An expression that produces a numerical value is therefore not allowed at this point.

If the `select` attribute is omitted, all child nodes of the current node are selected. In accordance with the determination of node types and properties of XPath this means that attribute nodes and namespace nodes are not included in the automatic processing. If, for example, fragments of the input tree are to be copied, `<xsl:apply-templates />` alone is not sufficient. For the attributes to be included by the template being executed, the instruction would have to read `<xsl:apply-templates select="@*|* " />`.

Using `<xsl:apply-templates>` the instruction part of the matching template is activated and the property "current node" skips the nodes of the selected node set that is already being processed. Within this set, the position of the current node can be determined using the `position()` function, and the number of nodes in the selected set can be determined using the `count()` function. With each entrance into the instruction part of the template that was activated by `<xsl:apply-templates>`, a context is built up using `current node list`, `current node` etc.

If an `<xsl:sort>` instruction was defined within `<xsl:apply-templates>`, the selected nodes are sorted before they are processed. How does the processing of the other nodes now proceed?

For each node of the selection, a template is selected that specifies how it is to be processed. This selection is controlled by the `match` attribute of the template. If no suitable template is found, the XSLT processor uses a default template (`built in template rule`). However, a template is always used if its `mode` attribute is identical to the `mode` attribute of the `<xsl:apply-templates>` call. If neither have a `mode` they are considered to be identical.

Using the instruction `<xsl:with-param>`, the called template can be passed a parameter. The value of the parameter is passed to a parameter variable with the same name as the template. If there are only parameters with different names within the template, `<xsl:with-param>` is ignored.

The `<xsl:apply-templates>` instruction is most useful if the structure of the element to be processed is complex or has a lot of variants, or if frequent changes to the structure are expected. This is because the instruction leaves the control of the processing up to the template (`template rules`) or the XSLT processor. If a defined, known, or rarely changed element structure is to be processed, `<xsl:for-each>` can be used.

A.2.3 `<xsl:call-template>`

The `<xsl:call-template>` instruction is used to call a named template.

```
<xsl:call-template name=QName>
   <xsl:with-param>*</xsl:with-param>
</xsl:call-template>
```

The mandatory `name` attribute must be identical to the name of the `<xsl:template>` element that is called.

The treatment of the optional parameters is similar to that of optional parameters of the `<xsl:apply-templates>` instruction.

In contrast to the `<xsl:apply-templates>` instruction, no new context is created by means of `<xsl:call-template>`, i.e., the `current node` remains the same. Because of this, this instruction is more like the functions of procedural programming languages. Application logic which is needed at various points in the processing can be implemented meaningfully using named templates. In order to achieve effects similar to the return value of a function, the `<xsl:call-template>` instruction can be called during the creation of an XSLT variable.

```
<xsl:variable name="temp_value">
   <xsl:call-template name="number_in_list" />
</xsl:variable>
```

From now on, the variable $temp_value contains the value that was created by the template number_in_list. This value can be used, for example, to influence conditional processing (<xsl:if test="$temp_value=3">).

A.3 Elements for the structuring of style sheets

A.3.1 <xsl:stylesheet>

<xsl:stylesheet> is used to refer to the root element of an XSL document. <xsl:transform> can also be used.

```
<xsl:stylesheet
id="identification"
version="1.0"
xmlns:xsl="http://www.w3.org/1999/XSL/Transform"
extension-element-prefixes="prefix list"
exclude-result-prefixes="prefix list"
>
<!-- Top-level elements-->

</xsl:stylesheet>
```

The instruction must contain at least one namespace declaration, or possibly several. For example, if formatting objects are to be output, the following declaration has to be incorporated:

```
xmlns:fo="http://www.w3.org/1999/XSL/Format"
```

The version attribute must be given, and, at present, can only carry the number 1.0, whilst the other attributes are optional.

Using the extension-element-prefixes attribute, a method is defined for marking and addressing an XSLT processor's function extensions, even though these were still unknown at the time of the XSLT Specification. The attribute dictates which namespace prefix marks function extensions. For example, the XSLT processor Xalan, which is used in the book, has extended functions that allow it to create several output files by processing one style sheet. In order to use these, the following declarations in the style sheet are necessary:

```
<?xml version="1.0" encoding="UTF-8"?>
<xsl:stylesheet version="1.0"
xmlns:xsl="http://www.w3.org/1999/XSL/Transform"
xmlns:xalan="org.apache.xalan.xslt.extensions.Redirect"
extension-element-prefixes="xalan">
```

```
. . . . . . .
</xsl:stylesheet>
```

Accordingly, the extensions are activated within the style sheet:

```
<xalan:write select="$Naming variable">
<xsl:value-of select="."/>
</xalan:write>
```

However, this attribute should only be used if a style sheet actually uses the extensions. The mere existence of additional functions in an XSLT processor does not create the need to declare extension-element-prefixes. Extension functions can be made available by the manufacturer of the XSLT processor or by third parties, including users themselves. The details of this depend on the APIs of the manufacturer. Even in this case, however, the prefixes for the extensions have to be declared.

Using the exclude-result-prefixes attribute, specified namespace declarations can be excluded from being sent to the output document by means of a transformation. For example, a template such as the following:

```
<xsl:template match="web-design:Chapter">
   <testprint>
     <xsl:value-of select="*">
   </testprint>
</xsl:template>
```

would automatically write the namespace prefix into the output document. Using the exclude-namespace-prefixes="web-design" attribute within the <xsl:stylesheet> element, this would be suppressed in the whole of the style sheet.

A.3.2 <xsl:import>

This top-level element is used for the modularisation of style sheets. It imports the definitions of a second style sheet into the style sheet that contains the instruction.

```
<xsl:import href="URI" />
```

The style sheet that contains the <xsl:import> instruction will be referred to in this section as a *parent style sheet (P)*, and the integrated style sheet as the *child style sheet (C)*.

Because of its effect on the priority rules when there are imported instructions, <xsl:import> must be given as the first child element of <xsl:stylesheet>. It is thus the only top-level element whose position in the style sheet is important. All top-level elements of (C) are inserted at the position of the <xsl:import> instruction in the parent style sheet. The child style sheet may contain further <xsl:import> and <xsl:include> instructions. However, in any event, relative path specifications in the `href` attribute are evaluated relatively to the position of the style sheet in which the `<xsl:import>` instruction is. It can become very confusing as to which style sheet incorporates which other one. There is also the danger of creating chains of circular `<xsl:import>` instructions, which are explicitly forbidden.

If there are identical elements in the parent and child style sheet, a priority rule comes into effect. The priority rule for imported top-level instructions stipulates that they have as low a priority as those that are coded in the parent style sheet. If several style sheets are imported, the style sheet that was imported first has a lower priority level than the next.

A.3.3 <xsl:include>

This top-level element is used for the modularisation of style sheets. It integrates the definitions of a second style sheet into the style sheet containing the instruction.

```
<xsl:include href="URI" />
```

In contrast to the elements that can be accessed through `<xsl:import>` from other style sheets, with `<xsl:include>` integrated elements have the same priority as those defined within the parent style sheet. They therefore work as if they were coded somewhere in the parent style sheet. The external templates behave as if they had been copied in as text at the position of the `<xsl:include>` instruction. For the sake of clarity, `<xsl:include>` instructions should be put at the start of the style sheet if this does not have any effect on the processing logic.

A.4 Output oriented elements

A.4.1 <xsl:value-of>

The `<xsl:value-of>` instruction writes a character string to the output data stream.

```
<xsl:value-of select="expression"
              disable-output-escaping="yes" | "no" />
```

The character string written by the instruction is the result of evaluating the `select` expression. The declaration of a `select` expression is mandatory. If the optional `disable-output-escaping` attribute is set to `"yes"`, the symbols that are reserved in XML such as & or < are output without coding (`&amp;` or `&lt;`) having to be used. The default value of this attribute is `"no"`. If `"yes"` is specified, the attribute works in the same way as `<xsl:text>`.

Before the output of the character string, a conversion may take place, depending on what value the `select` expression produces. The way that the `<xsl:value-of>` instruction works with the output of the `select` expression will be shown with a small example style sheet that uses the slides example as a source file.

```
<?xml version="1.0" encoding="ISO-8859-1"?>
<xsl:stylesheet version="1.0"
    xmlns:xsl="http://www.w3.org/1999/XSL/Transform">
<xsl:output method="text" />
<xsl:template match="slides">
(1)logic expression: <xsl:value-of select="1=2"/>
(2)node set:<xsl:value-of select="//title" />
(3)single node:<xsl:value-of select="slide[2]" />
(4)numerical: <xsl:value-of
          select="count(descendant::node())" />
</xsl:template>
</xsl:stylesheet>
```

1. A logical expression returns the boolean values `true` or `false`. They are re-turned from the instruction as a character string `"true"` or `"false"`. Output of (1):

   ```
   (1) logic expression: false
   ```

2. The `select` expression returns a node set, namely all `<title>` elements. If the expression produces a node set, only the value of the first node (referring to the document order) is returned as a character string. All subsequent `<title>` elements are ignored! Output of (2):

   ```
   (2) node set: summary of slides
   ```

3. The `select` expression returns a single node, namely the second `<slide>` ele-ment within the document. In this case, the values of all child elements, i.e. all text nodes of all child elements, are output. Output of (3):

   ```
   (3) single node: Motive for the use of a CMS A large
   amount of content has to be dealt with Different groups
   of people work together on the documents
   ```

4. If the value of the expression is numerical, a conversion into a character string takes place. Output (4) shows the number of all child nodes of the root:

   ```
   (4) numerical: 82
   ```

A.4.2 <xsl:element>

In order to create an XML element in the output, it can simply be coded directly in the style sheet, as long as the name and the structure of the element are known. However, if the formation of the element depends on data in the input document, without being identical to the input elements, the flexibility provided by the `<xsl:element>` instruction can be used.

```
<xsl:element name="QName" namespace="URI"
     use-attribute-set="QNames">
```

```
      *
</xsl:element>
```

The declaration of the `name` attribute is mandatory, but that of namespace and attribute sets is optional. Both `name` and `namespace` can be written as attribute value templates. The content of the element consists of child elements, which are produced by further instructions and literal result elements. Attributes can be assigned to the element either through the `use-attribute-set` attribute or through `<xsl:attribute>`, `<xsl:copy>` or `<xsl:copy-of>`. As an example of this instruction's use, suppose the representation of XML is to be rendered directly using Cascading Style Sheets. Cascading Style Sheets can be used to define the formatting of XML elements, but not attributes, however. To overcome this problem, a transformation that generates CSS in an output file can also convert all attributes into elements. As a result, the CSS style sheet is able to cope with all the contents of an XML file. A template can, for example, look as follows:

Transformation of attributes into elements

```
<xsl:template match="@" mode="a2e" >
  <xsl:element name="{name()}">
    <xsl:value-of select="." />
  </xsl:element>
</xsl:template>
```

The template overwrites the default template for attributes and creates an element on the basis of the attribute name. So as not to define this behaviour globally, the `mode` attribute is used. The value of the new element is taken from the attribute value using `<xsl:value-of>`. Within a template that processes elements, the above template can then be activated using

```
<xsl:apply-templates select="@*" mode="a2e" /
```

A.4.3 <xsl:attribute>

This instruction creates an attribute name and a value in the current element that is to be output.

```
<xsl:attribute name="QName" namespace="URI">
  Attribute value
</xsl:attribute>
```

The attribute name and value have to be created before other attributes or child elements are added to the current element. The declaration of the `name` attribute is obligatory. The value of the newly created attribute consists of the character string that is given within the element.

The instruction is useful on occasions when an attribute cannot be hard coded, but instead depends on the content of the input document. For example, if an HTML link is to be produced from this input

```
<page title="Web design" src="wd.xml" />
```

the template that produces it can look as follows:

```
<xsl:template match="page">
   <a>
     <xsl:attribute name="href">
         <xsl:value-of select="@src" />
     </xsl:attribute>
     <xsl:value-of select="@title" />
   </a>
</xsl:template>
```

It would be an error if the `<xsl:value-of>` instruction were to be put in front of the output of the `href` attribute.

A.4.4 `<xsl:attribute-set>`

This top-level element allows a set of attribute names and values to be given a name. By using this name, the attributes can be assigned to an arbitrary output element as a packet.

```
<xsl:attribute-set name="QName"
   use-attribute-sets="QNames">
   <xsl:attribute>*</xsl:attribute>
</xsl:attribute-set>
```

The declaration of the name attribute is mandatory. With the help of the optional `use-attribute-sets` attribute, attribute set definitions can be built up in modules. Each of the attributes of the set are defined using either zero or more `<xsl:attribute>` instructions. The following example defines an attribute set for the default font.

```
<xsl:attribute-set name="default font">
<xsl:attribute name="font-name">Verdana</xsl:attribute>
<xsl:attribute name="font-size">12pt</xsl:attribute>
</xsl:attribute-set>
```

The following example shows the use of the attribute set to create an HTML table element:

```
<xsl:template match="topic">
   <xsl:element name="td"
         use-attribute-sets="default font">
   <xsl:value-of select="." />
   </xsl:element>
</xsl:template>
```

If the output element is not created using `<xsl:element>`, the instruction needs a namespace prefix:

```
<td xsl:use-attribute-sets="default font">
    <xsl:value-of select="." />
</td>
```

A.4.5 `<xsl:comment>`

This instruction allows a comment to be written in the output.

```
<xsl:comment>
    comment text
</xsl:comment>
```

The instruction simply produces a text node for the content of the comment. It is not possible for this text to contain the string `<!--` or `-->`, the comment delimiters for XML or HTML.

A.4.6 `<xsl:processing-instruction>`

Using this instruction, a processing instruction is written in the output tree.

```
<xsl:processing-instruction name="QName">
    *
</xsl:processing-instruction>
```

The `name` attribute is mandatory and must not contain of the character string `"xml"` in any form. The instruction cannot therefore be used to create an XML declaration at the start of the output file – the declaration is also not valid as a processing instruction. It is produced by the XSLT processor with an appropriate parameterisation of the `<xsl:output>` element. The instruction can be used to transmit information to subsequent processes or transformations, for example, when using style sheets.

```
<xsl:processing-instruction name="xml-stylesheet">
    <xsl:text>href="web-design.css"
        type="text/css" </xsl:text>
</xsl:processing-instruction>
```

In environments such as those that are used in the book in hand, the generation of PIs is not of great significance. However, in server-based production environments, which often carry out several transformation steps one after the other, they are an important means of control. For example, the different server-side processing steps within the publishing framework of Apache Cocoon are controlled by processing instructions. In the case of multi-level transformations, depending on the application logic or user request, an appropriate processing instruction can be generated which informs the following process about what is to be done. An example of this is the access to an identical URL, once by a conventional browser, and another time using a WAP device. A first transformation can select the correct data set for the respective end device. It also creates the PI for the second processing step. In this processing instruction a suitable style sheet is then activated, which produces HTML or WML.

A.4.7 <xsl:text>

This instruction is used to control the output of whitespace and special characters such as & or <.

```
<xsl:text disable-output-escaping="yes" | "no" >
   text
</xsl:text>
```

Primarily, the instruction has an effect on the output of blank space. A node that only contains blank space is only written in the output tree if it is produced within an <xsl:text> instruction. The instruction is therefore used most frequently to create blank space between two output elements. For example, in the case of the output of

```
<xsl:value-of select="surname" />
<xsl:value-of select="date of birth" />
```

the blank space between the two elements is suppressed. In order to make sure this space exists, <xsl:text> can be used:

```
<xsl:value-of select="surname" />
<xsl:text> </xsl:text>
<xsl:value-of select="date of birth" />
```

Another use is to control of the output of special characters that could be output by the XSLT processor only by means of coding. This is controlled using the disable-output-escaping attribute. If the target output is not pure XML or XHTML but, for example JSP, often these characters are required.

```
<%@ page errorPage="errp.jsp" session="true"%>
```

In order to prevent < instead of < from appearing in the output, the <xsl:text> instruction is constructed as follows:

```
<xsl:text disable-output-escaping="yes">
   &lt;%@ page errorPage="errp.jsp" session="true"%>
</xsl:text>
```

A.4.8 <xsl:copy>

Using this instruction, the current node of the input tree is copied into the output. The instruction produces a shallow copy of the current node, which means that child elements are not copied as well. Because of this, this instruction has the same effect as <xsl:element>.

```
<xsl:copy use-attribute-sets="QNames" >
    *
</xsl:copy>
```

During the copying, using the optional use-attribute-sets attribute, a set of predefined attributes can be assigned to the new element. The instruction works differently depending on which kind of current node it is dealing with.

Element nodes: The node is copied, its name is transferred along with possible namespace definitions, and the assigned attribute sets are output. Child nodes are not copied along with this node. If, for example, there is an <xsl:apply-templates> given in the template body, this is evaluated. This means that if no other templates determine further details, then the text of all child elements is output by means of the built-in default templates.

Text nodes: A new text node is created in the output tree. Only the value is transferred. Possible attribute set declarations are ignored, since by definition, text nodes have neither names nor attributes.

Attribute nodes: The name and the value of the node are transferred into the output. If there is no current node in the output tree that can incorporate the attribute, an error is output. Attribute set declarations are ignored.

Processing Instructions and comments: An appropriate node is created in the output. Attribute set declarations are ignored, and a possible template body within <xsl:copy> is likewise ignored.

A template with a recursive call can be created for copying subtrees of the input document. The effect of the following example is identical to that of the <xsl:copy-of> instruction in that it executes recursive copying.

Recursive copying of subtrees using <xsl:copy>

```
<xsl:template match="@*node()" mode="copy">
    <xsl:copy>
        <xsl:apply-templates select="@*" mode="copy" />
        <xsl:apply-templates mode="copy" />
    </xsl:copy>
</xsl:template>
```

Using the first <xsl:apply-templates> instruction, the template calls itself recursively by selecting the attribute nodes that, without this line, would disappear. In the second <xsl:apply-templates>, this call takes place for the child elements. As has already been mentioned, this example is equivalent to the deep-copy of <xsl:copy-of>. With a little manipulation, the above example can take on specific attributes. If the lines for copying the attributes are changed as follows, only the attributes called ident are copied.

```
<xsl:apply-templates select="@*[name()='ident']"
                     mode="copy" />
```

A.4.9 <xsl:copy-of>

This instruction copies a node and all its descendants recursively into the output tree.

```
<xsl:copy-of select="expression" />
```

This instruction works in the same way as `<xsl:value-of>` if the expression does not produce a node set. Otherwise, all attribute nodes and child nodes are copied. This property is used if parts of the input document are to be copied without being changed.

A further application case is the use of `<xsl:copy-of>` in order to access the output tree. This can be created in the expression with the help of a variable and a variable reference. For example, if a table caption is to be used several times in the output, a variable can be created.

Variables as a
memory for
output structures

```
<xsl:variable name="caption" >
   <tr>
      <td>Name</td>
      <td>Date of birth</td>
   </tr>
</xsl:variable>
```

This structure can now be reproduced in the template that is used to construct tables using `<xsl:copy-of>`:

```
<xsl:template match="..." >
.....
   <table>
      <xsl:copy-of select="$caption" />
      <tr>

         <td><xsl:value-of .../></td>
         <td><xsl:value-of .../></td>
      </tr>
   </table>
</xsl:template>
```

A.4.10 <xsl:output>

This top-level element makes it possible to control the output format of a style sheet. This instruction has a direct effect on the serialization of the result tree i.e., normally on the writing of output in files. In environments that allow the dynamic publishing of, for example, Web sites, it may be the case that no serialization takes place, but instead, the result tree or a structure that conforms to the DOM may be passed on to subsequent processes. In these kinds of environment, `<xsl:output>` can be ignored.

```
<xsl:output
    method="xml" | "html" | "text" | "QName"
    version="string"
    encoding="string"
    indent="yes" | "no"
    omit-xml-declaration="yes" | "no"
    cdata-section-elements="QNames"
    doctype-public="string"
    doctype-system="string"
    standalone="yes" | "no"
    media-type="string"/>
```

All attributes are optional, however if the `method` attribute is being used its value determines which of the other attributes must be present. As a rule, it is not necessary to use the `<xsl:output>` instruction in an XSLT script. The default is always that XML is to be output. If the first output instruction that the XSLT processor comes across is `<html>`, then `"html"` is assumed to be the `method` attribute. Owing to there being so many possible combinations of attributes, we will only look at a few of these here.

• **Method xml:** If the value of the `method` attribute is `"xml"`, the `version` attribute is obligatory and is at present set to `"1.0"`. The `encoding` attribute is optional, since all processors have to support at least UTF-8 which, as a result, guarantees that all Unicode characters are processed. If the `omit-xml-declaration` attribute is set to `"yes"`, then no `<?xml version="1.0"?>` declaration is written in the output document.
The `standalone`, `doctype-public` and `doctype-system` attributes produce corresponding document type declarations (e.g. `doctype-system-="test.dtd"` creates `<!DOCTYPE test SYSTEM "test.dtd">`) if the name of the DTD is given as the value of the attribute, or even in a `standalone` declaration. Using the `cdata-section-elements` attribute, elements that are to be output as CDATA sections can be referred to by name. For example,

```
cdata-section-elements="code"
```

can be used to specify that the element

```
<code> a &lt; b </code>
```

will be output as

```
<![CDATA[ a < b ]]>
```

- **Method html:** By default, this declaration produces output that conforms to HTML 4.0. As a result, most notably, characteristics of some HTML elements that are not well-formed XML are supported such as, for example, `<br>`, `<hr>`, `<img>` and a few others. When they are output, the elements `<script>` and `<style>` are treated in such a way that the opening angle bracket remains unchanged and is not recoded into `&lt;`. `href` or `src` attributes are identified and the blank spaces that they contain are appropriately output as `"%20"`. In order to support older browsers, some HTML elements are output in an abbreviated form (e.g. `<OPTION SELECTED>` instead of `<OPTION SELECTED="se-lected">` and so on). The `cdata-section-elements`, `omit-xml-declaration` and `standalone` attributes cannot be used for the output of HTML. The `doctype-system` and `doctype-public` attributes produce a declaration called `"html"`.

- **Method text:** This method has the effect that only the text nodes corresponding to the character set given in the `encoding` attribute are written in the output file.

A.4.11 `<xsl:preserve-space>` and `<xsl:strip-space>`

These top-level elements are used to control the treatment of whitespace in input documents.

```
<xsl:preserve-space elements="List of element names" />
<xsl:strip-space elements="List of element names" />
```

If these instructions are not used, empty text nodes in the input document are kept when this document is processed and output. The `<xsl:preserve-space>` instruction therefore should only be used if `<xsl:strip-space>` has been used to nominate elements that are to be omitted if they only consist of blank space. The following characters are treated as whitespace: spaces, tabs, carriage return and line-feed. A text node that only contains blank space consists exclusively of such characters. The elements only have an effect on these kinds of node.

If a `<topic>` element that only contains blank space is removed from the input using `<xsl:strip-space elements="topic" />`, it cannot be processed by `<xsl:template>` instructions. This means that it is not copied into the output and thus is also not included by any `<xsl:number>` instructions that may exist. Jumps in numbering using `<xsl:number>` are often due to blank space elements that have been taken on.

A.5 Elements for the production of variables and parameters

A.5.1 `<xsl:variable>`

This instruction is used to create a named variable and to assign a value to it. If `<xsl:variable>` is used as a top-level element it defines a global variable. For variables which have a local scope, the instruction can also be given in the body of other instructions.

```
<xsl:variable name="QName" select="expression">
    template body
</xsl:variable>
```

A name is mandatory, but the formulation of a select attribute for the determination of the value of the variable is optional. If the select attribute is not used, the XSLT processor generates the value of the variable from the template body. However, if the select attribute is used, the template body can remain empty. If both parts are empty, the variable contains an empty character string as its value.

In contrast to variables in other programming languages, with XSLT variables it is not possible to change the value that was assigned at the start during the course of the XSLT script. Because of this, XSLT variables are more like the constants of other programming languages. Since this takes a lot of getting used to, some manufacturers of XSLT processors have changed this by installing extensions in their products (e.g. Saxon) which allows the values of variables to be changed by assignment, although the Specification does not provide for such behaviour.

In order to assign a character string to a variable, you have to make sure that, depending on the kind of assignment, the single quotation mark is used correctly. The following instructions are all equivalent, and are also all correct:

```
<xsl:variable name="booktitle" select="'Web-Design'" />
<xsl:variable name="booktitle" select='"Web-Design"' />
<xsl:variable name="booktitle">Web-Design< xsl:variable>
```

If the value is coded in the template body, it is converted into a character string. If the value is written inside the select attribute, there has to be an indication that it is a character string, because otherwise the value is interpreted as an XPath expression.

```
<xsl:variable name="booktitle" select="Web-Design" />
```

This variable has an XPath expression as a value, which selects a set of nodes that have the name Web-Design. If a variable contains a selection expression or a calculation, it can be used in a similar way to an SQL view. However, the restrictions of scope must be taken into account.

The scope of variables within the style sheet is also unusual. Any <xsl:variable> instructions which are formulated as top-level elements have global scope, and this also extends to style sheets integrated using <xsl:include> or <xsl:import>. Global variables can therefore be used before their declaration.

Variables that are defined within templates only have local scope, i.e. only within the element in which they are defined. Their validity extends to the successor axis, but not to their own descendants! The most frequent problem with variables in style sheets are the results of misunderstandings concerning scope. A problem also arises during the definition of variables with the same name if their scope clashes.

A.5.2 <xsl:param>

`<xsl:param>` can be used to create a named parameter and assign a default value to it. The instruction can be used as a top-level element or a first child element within an `<xsl:template>` instruction.

```
<xsl:param name="QName" select="expression">
   template body
</xsl:param>
```

A name is mandatory, but the formulation of a `select` attribute for the determination of the value is optional.

Parameters are very similar to variables, the difference being that they can get a new value when the template or style sheet in which they are declared is invoked, not just within the declaration. Nevertheless, they are not variables in the sense of conventional programming languages, whose value can be assigned as often as desired.

Global parameters may obtain their value from parameter values provided during the call of the style sheet. Since the XSLT Specification leaves the method of passing parameters to style sheets up to the providers of XSLT processors, the way in which global parameters obtain their value has to be looked up in the documentation for the product. Local parameters receive their value through an `<xsl:with-param>` child element of the parent element.

A.5.3 <xsl:with-param>

This instruction can be used to pass parameter values to templates that were activated by `<xsl:call-template>` or `<xsl:apply-templates>`.

```
<xsl:with-param name="QName" select="expression">
   template body
</xsl:with-param>
```

The declaration of the `name` attribute is obligatory, the `select` attribute is optional. The instruction can only be used as a child element of `<xsl:call-template>` or `<xsl:apply-templates>`. Within the called template, there must be a parameter whose name matches the one given in `<xsl:with-param>`. If such a parameter is not available, the instruction is ignored, and a reference to this parameter within the template then leads to an error message.

A.6 Elements for the control of conditional processing

A.6.1 <xsl:if>

This instruction tests a condition. If the result of the evaluation is `true`, the template body is executed. If the result of the evaluation is `false`, no action is taken since an else part, as found in other programming languages, is missing.

```
<xsl:if test="expression" >
   template body
</xsl:if>
```

The declaration of an expression for the test attribute is obligatory. The result of evaluating this XPath expression is converted into a boolean value. If the evaluation produces a node set, a character string or a result tree fragment which are not empty, the expression is evaluated as true. If the result is numerical, all values apart from 0 are true.

In the following example, a comma is output, so long as the node that is being processed is not the last:

Checking for
the end of a list

```
<xsl:for-each select="topic" >
   <xsl:if test="not(position()=last)" >, </xsl:if>
</xsl:for-each>
```

A.6.2 <xsl:choose>,<xsl:when>, <xsl:otherwise>

<xsl:choose> can be used to choose from a number of alternatives.

```
<xsl:choose>
   <xsl:when test="expression">+
   <xsl:otherwise>
</xsl:choose>
```

The <xsl:choose> instruction does not have any attributes and can contain one or more <xsl:when> instructions, but no more than one single <xsl:otherwise> instruction, which can only appear as the last one in the list.

The contents of the first <xsl:when> element whose test expression evaluates as true are evaluated. All subsequent <xsl:when> instructions are ignored, regardless of whether their test expression would also be evaluated as true. If none of the <xsl:when> elements has an expression that is evaluated as being true, <xsl:otherwise> is selected. If this is not available, the entire <xsl:choose> instruction does nothing. An <xsl:choose> instruction that only contains one <xsl:when> child element and no <xsl:otherwise> instruction is equivalent to an <xsl:if> instruction.

A.6.3 <xsl:for-each>

With <xsl:for-each> the processing instructions of the template body are used on a set of selected nodes.

```
<xsl:for-each select="expression">
   <xsl:sort>
   template body
</xsl:for-each>
```

The declaration of the select attribute is obligatory, and the select expression must produce a node set as the result of the evaluation. This node set is run through using `<xsl:for-each>`, and the instructions in the template body are executed once for each node.

The following example selects all `<topic>` nodes of the document, copies each element, creates a number attribute, and assigns the current position within the selection to this:

Copying and numbering elements

```
<xsl:for-each select="//topic">
    <xsl:copy>
        <xsl:attribute name="number">
            <xsl:value-of select="position()" />
        </xsl:attribute>
    </xsl:copy>
</xsl:for-each>
```

If no sorting instruction is entered, the nodes are processed in document order. If an `<xsl:sort>` element is given, the selected nodes are sorted before they are processed.

A.7 Elements for sorting and numbering

A.7.1 `<xsl:sort>`

`<xsl:sort>` determines the sequence in which the nodes that were selected using a `<xsl:for-each>` or a `<xsl:apply-templates>` instruction will be processed.

```
<xsl:sort
    select="expression"
    order={"ascending" | "descending"}
    case-order={"upper-first" | "lower-first"}
    lang="country code"
    data-type={"text" | "number" }
/>
```

The `<xsl:sort>` instruction has to be written at the start of the template body of `<xsl:for-each>` and can appear next to `<xsl:apply-templates>` before the `<xsl:with-param>` declaration. Several `<xsl:sort>` instructions can even be given, which define the first, second,... nth sort order key in the sequence that they are written.

All attributes are optional. The select attribute describes the sort key. The evaluated expression is converted into a character string. The treatment of this character string can be determined by further attributes. The order attribute is used to specify an ascending or descending sorting sequence. The case-order attribute is used to specify the treatment of identical characters that are written differently in upper or lower case. The attribute value "upper-first" is used to specify that upper case letters are sorted to the front. Conversely, lower case letters are sorted to the front if "lower-first" is set. The attribute lang is used to take into account the characteristics of each language during the sorting process. Unfortunately, sorting order is not standardized, even within a single language but changes from library to library and is subject to historical fluctuations.

If "number" is specified for data-type, a further conversion of the evaluated expression into a number takes place.

The following example shows two sorting methods for the slide example. In the first, the sorting is carried out using the character string of the select attribute. In the second, the numerical values of the evaluated select="position()" expression are used.

Sorting a list of elements

```
<?xml version="1.0" encoding="ISO-8859-1"?>
<xsl:stylesheet version="1.0"
    xmlns:xsl="http://www.w3.org/1999/XSL/Transform" >

<xsl:template match="/">
   <topiclist>
      <xsl:comment>
            ascending alphabetically according to topic
      </xsl:comment>
      <xsl:for-each select="//topic">
          <xsl:sort order="ascending"/>
          <xsl:call-template name="topic-out" />
      </xsl:for-each>

      <xsl:comment>
            Now in the reverse document order

      </xsl:comment>
      <xsl:for-each select="//topic">
          <xsl:sort select="position()"
                 data-type="number" order="descending"/>
          <xsl:call-template name="topic-out" />
      </xsl:for-each>
   </topiclist>
</xsl:template>
<xsl:template name="topic-out">
   <topic>
      <xsl:attribute name="position">
            <xsl:value-of select="position()" />
      </xsl:attribute>
      <xsl:value-of select="." />
```

```
        </topic>
      </xsl:template>
    </xsl:stylesheet>
```

A.7.2 <xsl:number>

This instruction is used for creating and formatting a counting number. As the result of its calculation, it outputs a formatted character string as a text node.

```
<xsl:number level="any" | "multiple" | "single"
count="pattern"
from="pattern"
value="expression"
format="Format character string"
lang="Country code"
letter-value="alphabetic" | "traditional"
grouping-separator="Character"
grouping-size="number" />
```

The declarations of the attributes are optional, but the details of the implementation are in many cases left up to the manufacturers of XSLT processors. The way in which the attributes work with one another is complex.

The instruction determines a number for the nodes of the source tree. With the instruction `<xsl:number />` (which is not specified further) the position number is assigned to each node within its sibling nodes. The method of numbering can be controlled by the attributes `level`, `count`, `from` and `format`. The default value for `level` is "single", i.e., a single sequence number will be output. If the value of the attribute is set to "multiple", on the other hand, the numbering proceeds in a hierarchical way, according to the hierarchy of the nodes (1., 1.1, 1.2,...). Problems arise if nodes whose number is to be used are hierarchically nested elements without any gaps. In the example document used throughout the book, each `<slide>` element contains a `<title>` element and a `<topiclist>` element. The `<topic>` points are in turn formed as child elements of `<topiclist>`, i.e., hierarchically, `<topiclist>` is one level between `<title>` and `<topic>`. A hierarchical numbering which allocates a running number for the title and, for the next level, allocates a sequence number for all associated topics, is not possible with these means. The following template

Hierarchical numbering

```
<xsl:template match="title | topic">
    <entry>
      <xsl:number level="multiple" format="1.1"/>
          <xsl:text> </xsl:text>
          <xsl:value-of select="."/>
    </entry>
</xsl:template>
```

outputs entries in this form:

```
<entry>1.1.1 Overview of slides</entry>
<entry>1.1.2.1 What must a CMS be able to do?</entry>
<entry>1.1.2.2 Who should use a CMS?</entry>
```

It is clear that the upper hierarchical levels, or the levels that lie between the elements and are not of interest, are also included in the numeration. Setting the attribute `from="title"` leads to the counting beginning again with this element, and to the `<title>` elements not carrying a number. Everything else is dealt with in the way that is described above.

The results are a little more predictable if it is not left up to the processor to find a number, but if the `value` attribute is used to assign numbers to the instruction (for example using the `position()` function), which only have to be formatted. The `format` attribute allows a character string to be given, which specifies how the number is displayed. Using `format="I"` roman numbering is produced, and using `format="a"` alphabetic numbering.

A.8 Further elements

A.8.1 <xsl:decimal-format>

The instruction controls the presentation of decimal numbers that are output using the `format-number()` function. The instruction has no effect on `<xsl:number>`!

```
<xsl:decimal-format
    name="QName"
    decimal-separator="character"
    grouping-separator="character"
    infinity="Infinity"
    minus-sign="character"
    NaN="character sting"
    percent="character"
    per-mille="character"
    zero-digit="character"
    digit="character"
    pattern-separator="character" />
```

Without exception, the optional attributes describe characters and character strings that can be determined as decimal points (`decimal-separator`), zeros, indicators for non-numerical entries (`NaN` – Not a Number) etc. The use of the `name` attribute makes it possible to activate a decimal format specification within a `format-number()` call.

A.8.2 <xsl:key>

Using this top-level element, a search code is defined that can be used with the key() function.

```
<xsl:key name="QName" match="pattern" use="expression" />
```

The specification of all attributes is obligatory. Using the name attribute, the name under which the search code can be activated within the key() function is specified. Using match a search pattern is indicated, which specifies the node set to be selected. The use attribute specifies the value of the node that is being indexed on. The following example defines an index for slides. The selection of <slides> elements is limited to those whose ident attribute is equivalent to the value passed to key().

```
<xsl:key name="getslide" match="slide" use="@ident"/>
```

The key() function can use this definition as follows:

```
<xsl:value-of
    select="key('getslide', 'access')/title" />
```

Using the <xsl:value-of> instruction, the title of the slide is selected using the ident attribute "access". Of course, access to this node can also be obtained using an XPath expression:

```
<xsl:value-of
    select="//slide[@ident='access']/title" />
```

Manufacturers of XSLT processors are however required to construct an index, if a search code was defined using <xsl:key>. The access using using the key() function should consequently be faster than it is with a normal XPath expression.

The fastest access can certainly be achieved using the id() function. But this require the presence of a DTD, which also actually combines id attributes with the XML datatype ID. The key() function is therefore also intended as a substitute for the id() function, since XSLT processing can get by without DTDs and in practice is indeed frequently carried out without them. If an appropriate DTD is available, the id() function is certainly preferable, thanks to its simplicity and speed. However, if it cannot be assumed that a DTD is available the key() function should be used.

A.8.3 <xsl:message>

This instruction outputs a message and may possibly terminate the processing of the style sheet.

```
<xsl:message terminate="yes" | "no">
    template body
</xsl:message>
```

The optional specification of the `terminate` attribute with `"yes"` leads to the termination of the processing of the style sheet. The default value is `"no"`. The instruction outputs the text produced in the template body as a message. Whether this happens in a dialog box on the screen or in a log file is not specified. The behaviour of this instruction has therefore to be determined from the specifications of the XSLT processor's manufacturer.

A.8.4 <xsl:fallback>

This instruction specifies what happens if the template body in which it is written cannot be executed.

```
<xsl:fallback>
    template body
</xsl:fallback>
```

The instruction takes into account that alterations and extensions can be made to future versions of XSLT that are not yet supported by existing XSLT processors. In this case, `<xsl:fallback>` can be used to describe what is to be done in place of instructions that are not yet supported. Likewise, using this instruction, a style sheet that uses manufacturer-dependent extensions can give an indication if it is not capable of running in other environments.

A.8.5 <xsl:namespace-alias>

The top-level element `<xsl:namespace-alias>` can specify that a namespace prefix that is written within the style sheet should be converted into another namespace definition when it is output in the target document. This is necessary, for example, if a transformation is to produce an XSL style sheet. The `xsl:` namespace cannot then be used directly as a literal result element.

```
<xsl:namespace-alias stylesheet-prefix="Prefix"
        result-prefix="Prefix" />
```

The specification of both attributes is obligatory. What happens when the namespace prefix is changed is not defined. The instruction intervenes in the serialization of the output tree to the output files. Some processors (e.g. Xalan and XT) keep the `stylesheet-prefix` and only assign the namespace that corresponds to the `result-prefix` to the `stylesheet-prefix` in the output.

The following style sheet produces a skeleton for an arbitrary XML file and, in order to do this, uses the namespace prefix "out", so as not to confuse the XSLT processor. It contains an `<out:template>` instruction for all element names, and within this, an `<out:apply-templates>` entry for each child element. If the element has no further child elements, an `<out:value-of select=".">` is created. The namespace prefix in the output style sheet file is then also `'out:'`. For the functionality of the style sheet that is produced, it does not matter whether the namespace contraction "out" is kept or not, as long as the correct XSLT namespace is assigned to it.

*Creation of
one style sheet
from another*

```xml
<?xml version="1.0" encoding="ISO-8859-1"?>
<xsl:stylesheet version="1.0"
    xmlns:xsl="http://www.w3.org/1999/XSL/Transform"
    xmlns:out="test.xsl">
    <xsl:namespace-alias stylesheet-prefix="out"
        result-prefix="xsl"/>
<xsl:template match="/">
    <out:stylesheet version="1.0">
        <xsl:for-each select="//*">
            <xsl:variable name="nm" select="name()"/>
        <xsl:if test="not(preceding::node()[name()=$nm])">
                <out:template>
                <xsl:attribute name="match">
                        <xsl:value-of select="name()"/>
                </xsl:attribute>
            <xsl:call-template name="get-subelements"/>
                </out:template>
            </xsl:if>
        </xsl:for-each>
    </out:stylesheet>
</xsl:template>
<xsl:template name="get-subelements">
<xsl:choose>
    <xsl:when test="not(*)">
        <out:value-of select="."/>
    </xsl:when>
    <xsl:otherwise>
        <xsl:for-each select="*">
                <xsl:variable name="nm" select="name()"/>
        <xsl:if test="not(preceding::node()[name()=$nm])">
                    <out:apply-templates>
                        <xsl:attribute name="select">
                            <xsl:value-of select="name()"/>
                        </xsl:attribute>
                    </out:apply-templates>
                </xsl:if>
        </xsl:for-each>
    </xsl:otherwise>
</xsl:choose>
</xsl:template>
</xsl:stylesheet>
```

In order to prevent elements of the input document that appear frequently from being given an `<out:template>` template every time they appear, in the above style sheet it is checked whether the node name has already appeared before. Initially, using

```
<xsl:for-each select="//*">
```

a set of all nodes is created and a current node is determined. Its name can be seen in the variable $nm, which is subsequently used before each write operation to check whether this name has already appeared in the list of the predecessors.

```
<xsl:if test="not(preceding::node()[name()=$nm])">
```

In this case, a template had already been created for this element. If a node with this name already exists, another template will not be created for it.

A.9 XSLT functions

A.9.1 current()

This function returns a node set that only contains the current node. As a rule, the current node is identical to the context node. The context node can be obtained using the XPath expression " . ". Within a normal XPath expression, `current()` and " . " are identical; within a predicate however, they are not absolute. Whereas the context node can change when a predicate is evaluated, the current node remains unchanged.

A very good description of this complex concept can be found in [KAY00], which can be loosely paraphrased as follows:

The current node is created in the following way:

- During the evaluation of a global variable, the current node is the root node of the document.

- If an `<xsl:apply-templates>` instruction is executed in order to process a node set, each of the selected nodes becomes the current node, one after the other. If a template is activated, the current node is always the one that leads to the template being selected. On return from the `<xsl:apply-templates>` processing, the current node is reset to its previous value.

- In a similar way, the root node of the source document becomes the current node if the system implicitly calls a template that processes the root node of the document.

- If `<xsl:for-each>` is used to process a selected node set, each of the selected nodes becomes the current node, one after the other. If the processing of the `<xsl:for-each>` loop ends, the current node is reset to its previous value.

- The instructions `<xsl:call-template>` and `<xsl:apply-imports>` leave the current node unchanged.

- The current node does not change – in contrast to the context node – if a predicate is evaluated within an XPath expression.

The context node is returned by the XPath expression " . ". Within a simple XPath expression, the evaluations of "." and current () produce the same result. If however they are used within a predicate, the result values are usually different. ([KAY00], Page 437).

A.9.2 document()

The document () function opens an external document, constructs an input tree, and returns its root node. The main area of use for the function is to open other XML documents during a transformation in addition to the default input document. For example, a reference to a file can look as follows:

```
<page id="access" href="xml_access.xml" />
```

During the processing of the source file containing this entry, using

```
<xsl:apply-templates select="document(@href)" />
```

the referenced document can be opened, and the processing of the elements of this file is activated by the templates of the current style sheet. If tags are contained in the opened file and have the same name as elements of the source file, they are accordingly processed by the defined templates of the style sheet. If, however, other templates are to be used, depending on their origin, this can be done, for example, by using the mode attribute during the <xsl:apply-templates> call.

In the example just given, it is assumed that the file is in the same directory as the style sheet file in which the document () function is called. Other directories can also be specified however. It is also possible to specify files directly using character strings like, for example

```
document('xml_access.xml')
document('../text/xml_access.xml')
```

The call document (' ') returns the root node of the current style sheet. A style sheet could therefore analyse itself.

A.9.3 element-available()

This function is used to determine whether an XLST element is available or not. Currently, this only concerns extension elements that manufacturers build in to XSLT procesors; element-available() will however be able to be used in future versions to check whether the processor being used supports an element or not. The expression

```
element-available('xsl:apply-templates')
```

should prove to be true, as should the test of all other elements defined in XSLT version 1.0.

A.9.4 format-number()

The `format-number()` function is used for the conversion of numerical values into character strings. The formatting of the character string that is produced is controlled by `<xsl:decimal-format>`. There is no connection with and no effect on the `<xsl:number>` element. The value and the format pattern are given as parameters. This is most easily explained using an example:

```
<xsl:value-of
        select="format-number(76542.127, '£#,##0.00')" />
```

This instruction produces the output

```
£76,542.13
```

If the first parameter is not a numerical value but a character string, it will first of all be converted into a numerical value. The format pattern has to be written using the American separators for thousands or decimal separators (, and ., respectively), unless something else is provided within a named `<xsl:decimal-format>` instruction (for example, to accommodate German conventions). The connection to such an instruction takes place via a third possible parameter during the call of `format-number()`. The name of an `<xsl:decimal-format>` instruction which determines other separators, etc. can be given here.

The value parameter is always rounded to the number of decimal places of the format pattern. The format pattern is constructed using the following special characters:

#	a digit, leading zeros are not output
0	a digit, zeros always appear as 0
,	grouping separator
.	decimal point
-	negative tag
%	displays a value as a percentage

The format pattern may consist of two parts, separated from each other by a semicolon ;. The left part of the pattern specifies the format for the positive number range, the right part the negative range.

A.9.5 function-available()

In a similar way to `element-available()`, `function-available()` can be used to check whether the function whose name is given as a parameter is available within the XSLT processor.

A.9.6 generate-id()

This function produces a character string that uniquely identifies a node. If the function is called several times for the same node, e.g. during the course of the style sheet processing, an identical character string is produced each time for that node. However, the way the string is produced is dependent on the implementation of the function in the particular processor. This means that it does not make any sense to write a character string produced using `generate-id()` into an XML output stream that will then be processed by a different XSLT processor.

The most important area of use of the function is the production of names that are to be used as HTML link targets, and associated links. For example, the first time an input document is gone through, a list of links can be created.

```
<xsl:for-each select="//topic" >
    <a href="#{generate-id(.)}">
        <xsl:value-of select="@title"/>
    </a>
</topic>
```

During this pass through the document, the corresponding `<a name>` element does not yet exist in the output file. It is however guaranteed that, when the identical node is gone through at a later time, an identical `id` will be created using `generate-id()`. In a subsequent pass through the source file, the corresponding named anchor is therefore generated using

```
<a name="{generate-id(.)}">
```

The `generate-id()` function has no connection to the XML data type ID, which can be defined in a DTD. Neither the `id()` nor the `key()` function can be used to find a node again whose identification was created using `generate-id()`. It is only possible to store the value returned by the `generate-id()` function in a variable and to test this variable in an XPath predicate by comparing it with the value returned by the `generate-id()` function (e.g. `[generate-id() = $generated]`).

A.9.7 key()

This function is a search function that is able to find nodes that correspond to the value of a named `<xsl:key>` element. If, using the top-level instruction

```
<xsl:key name="fsearch" match="slide" use="@ident" />
```

a named key called `fsearch` is produced, using the function call

```
<xsl:value-of select="key('fsearch', 'background')"/>
```

the slide whose `ident` attribute is equivalent to the character string 'background' is found. In contrast to the `id()` function, the `key()` function does not require the existence of a DTD. The `match` attributes that are used thus do not have to be from the ID data type.

A.9.8 system-property()

The function `system-property()` outputs information about the environment of the XSLT processor. The only parameters that are currently possible are `xsl:version`, `xsl:vendor` and `xsl:vendor-url`. The XSLT version is obtained as follows:

```
<xsl:value-of select="system-property('xsl:version')"/>
```

A.9.9 unparsed-entity-uri()

This function returns the file name of an entity that was defined within a DTD using the NDATA type. The entity reference of the entity that was searched for is given as a parameter.

In addition to the id() function, this is one of the few and limited ways of using information from DTDs within XSLT style sheets.

A.10 XPath functions

Within XPath, the following functions are available.

A.10.1 Functions that refer to node sets

last() returns the position of the last node of the current set

count(node set) returns the number of nodes that are contained in the node set of the function's argument.

position() returns the position of the current node within the current node set.

id(ID) returns a node at an arbitrary depth of nesting on the basis of its ID. The function can only be used if there is a DTD in which an attribute was defined with the data type ID.

local-name(node set) returns the local part of the name of a node.

namespace-uri(node set) returns the namespace URI of the node.

name(node set) returns the name of the current node.

A.10.2 Functions that refer to strings

string(object) converts an arbitrary object into a string.

concat(string, string, string*) concatenates two or more given strings to each other and returns the resulting string.

starts-with(string1, string2) tests whether string1 starts with the string string2. If it does, true is returned.

contains(string1, string2) returns true if string2 is contained in string1.

substring-before(string1, string2) returns the portion of string1 before the first occurrence of string2 within string1. For example, substring-before("dog and cat", " and ") returns "dog".

substring-after(string1, string2) returns the portion of string1 after the first occurrence of string2 within string1. For example, substring-after("dog and cat", " and ") returns "cat".

substring(string, start, n) returns the portion of string that starts at the start position and is n characters long. If the length parameter n is not supplied, the remainder of the string from the starting position onwards is returned.

`string-length(string)` outputs the number of characters in this character string.

`normalize-space(string)` removes all leading and trailing whitespace characters and reduces runs of several whitespace characters within the string to just one space.

`translate(string1,string2, string3)` replaces all occurrences of characters in `string2` in `string1` by the corresponding character in `string3`. Thus `translate("1.1.2000", ".", "-")` replaces all date separators by a hyphen.

A.10.3 Functions that produce logical values (XPath 4.3)

`boolean(object)` converts the argument into a truth value. Depending on the data type of the object, the following conversion takes place:
Numbers that are equal to 0 become `false`, all other numerical values become `true`.
Strings that have a length of 0 become `false`, otherwise `true`.
An empty node set becomes `false`, otherwise `true`.
A result tree fragment becomes `false` if it does not contain any text nodes, otherwise `true`.

`not(logic expression)` returns the negation of the logical expression.

`true()` returns `true`.

`false()` returns `false`.

`lang(string)` checks whether the `lang` attribute of the context matches the string that is given.

A.10.4 Numerical functions

`number(object)` converts the argument into a numerical value. If no argument is given, the string representation of the context node is converted. Depending on the type of the argument, `false` becomes 0, `true` becomes 1. If a given string cannot be converted into a number, `NaN` (not a number) is returned. A node set argument is first of all converted into a string (as if by `string()`), and then dealt with accordingly. The same applies to result tree fragments.

`sum(node set)` calculates the sum of all numerical values of the given node set. During the execution of the function, non-numeric nodes are converted into numerical nodes, as long as this is possible.

`floor(number)` returns the largest integer that is smaller than or equal to the numerical value of the argument.

`ceiling(number)` returns the smallest integer that is larger than or equal to the numerical value of the argument.
`ceiling(1.2) = 2`
`ceiling(-1.2) = 1`

`round(number)` rounds the value of the argument to the nearest integer.

Complete style sheets

In the following section, you will find two complete listings of XSLT style sheets, parts of which were discussed in the text of the book. A full length summary of the total structure of the style sheet is also given here.

B.1 Structure of a hierarchical navigation, page 147

Style sheet for the creation of a site with a hierarchical navigation structure. The navigation and the structure of the style sheet is described in detail on page 147.

```xml
<?xml version="1.0" encoding="ISO-8859-1"?>
<!-- page.xsl -->
<xsl:stylesheet version="1.0"
   xmlns:xsl="http://www.w3.org/1999/XSL/Transform">
<xsl:output method="html" version="1.0"
   encoding="UTF-8" indent="yes"/>

<!-- global parameters and variables -->
<xsl:include href="content.xsl" />

<!-- Variables for menu width and extension of the main
menu
calculated as a number of top-level menu elements
-->
<xsl:variable name="menu-width">140</xsl:variable>
<xsl:variable name="content-span">
   <xsl:value-of select="count(site/page)"/>
</xsl:variable>

<!-- Allocate selection parameters and
save access path to contents file in variable
-->
<xsl:param name="selpar" select="'Home'"/>
```

```
<xsl:variable name="content-file">content\
   <xsl:value-of select="//page[@id=$selpar]/@src"/>
</xsl:variable>

<!-- Attribute set for the navigation table -->
<xsl:attribute-set name="navtable-atts">
   <xsl:attribute name="border">0</xsl:attribute>
   <xsl:attribute name="cellspacing">0</xsl:attribute>
   <xsl:attribute name="cellpadding">4</xsl:attribute>
</xsl:attribute-set>
<xsl:attribute-set name="navtable-atts-down"
   use-attribute-sets="navtable-atts">
   <xsl:attribute name="class">down_menu</xsl:attribute>
   <xsl:attribute name="width">140</xsl:attribute>
</xsl:attribute-set>

<!-- Start of the processing
Construction of the HTML page structure, setting of METAs
and page title, attachment of a CSS stylesheet
-->
<xsl:template match="site">
   <html>
   <head>
   <META HTTP-EQUIV="Content-Type" CONTENT="text/html;
   charset=iso-8859-1"/>
   <META NAME="description" CONTENT="XML-WEB"/>
   <META NAME="keywords" CONTENT="XML XSL XSLT"/>
   <TITLE>
   <xsl:value-of select="@title"/>
   <xsl:text>  /   </xsl:text>
   <xsl:value-of select="$selpar"/>
   </TITLE>
   <LINK REL="stylesheet" TYPE="text/css"
   HREF="xml-web.css"/>
   </head>

   <body>
<!-- Always display main menu from left to right -->
   <table xsl:use-attribute-sets="navtable-atts">
   <tr>
   <td width="{$menu-width}">
   <img src="logo.gif" border="0"
   width="113" height="41"/>
   </td>
```

```
    <xsl:apply-templates select="page"
    mode="top_toc"/>
    </tr>

<!-- Construct menu in the left border column within the
    embedded table
-->
    <tr>
    <td width="{$menu-width}" valign="top">
    <table
    xsl:use-attribute-sets="navtable-atts-down">
    <xsl:apply-templates
    select="//page[@id=$selpar]"
    mode="down_toc"/>
    <tr>
    <td width="{$menu-width}">
    <a href="mailto:webm@xml-web.de">
    <i>Contact</i>
    </a>
    </td>
    </tr>
    </table>
    </td>

<!-- Copy in content from file -->
    <td valign="top" colspan="{$content-span}">
    <xsl:apply-templates
    select="document($content-file)"
    mode="cont_base"/>
    </td>
    </tr>
    </table>
    </body>
    </html>
    </xsl:template>

<!-- Template for the main menu -->
<xsl:template match="page" mode="top_toc">
    <td>
    <div class="right_menu">
    <xsl:call-template name="create-link-mark"/>
    </div>
    </td>
</xsl:template>
```

```
<!-- Template for left border column -->
<xsl:template match="page" mode="down_toc">

   <xsl:variable name="level">
   <xsl:value-of select="count(ancestor::node())"/>
   </xsl:variable>
   <xsl:call-template name="empty-tr"/>
   <xsl:choose>

<!-- Main element selected:
   list corresponding child pages
-->
   <xsl:when test="$level = 2">
   <xsl:for-each select="page">
   <xsl:call-template name="down_toc"/>
   </xsl:for-each>
   </xsl:when>

   <!-- 2nd level selected: display siblings -->
   <xsl:when test="$level = 3">
   <xsl:for-each select="../page">
   <xsl:call-template name="down_toc"/>
   </xsl:for-each>
   </xsl:when>
   </xsl:choose>
   <xsl:call-template name="empty-tr"/>
</xsl:template>

<xsl:template name="down_toc">
   <tr>
   <td valign="top">
   <xsl:call-template name="create-link-mark"/>
   </td>
   </tr>
</xsl:template>

<xsl:template name="create-link-mark">
   <a>
   <xsl:attribute name="href">
   <xsl:value-of select="@id"/>.html
   </xsl:attribute>
   <xsl:if test="@id=$selpar or page[@id=$selpar]">
   <img src="open.gif" border="0"/>
   </xsl:if>
   <xsl:value-of select="@title"/>
```

```
        <xsl:if test="@id=$selpar or page[@id=$selpar]">
        <img src="close.gif" border="0"/>
        </xsl:if>
        </a>
</xsl:template>

<!-- Make an empty table row -->
<xsl:template name="empty-tr">
        <tr><td valign="top">  </td></tr>
</xsl:template>

</xsl:stylesheet>
```

B.2 Creating FO documents, page 166

Style sheet for the creation of the booklet in FO format. Details of the XSLT style sheet are given in the appropriate chapter. The notes in the margin refer to these explanations, which are likewise marked in the margin in the chapter on FO.

```
<?xml version="1.0"?>
<!-- Begin stylesheet with namespace declarations -->
<xsl:stylesheet version="1.0"
    xmlns:xsl="http://www.w3.org/1999/XSL/Transform"
    xmlns:fo="http://www.w3.org/1999/XSL/Format">

<xsl:template match="slides">
    <fo:root xmlns:fo="http://www.w3.org/1999/
    XSL/Format">

        <!-- Definition of page construction and page order
    -->

        <fo:layout-master-set>

        <!-- Definition of the page geometry -->

        <!-- title page -->
        <fo:simple-page-master master-name="cover
          page"
          page-height="29.5cm" page-width="20.9cm"
          margin-top="2cm" margin-bottom="2cm"
          margin-left="2.5cm" margin-right="2.5cm">
          <fo:region-body margin-top="4cm"
            margin-left="2cm" margin-right="2cm"/>
        </fo:simple-page-master>
```

*See also
explanation to
FO fragment 2*

```
<!-- table of contents -->
<fo:simple-page-master master-name="toc"
  page-height="29.5cm" page-width="20.9cm"
  margin-top="2cm" margin-bottom="2cm"
  margin-left="2.5cm" margin-right="2.5cm">
  <fo:region-before extent="6cm"/>
  <fo:region-body margin-top="3cm"/>
  <fo:region-after extent="2cm"/>
</fo:simple-page-master>

<!-- Content pages -->
<fo:simple-page-master master-name="rest"
  page-height="29.5cm" page-width="20.9cm"
  margin-left="2cm" margin-right="2cm"
  margin-top="2.5cm" margin-bottom="2.5cm">
  <fo:region-before extent="2cm"/>
  <fo:region-body margin-top="2cm"/>
  <fo:region-after extent="2cm"/>
</fo:simple-page-master>

<!-- Definition of the page order -->
```

See also
explanation to
FO fragment 3

```
<!-- title page on a single page-->
<fo:page-sequence-master master-name="leading
text">
  <fo:single-page-master-reference
    master-name="cover page"/>
</fo:page-sequence-master>

<!-- Table of contents, possibly several pages -->
<fo:page-sequence-master master-name="content">
  <fo:repeatable-page-master-reference
    master-name="toc"/>
</fo:page-sequence-master>

<!-- Content pages over several pages -->
<fo:page-sequence-master master-name="all">
  <fo:repeatable-page-master-reference
    master-name="rest"/>
</fo:page-sequence-master>
    </fo:layout-master-set>

<!-- Filling the page order -->
```

*See also
explanation to
FO fragment 10*

```
<!-- filling the title page with static content -->
<fo:page-sequence master-name="leading text">
  <fo:flow flow-name="xsl-region-body">
    <fo:block text-align="center"
      line-height="30pt" font-size="22pt"
      space-after.optimum="22pt"
      space-before.optimum="22pt"
      padding-end="30pt">
        Content Management Systems
    </fo:block>
    <fo:block text-align="center"
      font-size="16pt" padding-end="24pt">
        slides on the problems of content management
    </fo:block>
  </fo:flow>
</fo:page-sequence>

<!-- Filling table of contents -->
<fo:page-sequence master-name="content">
```

*See also
explanation to
FO fragment 11*

```
  <!-- footer line and page number -->
  <fo:static-content flow-name="xsl-region-after">
    <fo:block text-align="center" font-size="10pt"
      font-family="serif" line-height="14pt">
      - <fo:page-number/> -
    </fo:block>
  </fo:static-content>
```

*See also
explanation to
FO fragment 12*

```
  <!-- Header line with graphic and line -->
  <fo:static-content flow-name="xsl-region-before">
    <fo:block text-align="start">
      <fo:external-graphic src="file:web-design.gif"
        width="8cm" hight="3.5cm"/>
    </fo:block>
    <fo:block>
      <fo:leader leader-pattern="rule"
        space-before.optimum="12pt"
        space-after.optimum="12pt"/>
    </fo:block>
  </fo:static-content>

<!-- Place table contents in table of contents text
column-->
<fo:flow flow-name="xsl-region-body">
```

```
<fo:block>
  <fo:block font-size="22pt"
    space-after.optimum="24pt"
    space-before.optimum="32pt">
    Summary of the slide title
  </fo:block>
```

*See also
explanation to
FO fragment 13*

```
<!-- Positioning title and page reference with tables -->
    <fo:table space-before.optimum="32pt">
        <fo:table-column column-width="12cm"/>
        <fo:table-column column-width="1cm"/>
        <fo:table-body font-size="12pt">
        <xsl:for-each select="slide[@status='active']">
           <fo:table-row>
           <fo:table-cell  padding="6pt" spacing="6pt">
             <fo:block>
                <xsl:number value="position()"/>
                <xsl:text> </xsl:text>
                <xsl:value-of select="title"/>
                <xsl:text> </xsl:text>
             </fo:block>
           </fo:table-cell>
           <fo:table-cell padding="6pt" spacing="6pt">
             <fo:block>
                <fo:page-number-citation>
                <xsl:attribute name="ref-id">
                 <xsl:value-of select="generate-id(.)"/>
                </xsl:attribute>
                </fo:page-number-citation>
             </fo:block>
           </fo:table-cell>
           </fo:table-row>
        </xsl:for-each>
        </fo:table-body>
      </fo:table>
    </fo:block>
  </fo:flow>
</fo:page-sequence>
<!-- End page filling of table of contents -->

<!-- Filling of content pages  -->
<fo:page-sequence master-name="rest">

<!-- Header line with static text and dividing rule-->
```

```
                    <fo:static-content flow-name="xsl-region-before">
                      <fo:block text-align="end" font-size="10pt"
                         font-family="serif" line-height="14pt">
                          XSL-FO Example: slides as brochures
                      </fo:block>
                      <fo:block>
                          <fo:leader leader-pattern="rule"
                              space-before.optimum="12pt"
                              space-after.optimum="12pt"/>
                      </fo:block>
                    </fo:static-content>

                 <!-- footer line with page nnumber -->
                    <fo:static-content flow-name="xsl-region-after">
                      <fo:block text-align="center" font-size="10pt"
                         font-family="serif" line-height="14pt">
                          - <fo:page-number/> -
                      </fo:block>
                    </fo:static-content>

                 <!-- Filling in content from data source,
                      page break after every third slide
                 -->
                    <fo:flow flow-name="xsl-region-body" >
                      <xsl:for-each select="slide[@status='active']">
                          <fo:block>
                            <xsl:if test="position() mod 3 = 0 ">
                                <xsl:attribute name="break-after">
                                   page
                                </xsl:attribute>
                            </xsl:if>
                            <xsl:attribute name="id">
                                <xsl:value-of select="generate-id(.)"/>
                            </xsl:attribute>
                            <xsl:call-template name="postable"/>
                          </fo:block>
                      </xsl:for-each>
                    </fo:flow>

                 </fo:page-sequence>

                 </fo:root>

                 /xsl:template>
```

*See also
explanation to
FO fragment 15*

```
<!-- named template for positioning content and lines
-->
<xsl:template name="postable">
    <fo:table space-before.optimum="32pt">
        <fo:table-column column-width="3in"/>
        <fo:table-column column-width="3in"/>
        <fo:table-body font-size="12pt">
            <fo:table-row>
                <fo:table-cell border-width="1pt"
                  border-style="solid" padding="6pt"
                  spacing="6pt">
                  <xsl:apply-templates/>
                </fo:table-cell>
                <fo:table-cell padding="6pt" spacing="6pt">
                    <xsl:call-template name="make_empty_
                        lines"/>
                </fo:table-cell>
            </fo:table-row>
        </fo:table-body>
    </fo:table>
</xsl:template>

<!-- Output content of slides -->
<xsl:template match="title">
    <fo:block font-size="16pt" font-family="serif"
        line-height="16pt" space-after.optimum="15pt">
        <xsl:apply-templates/>
    </fo:block>
</xsl:template>
```

*See also
explanation to
FO fragment 16*

```
<xsl:template match="topiclist">
    <fo:list-block font-size="12pt" start-indent="1cm">
        <xsl:apply-templates/>
    </fo:list-block>
</xsl:template>

<!-- Output topiclist with special character as a
label -->
```

*See also
explanation to
FO fragment 17*

```
<xsl:template match="topic">
    <fo:list-item>
        <fo:list-item-label>
            <fo:block>&#x2022;</fo:block>
        </fo:list-item-label>
        <fo:list-item-body>
```

*See also
explanation to
FO fragment 18*

```
            <fo:block>
              <xsl:apply-templates/>
            </fo:block>
          </fo:list-item-body>
        </fo:list-item>
      </xsl:template>
      <!-- Output 5 empty lines with ruling -->
      <xsl:template name="make_empty_lines">
        <xsl:call-template name="make_empty_line"/>
        <xsl:call-template name="make_empty_line"/>
        <xsl:call-template name="make_empty_line"/>
        <xsl:call-template name="make_empty_line"/>
        <xsl:call-template name="make_empty_line"/>
      </xsl:template>

      <!-- Template for the creation of a ruled empty line
      -->
      <xsl:template name="make_empty_line">
        <fo:block start-indent="1cm">
          <fo:leader leader-pattern="rule"
            space-before.optimum="0.5cm"
            space-after.optimum="0.5cm"/>
        </fo:block>
      </xsl:template>

      </xsl:stylesheet>
```

Further information

Of the vast amount of literature on the topic of XML that is available today, only documents that were essential for the authors were selected. Publications that attach more importance to XML and the related fields have not been listed.

[AND00]   Anderson, Richard; Birbeck, Mark u.a.: *XML professionell. Deutsche Ausgabe*, MITP Verlag, 2000.

[BAC00]   Bach, Mike: *XSL und XPath, Transformation und Ausgabe von XML-Dokumenten mit XSL*. Addison-Wesley, 2000.

[BOS99]   Bos, Bert: *CSS & XSL, which should I use?*
          http://www.w3.org/Style/CSS-vs-XSL, 1999.

[BOS99a] Bos, Bert; Lie, Håkon Wium: *Cascading stylesheets: Designing for the Web*. Addison-Wesley, 1999.

[BOX00]   Box, Don; Skonnard, Aaron; Lam, John : *Essential XML, Beyond Markup*. Addison-Wesley, 2000.

[BRA00]   Bradley, Neil: *The XSL companion*. Addison-Wesley, 2000.

[CLA99]   Clark, James: *XML Namespaces*.
          http://www.jclark.com/xml/xmlns.htm. 1999

[ECK00]   Eckstein, Robert: *XML kurz und gut. Übersetzung v. N. Klever*. O'Reilly, Köln, 2000.

[HAR99]   Harold, Eliotte Rusty: *The XML Bible*. IDG Books, 1999.

[HOL00]   Holman, Ken: *Practical Transformation using XSLT and XPATH*.
          CraneSoftwrights Ltd. http://www.CraneSoftwrights.com, PDF document to download. Parts of this are freely available as a preview. Future revisions of the full document are also available, at a charge.
          The first coherent representation of transformations using XSLT. Many examples and graphics make the topic more accessible, although the approx. 300 pages do not contain any prose, just keywords.

[HOM99]   Homer, Alex: *XML IE5 Programmer's Reference*. Wrox Press 1999.

[KAY00]   Kay, Michael: *XSLT Programmer's Reference*. Wrox Press 2000.
            In a total of 700 pages, the developer of the XSLT processor Saxon
            describes the transformation language XSLT. It is obvious from the book
            that this is someone who had to convert the ideas of XSLT into program
            code. The background information, the examples and the explanations
            probably cannot be represented any better than they are in this book. The
            passages in which Kay points out errors in the XSLT standard document
            are also pleasant to read. This is a must read for all those who are serious
            about XSLT, even for the future, because Michael Kay has been appointed
            to the working team in order to develop the XSLT standard further.

[MEY00]   Meyer, Eric: *Cascading Stylesheets: The Definitive Guide*. O'Reilly, 2000.

[NOR99]   North, Simon und Hermans, Paul: *XML in 21 Days*. Markt und Technik,
            1999.

[TOL00]   Tolksdorf, Robert: *Die Sprachen des Web: HTML und XHTML*. Processing
            information and presenting it on the Internet. 4th revised edition.
            dpunkt.verlag, 2000.

[XMLSY]   XML-Syntax. *Syntax der Extensible Markup Language (XML)* 1.0. http://
            members.aol.com/xmldoku.
            The document gives a brief insight into the XML syntax in the German
            language. Because it is short, it is more suitably used as a source of
            reference. The ENTITY topic is presented particularly briefly and well.

C.1 Specifications

[XML10]   *Extensible Markup Language (XML) 1.0,*
            W3C Recommendation 10 February 1998.
            http://www.w3.org/TR/1998/REC-xml-19980210

[XMLNS]   *Namespaces in XML,*
            World Wide Web Consortium 14 January 1999
            http://www.w3.org/TR/REC-xml-names

[XMLS1]   *XML Schema Part 1: Structures,*
            W3C Working Draft 25 February 2000
            http://www.w3.org/TR/xmlschema-1/

[XMLS2]   *XML Schema Part 2: Datatypes,*
            W3C Working Draft 25 February 2000
            http://www.w3.org/TR/xmlschema-2/

[XMLSP]   *XML Schema Part 0: Primer,*
            W3C Working Draft 5 April 2000
            http://www.w3.org/TR/xmlschema-0/

[XMLST]   *Associating stylesheets with XML Documents Version 1.0,*
            W3C Recommendation 29 June 1999
            http://www.w3.org/TR/xml-stylesheet/

[XPATH]   *XML Path Language (XPath) Version 1.0*
            W3C Recommendation 16 November 1999.
            http://www.w3.org/TR/xpath

[XSL]   *Extensible stylesheet Language (XSL) Version 1.0,*
            W3C Working Draft 1 March 2000.
            http://www.w3.org/TR/xsl/

[XSL99]   *Extensible stylesheet Language (XSL) Version 1.0,*
            W3C Working Draft April 1999.
            http://www.w3.org/TR/1999/WD-xsl-19990421

[XSLT]   *XSL Transformations (XSLT) Version 1.0,* W3C Recommendation
            16 November 1999.
            http://www.w3.org/TR/xslt

Index